By Mu Qinghan
沐青涵 著

Notes on Depression Self-help

抑郁
自救笔记

Billson International Ltd.

Published by
Billson International Ltd
27 Old Gloucester Street
London
WC1N 3AX
Tel:(852)95619525

Website:www.billson.cn
E-mail address:cs@billson.cn

First published 2025

Produced by Billson International Ltd
CDPF/01

ISBN 978-1-80377-161-8

©Hebei Zhongban Culture Development Co.,Ltd All rights reserved.

The original content within this product remains the property of Hebei Zhongban Culture Development Co.,Ltd, and cannot be reproduced without prior permission. Updates and derivative works of the original content remain the property of Hebei Zhongban. and are provided by Hebei Zhongban Culture Development Co.,Ltd.

The authors and publisher have made every attempt to ensure that the information contained in this book is complete, accurate and true at the time of printing. You are invited to provide feedback of any errors, omissions and suggestions for improvement.

Every attempt has been made to acknowledge copyright. However, should any infringement have occurred, the publisher invites copyright owners to contact the address below.

Hebei Zhongban Culture Development Co.,Ltd
Wanda Office Building B, 215 Jianhua South Street, Yuhua District, Shijiazhuang City, Hebei province, 2207

前言

　　我拿起笔，写下这些文字，是想探寻一个更加真实、未经修饰的自我。这本书不仅是对抗抑郁经历的回顾，更是我与自己对话、尝试理解和接纳这段过去的方式。我的目的很简单，却又充满力量：通过分享个人的挣扎与成长，我希望能够给予那些在黑暗中摸索的人们一些指引和慰藉，告诉他们——你并不孤单。

　　促使我提笔的动机，源自内心深处的共鸣和渴望。我经历过抑郁症带来的痛不欲生，那种仿佛身陷无底深渊、四周一片漆黑的无助感，让人难以言说。正是这些深刻的痛苦体验，让我意识到，沉默不再是解决问题的方法。我必须打破沉默，发声，为那些与我有着相同遭遇的人们，为那些还在默默忍受痛苦的灵魂。

　　在这个过程中，我发现了文字的力量。它们可以描绘出最细微的情感波动，勾勒出抑郁症背后的复杂纹理。它们可以成为我与外界沟通的桥梁，也可以是我自我疗愈的工具。所以，我选择了写作，用我最真挚的情感和最直接的语言，去还原那段刻骨铭心的岁月。

　　抑郁症，听起来好像离我们很远，但其实它就像一位不请自来的访客，有时甚至会悄无声息地住进我们的心里。它不是简单的"心情不好"或者"性格缺陷"，而是一种真实存在的心理疾病。想象一下，有一天你突然发现自己对曾经热爱的事物失去了兴趣，笑容变得越来越少，连日常的社交都变得困难重重。你开始感到疲惫、无力，不再想出门与外界接触，仿佛整个世界都失去了色彩。这就是抑郁症可能带来的感受。

　　它并不总是有明显的外在表现，有时甚至连患者自己都难以察觉。但随着时间的推移，抑郁症可能会逐渐侵蚀一个人的内心，让他们感到无助、绝望，甚至产生自杀的念头。

　　但请不要失去希望，抑郁症并不是一头无法战胜的怪兽。它虽然强大，但并非无敌。通过专业的治疗、心理辅导、药物治疗以及生活方式的调整，我们是可以逐渐走出抑郁症的阴影的。最重要的是，我们要学会倾听自己的内心，勇敢地面对自己的情绪，并寻求外界的帮助和支持。

　　回想起来，再没有摆脱抑郁以前，我曾将所有希望毫无保留地寄托于医生，那是一种近乎绝对的依赖。尽管医生的诊断与治疗无疑起到了至关重要的作用，但真正的康复之路，实则更多地依赖于我们自身的觉醒与自救。倘若内心缺乏这份自救的意识，渴望醒来、渴望解脱的愿望，那么，真正的康复便如同空中楼阁，遥不可及。确切地说，康复之路，尤其是完全的康复，绝非单凭外力所能达成，它需要我们自身的深刻觉醒与不懈努力。我很庆幸，在经历了长达二十年的艰难磨砺后，我终于迎来了内心的觉醒，踏上了自我救赎的道路。在这一过程中，我的身体、大脑乃至心灵都经历了深刻的转变，它们以一种前所未有的美好姿态呈现在我面前，我的韧性与抗压能力也因此得到了极大的提升。

　　所以，如果你或你身边的人正在经历这样的困境，请不要犹豫，及时寻求专业的帮助。记住，你不是一个人在战斗，我们永远都在你身边。

　　我期望这本书能带给读者一种共鸣，一种理解，甚至是一种启发。在这个看似冷漠和疏离的社会中，也许我们可以通过分享自己的故事，找到彼此的连接点，共同构建一个更加温暖、包容的环境。抑郁症并不是终点，而是一个转折点，是我们重新审视自己、重新定义生活意义的契机。希望我的故事，能够激励更多的人勇敢地面对自己的内心世界，去追寻属于自己的那份光明。

　　为保护个人隐私，本书中的一些姓名和身份细节已作更改。我尽力根据记忆重现事件、地点和对话，但为了维护匿名性，在某些情况下更改了人物和地点的名称，也更改了一些身份特征和细节，比如外貌特征、职业和居住地。书中如有与现实中的任何人相似之处，纯属巧合，并非有意为之。

Foreword

I took up the pen to write these words in search of a truer, unadorned version of myself. This book is not only a review of my experience with depression, but also a way for me to talk to myself and try to understand and accept this past. My purpose is simple, yet powerful: By sharing my personal struggles and growth, I hope to give guidance and comfort to those who are struggling in the dark and tell them that you are not alone.

What motivates me to write is a deep sense of empathy and longing. I have experienced the agony of depression, the indescribable feeling of helplessness in a bottomless pit of darkness. It was these deeply painful experiences that made me realize that silence is no longer the answer. I must break my silence and speak out for those who have been through the same thing and for the souls who are still suffering in silence.

In this process, I discovered the power of words. They can map out the most subtle of emotional fluctuations and outline the complex textures behind depression. They can be a bridge for me to communicate with the outside world, or a tool for my self-healing. Therefore, I choose to write, using my most sincere emotions and the most direct language, to restore that unforgettable time.

Depression, it sounds as if it is far away from us, but in fact it is like an uninvited visitor, sometimes even quietly living in our hearts. It is not simply a "bad mood" or a "character flaw" , but a real mental illness. Imagine that one day you suddenly find yourself losing interest in the things you once loved, smiling less and less, and having difficulty in everyday social interactions. You

抑郁自救笔记
Notes on Depression Self-help

begin to feel tired and powerless. You no longer want to go out and interact with the outside world. It's as if the whole world has lost its color. This is how depression can feel.

It's not always obvious on the outside, and sometimes it's hard even for the sufferer to notice. But over time, depression can gradually eat away at a person's insides, leaving them feeling helpless, hopeless and even suicidal.

But don't lose hope, depression is not an unbeatable monster. While it is powerful, it is not invincible. With professional therapy, counseling, medication and lifestyle adjustments, depression can be gradually overcome. The most important thing is that we learn to listen to our hearts, face our emotions bravely, and seek outside help and support.

Looking back, before I got rid of depression, I had placed all my hopes unreservedly on doctors, which was an almost absolute reliance. Although the diagnosis and treatment by doctors undoubtedly played a crucial role, the true path to recovery actually relied more on our own awakening and self-rescue. If there is no awareness of self-rescue in the heart, no desire to wake up and be liberated, then true recovery would be like a castle in the air, out of reach. To be precise, the path to recovery, especially complete recovery, cannot be achieved solely by external forces. It requires our own profound awakening and unremitting efforts. I am very fortunate that after twenty years of arduous struggle, I finally experienced an awakening in my heart and embarked on the path of self-redemption. During this process, my body, brain and even my soul underwent profound changes, presenting themselves to me in an unprecedentedly beautiful manner. My resilience and ability to withstand pressure have also been greatly enhanced.

So, if you or someone close to you is going through such a predicament, please don't hesitate to seek professional help in time. Remember that you are not alone in this fight and we are always here for you.

I expect this book to bring readers a sense of empathy, an understanding, and even an inspiration. In this seemingly cold and alienated society, perhaps we can find a connection with each other by sharing our own stories, and together build a more warm and inclusive environment. Depression is not an end, but a turning point, an opportunity for us to re-examine ourselves and redefine the meaning of life. I hope my story can inspire more people to bravely face their inner world and pursue their own light.

Some names and identifying details in this book have been changed to protect the privacy of individuals. I have tried to recreate events, locales, and conversations from my memories of them, but in order to maintain their anonymity 1 have in some instances changed the names of individuals and places and have also changed some identifying characteristics and details such as physical properties, occupations and places of residence. Any resemblance to persons living or dead is coincidental and not intended.

目 录

第一章 过往的回声 / 001

第二章 困兽笼中 / 013

    1. 病重 / 013

    2. 治疗初期 / 017

    3. 反复阶段 / 018

    4. "亦师亦友"的马医生 / 025

第三章 心理的轮廓 / 031

    1. 抑郁和焦虑的真相 / 031

    2. 与自我和解 / 033

    3. 缓解失眠 / 035

    4. 饮食疗法 / 036

    5. 公园效应 / 037

    6. 漂浮疗法 / 038

    7. 运动疗法 / 039

第四章 汗水的折光 / 043

    1. 爱上运动 / 043

    2. 运动中的思考 / 044

    3. 马拉松的新奇体验 / 050

第五章　孤岛之外　/ 058

1. 识于微时的老友　/ 058
2. 初心不再的旧友　/ 064
3. 朋友筛选法则　/ 067
4. 如何与抑郁症患者相处　/ 070

第六章　小手牵大手　/ 072

1. 截然相反的姐弟俩　/ 072
2. 孩子们教会我学习　/ 078
3. 平等的亲子关系　/ 083
4. 孩子身上的我　/ 086

第七章　自我的革命　/ 089

1. 做情绪的舵手　/ 089
2. 敏感的新内涵　/ 099
3. 破旧立新，解放思维　/ 103
4. 巧克力启示：珍惜当下　/ 104
5. 相信世界的善意　/ 106
6. 允许自己轻松　/ 107
7. 欲望：追求和满足的平衡　/ 108

第八章　随笔杂感　/ 113

《被讨厌的勇气》读后感　/ 113
《情归新泽西》观后感　/ 117
《运动改造大脑》读后感　/ 120

后记　/ 123

Chapter 1 Echoes of the past / 126

Chapter 2 Trapped in a Cage / 143

    1. Being seriously ill / 143

    2. Initial treatment / 148

    3. Recurring phases / 150

    4. "Mentor and Friend" Dr. Ma / 159

Chapter 3 The outline of the mind / 167

    1. The truth about depression and anxiety / 167

    2. Reconcile with yourself / 169

    3. Relieve insomnia / 172

    4. Diet therapy / 174

    5. The park effect / 175

    6. Float therapy / 176

    7. Exercise therapy / 177

Chapter 4 Refraction of Sweat / 182

    1. Fall in love with sports / 182

    2. Thinking in motion / 184

    3. The novelty experience of a marathon / 192

Chapter 5 Beyond the Island / 203

    1. An old friend who knows his time / 203

    2. An old friend whose heart has been lost / 212

    3. The Friend Filter / 215

    4. How do you deal with people with depression / 219

Chapter 6 Small Hands Hold Big Hands / 222

1. Diametrically opposed siblings / 222

2. My children teach me to learn / 230

3. An equal parent-child relationship / 237

4. The Me in my child / 241

Chapter 7 The Revolution of the Self / 245

1. Be the master of your emotions / 246

2. New connotations of sensitivity / 258

3. Break the old and break the new to free your mind / 263

4. Chocolate Inspiration: Cherish the moment / 266

5. Trust in the goodwill of the world / 268

6. Allow yourself to be easy / 269

7. Desire: The balance between pursuit and satisfaction / 271

Chapter 8 Miscellaneous Feelings / 277

After reading The Courage to Be Hated / 277

Feeling Back in New Jersey / 283

"Sports change the brain" after reading / 286

Postscript / 290

第一章　过往的回声

过往的岁月轻轻敲打着记忆的门，像是遥远山谷中的回声，时而模糊，时而清晰，却始终萦绕不去。这些回声构成了我——一个由经历塑造的个体，它们是故事的起点，也是理解我如今模样的钥匙。穿过时间的隧道，回到那些定义了我、挑战了我、最终塑造了我的时刻。

听大人们说，我出生后因被生父嫌弃性别而抛弃，生母亦无心照顾我，便支付了生活费委托别人代为照看。好在有人愿意照顾我，可是刚出生的我像瘦猴一样，胳膊只有大人的大拇指粗，还不吃东西，大家都怕养不活。于是，我被辗转寄养，这家养五天，那家看一周。

推来推去，就在我无处安身之时，庆幸，我的祖祖——我生父的奶奶，收留了我。我也总算有了安稳的"落脚处"，终于不用再像皮球一样被那些寄养家庭踢来踢去。家里原本已有七口人，包括祖祖、幺爷爷、幺奶奶以及他们的三个女儿和一个儿子——大爹、二爹、三爹和幺爸（在我老家，"爹"也用来指女性），现在又多了一个我。慈祥的幺爷爷作为家中的男性长辈，对于家中的琐事并不过多插手。而我，一个只会哭闹和需要照顾的婴儿，无疑给幺奶奶增加了不小的负担。幺奶奶总是很凶，不苟言笑，讲话大声，还喜欢骂人，满屋子回荡的都是她无法沉静的声音。

我当时不知道那是什么样的感情，也许是年幼的我心思敏感，时而感觉被欺凌，时而又觉得被亲人们宠爱如珍宝，时而又觉得自己像是被他们当作玩具来消遣。他们爱我但也可能有少许的讨厌我，觉得我是一个负担，又或者是一个可以随意摆布的玩偶……太复杂的情感。当然，我要感谢他们，谢谢他们在没有人愿意收养我的情况下，协助祖祖拉扯我长大。

不知道祖祖是怎样把我拉扯大的，她很老很老了，很瘦小，全身的皮都皱皱的，下巴和脖子处的皮已经松到完全垂下来了，我经常喜欢摸她下巴垂下来的皮，软软滑滑的很舒服，好好玩的样子。祖祖的脚很小，非常小，她从小就裹小脚，用裹布把脚裹得严严实实的。小脚趾弯曲着，就像一个驼背的人，紧紧地贴着第四脚趾上。而第四脚趾则倾斜着紧紧地贴向第三脚趾。这五个脚趾紧密地靠在一起，形成了一个不均匀的三角形。我和祖祖睡，我睡在另一头，就是对着祖祖只有五六岁孩子般大小的脚睡。哈哈，好小的脚。

祖祖经常和我说："不要怪你妈，是你爸爸的错，千万不记恨你妈妈……"其实和我说这些也没什么意义，我不知道什么是妈妈，什么是爸爸，对我来说只是一个模糊的代名词而已。比方说，妈妈就是那个偶尔会来看看我的人，奶奶就代表很凶，三爹就代表笑嘻嘻，对于别的家人我就比较模糊了，尤其是爸爸，那是什么？只有祖祖，慈祥，美丽，哪怕她皱皱的皮也是美丽的。她对着我没有脾气，只有耐心和慈祥的笑容。

后来我长大了，上学了，有次祖祖给我拿早餐钱的时候，她拿出裹了一层一层的手帕，打开后最里面裹的是钱，她把一张十块的当作两块给我了，我不动声色地接过钱去上学了，也不知道那时候把钱用来买了什么吃，或者买了什么、多久用完都不记得了，但是没有打算告诉祖祖。反而在想，祖祖下一次给我早餐钱的时候会不会又给错呢？那我下次应该买些什么好？貌似很期待下一次的十块钱。

记得有次大爹一直骂我，因为她抓住我把一根筷子点燃了当烟抽，还跑去漆黑的地方点燃筷子祭鬼。是的，我信鬼不信佛，因为我觉得世界都是丑恶的，没有什么是美好，所说的神能帮助你都是假的，真正存在的是鬼，黑暗中的鬼。那次，大爹是真的生气了，一直骂我，还要打我。祖祖看不过去了，找了一根竹竿，很大很长的竹竿，有一端被划破成一条一条的，说叫破响篙，具体用来干吗的我也不知道，只知道祖祖拿着破响篙打我，好像打在我身上又好像没有打到，因为我忘记了那时候痛不痛，那个破响篙的声音很大，很霸气的样子，我看着祖祖发飙的样子很惊讶，为什么那么慈爱的祖祖会打我呢？她打了两下就流泪了，她没有哭出声音，但是眼泪滑过她布满皱纹的脸颊落下。晚上睡觉的时候，她抱着我说："你要知道，我不是真的要打你，我是打气，我好气，我老了不能保护你，你要快长大保护自己。他们欺负你，不待见你，祖祖气，以后祖祖不在你身边你该怎么办呀？"此时此刻我还不能听出祖祖对我成长之路的焦虑。

有天，我看见祖祖挣扎着从地上爬起来，坐到她的藤椅上。我问她怎么了，为什么会摔倒。祖祖开始不愿意说，吞吞吐吐的。我一再追问："你不可能自己平地摔倒吧？"祖祖终于透露，是大爹和她发生争执后把祖祖推倒在地不管不顾的扭头就走。瞬间燃爆了我的小宇宙，怒火中烧的我，立马转身冲出家门，箭步般飞奔，沿着马路追赶刚吃过晚饭准备回家的大爹夫妻俩。大概跑了1公里多，我就看见他们两个的背影了。急不可耐地加速上前飞起就是一脚，踹向我大爹。那时，我大爹怀有身孕，她丈夫赶紧上前阻拦我，可我心中怒火无法平息，仍不依不饶地继续跳跃起身，踹过去。内心的愤怒都涌向踢出去的那条腿上。我恨她，祖祖上年纪了，身体早已不再灵活。她只能依靠那张藤椅来缓慢地挪动位置。每一次，她都要费力地推动藤椅，然后再向前伸出颤抖的脚，一点一点地往前挪动，每迈一步都需要费些力气。大爹竟然这么狠心，将祖祖推倒在地，还不扶起来。年幼时的我就已经开始以暴制暴，以牙还牙了。后来，大爹生下来的小孩有一点轻微的斗鸡眼，每次看到他我都在想，是不是我当时的一个飞踢把他踹坏了呢？我心里始终藏着一点小小的罪恶感。

现在想想我小时候大概确实淘气，总是喜欢在外面游荡，像男孩子一样上树掏鸟窝，下河摸螃蟹，钻黑洞，毕竟刚来到这个世界不久，很多都没见过，对生活充满了好奇。只是，每当我沉浸在这些冒险中时，总免不了幺奶奶的严厉斥责和惩罚。有次，我因为好奇跑去围观别人家杀黄鳝看到已近天黑过了晚饭的点，还是幺奶奶来菜市场找到我才回家，回家后被罚跪在屋顶。现在，我自己也成为一位母亲，才终于理解了当年幺奶奶为何会罚跪我。

祖祖那个时候吃饭都是吃白菜煮饭，没有肉，饭煮得很烂，菜也煮烂了，我觉得那饭还挺好吃的。我身体不好，非常瘦又不爱吃东西，祖祖就用明镜草、鸡菌子还有折耳根一起蒸汤，那汤是我喝过最好喝的汤，她说这汤养脾胃。还记得那时候我们是住在一个平房，房子建造得有点奇怪，因为房子是凹进去的，好像陷下去了一样。现在还能想起祖祖端着热腾腾的明镜草、折耳根和鸡菌子蒸的汤，站在门口喊我喝汤的场景：那个陷下去的房门让瘦小的她看起来更矮了，她小心翼翼地端着汤："过来，趁热把汤喝了，温温的刚刚好，这个养胃。"小步挪动脚步地边走边喊我，生怕汤洒了。

记得有次大雨下了很久很久，我们住的那个陷下去的房子里面灌满了水，我亲爷爷家就住隔壁一步之遥红砖砌的四层楼房的二层楼，也就是我幺爷爷的亲哥，有人过来接我们。只听祖祖用尽力气大声嘶喊着："你们先把她抱上去，要快点给她换套衣服，用被子裹起来，裹紧点哈！不要着凉了喔！"听见她用尽力气地嘶喊，我的心暖暖的，一字一句都灌满了祖祖对我的爱，我就是祖祖的心头肉，她不容我有半点的损伤。

祖祖，我爱您，很爱很爱，但当时幼小的我不懂生离死别，对于这份深厚的爱，却未知再过几年就会永远见不到我深爱的祖祖。

后来不知道几时我们搬家了，幺爷爷家自己盖的一座两层的小楼，二楼是他们一家人加上我生活的地方，一楼则被隔成了好几个小房间，用于出租。说起来真是有些戏剧性，抛弃我的生父、与每个月有负担我生活费的母亲就分别租住在这里。他们就住在我的楼下，却对我不闻不问、毫不关心，可以不过分地用形同陌路来比喻，也不明白各自都有各自的家，为什么会一起出现在这里。他们在楼下各过各的日子，母亲单身，生父带着他的各位相好。我曾经听见母亲跟三爹闲聊的时候提到生父："他老是找各种借口来我房间，不是借水，就是借纸……"

就在我即将接受我们是陌生人的现状的时候，生父忽然打破这表面的平静。那天，我照常从楼上下来要去找附近的小孩玩，路过一楼长长的走廊的时候，生父突然从他房间出来，一把拉着我，灿烂地笑着去他房间。

大概是第一次见生父对我露出笑容，现在想起来那笑容真是猥琐又狰狞，令人作呕，也是这个笑容导致我现在看见和他差不多长相的人就觉得恶心、厌恶。当时，我竟真傻乎乎地跟二愣子一样乖乖站那边。他的房间并不宽敞，而且有些杂乱。我站在未关上的房门口，整个房间越发弥漫着一股沉闷的气氛。我拘谨地站在门口，生怕自己哪个动作打破了这"亲密"的场景。他松开拉着我进门的手，走到床头，我才注意到床上的被子里还躺着一个女人。他坐下来，然后微笑着朝我招手："过来呀，站那么远干什么？"我小步挪蹭着，引来他不耐烦的一声"啧，快点过来"。我仍然没有加快步伐的意思，挪着小碎步，在床的一头远远望着。

"看看你小妈的咪咪，白不白，大不大？"说着话，他忽地掀开了女人身上的被子。赤裸的女人侧躺着，用胳膊支着脑袋，娇笑着，花枝乱颤。男人的笑声和女人的笑声交织在一起，像条毒蛇，追着我跑出了那个昏暗的房间。那时我五岁左右。

此后，每次我经过那个房间门口都是奔跑而过，生怕有只手，黑乎乎、毛茸茸且有着锋利爪子的手拉我进去。在后来的许多年里，那个昏暗的房间，都仿佛是一个黑暗的深渊，想要将我吞噬其中。以至于长大后的我时常怀疑，世界上的男人都像生父那样……不堪吗？

也是那时候，夜里十一点多，是的，深夜里的十一点多！他让我去火车站给她大咪咪女人买瓜子回来嗑，此时住他隔壁的生母也听见了，好在她认为我太小不应该去，及时制止了。

我母亲是很负面的人，她不喜欢沟通，我一说话她就会让我闭嘴，不要烦她。这种态度从我还是个小孩开始，一直延续至今。也许正因如此，我也养成了不喜欢过多啰唆、不善于主动沟通的习惯。无论遇到什么事情，她总是会以一种消极的视角去推测和解读。

我的母亲也不知道是几时再婚了。在我七岁那年，不明为何母亲带我离开了幺爷爷家，被带到了姥爷家，和姥爷、姨妈一家一起生活。也是从这一年开始，我几乎每天都受着不同程度的打骂，较好时只是一两记耳光，如果自己做错事或遇到她们心情不好的时候会满身淤青或紫红淤血，常态似的挨打比饭点还准时。很奇怪的一个现象是，姨妈开心地聊着天时会忽然笑着给我一个耳光……注意，这个耳光是用力扇下去的，扇得我的头扭向了另一方向的尽头，如果可以转动估计这头得旋转个五六圈，脸上的五指印清晰可见。这突如其来的耳光是，爱？

还记得到姥爷家的第一天我竟然失眠了，一个七岁的孩子失眠了。我端起一个小小的长方形四脚矮木凳到后院房门口，一米多距离是葡萄树架，院子里有很多花，有四季海棠、月季、栀子花等等，花香扑鼻。但此时年幼的我无心赏花，一手横放在膝盖上，一手托起下巴抬头看着高高的月亮，直到现在我仍然记得当晚的月亮特别的圆特别的亮。手托着的那侧脸感觉湿湿的，嗯，我哭了。眼泪止不住地流，顺着下巴流到脖子形成了一条线，不间断的线条一直流，滴答滴答地落在另外一只横放在膝盖上的手上和腿上。但是我一点声音都没有发出来，就像祖祖拿着破响篙打我时一样，那无声的泪如雨而下。顿感胸口处隐隐作痛，扯着痛，越来越痛。看着那晚皎洁的月亮仿佛看见了祖祖的笑脸，皱巴巴的笑脸，好想摸摸她下巴皱皱垂下的皮啊，还有那双孩童般的小脚，祖祖我好想你。我的祖祖肯定也非常地思念我。

接下来的一段时间，我的胸口一直很痛，感觉提不起气，胸闷气短。告知大人后，由姥爷决定给我喝一种糖浆，连续喝了大概两个多月就不再疼了。回忆起以前在祖祖身边的时候，我只是身体不好，并没有哪里疼痛又或者说是我不记得了。

姥爷腿脚不便，听说是年轻的时候受了伤。在我的童年记忆里，他是一个对我来说没有太多感情的亲人。因为他过世的时候，我没有感受到失去亲人的悲痛。姨妈家有两个儿子，我母亲再婚后又生了一个儿子，舅舅家也有个儿子。五个孩子里我作为家里唯一的女孩，理所当然地成了姥爷的"眼中钉"。姥爷的眼神，总是宛如冬日的疾风，锐利而冷峻。虽然那时的我尚且年幼，但我明白姥爷的眼神里是对我性别的无奈与不满。我在他对我性别嫌弃的打骂声中，没有感受到一个姥爷应有的慈祥。姥爷经常给表弟和我同母异父的弟弟吃维生素C片剂，然后看着他们俩被酸得扭曲的脸哈哈大笑。姥爷最喜欢的是大表弟也就是舅舅的儿子，因为他们同一个姓，称为内孙。三个表弟经常在姥爷床上打闹，内孙更是肆无忌惮地随意拿姥爷枕头边上信封里的钱和床头靠墙位置的桃酥和小零食。我心里暗自猜想，那床是不是比任何地方都好玩呢？他们好开心好快乐。虽然姥爷腿脚不便但是并不妨碍他打我，他喊我趴在他床角，他二女儿用力压着我的身体让我保持平衡不乱动，便于她爹操作，用他那一米多长硬拐拐的棕色龙头拐杖高高举起重重落下，一点也不手软。每次举起都能看见前一次落下时留下的大块淤紫，打到整个屁股淤青才罢休。他总是说："女儿是赔钱货，嫁出去的女儿就是泼出去的水，迟早都是别人的人……"

姥爷是北方人，不吃南方菜，只爱面食。他吃剩下的饺子和疙瘩汤总是会分给表弟们，偶尔他们都不吃了我也能吃上一两口。长大后，我讨厌饺子和疙瘩汤，也不吃桃酥。小时候分零食或者是水果都是由姥爷来分的，分成一份一份的，然后由我的表哥表弟们先选，选了剩下的那个就是我的。他们每个人都有三只手，在拿走属于他们那一份的同时每个人都会把我那一份顺走一点，最终剩下给我就不用再细说了。大人们相视而笑并没有打算说些什么，只是跷起二郎腿，一边嗑瓜子一边看着热闹。

话说真的是基因遗传，他大女儿也就是我母亲丝毫不比他逊色，让我挽起裤腿跪在地上，用藤条狠狠地抽我小腿。屁股上的瘀紫还没好，两条腿又全部变紫色了。这家人貌似酷爱紫色？也不知道我皮肤黑是不是因为小时候经常挨打，全身每一寸皮肤都淤紫过多，有所谓的色素沉淀？她没有想停下的意思，越打越上头，越打越用力，大概是找到了发泄的快感，而我已泣不成声。没必要形容我接下来是怎么走路，几天才能恢复的了。也因此，长大后的我非常讨厌紫色。

有次，姨妈让七岁的我和八岁的大表哥一起做饭。那个年代没有什么电饭锅之类的东西，都是灶火煮，但年幼的我们怎么能掌控得了灶火呢？完全没有任何经验，不出意料的，饭糊了。姨妈看到锅底焦黑的米，顿时怒不可遏，她竟操起菜板上的菜刀，冲我和大表哥砍过来："两个败家子，做个饭都做不好，你们还有什么用？老子砍死你们俩……"我和大表哥甚至都没有机会做出任何反应，我们做了什么要被乱刀砍死的事了？被吓得四处逃窜。我们跑到隔壁的舅舅家躲起来，舅舅的老婆在家。她出来在门口拦住姨妈，不停地劝说些毕竟他们太小之类的话。那时躲在屋里瑟瑟发抖的我竟还有些庆幸，还好姨妈没有只针对我一个人。

从那次，我心里种下了"做不好家务是要被刀砍"的种子，发芽后就认定"没有武力解决不了的问题"，只要你够凶、下手够狠就能征服所有。所以上学时我喜欢和暴力的男生一起玩耍，随时可能爆发一场搏斗，好展示她们言传身教给我的身手和狠辣。这也导致我隔三岔五就被请家长。

姨妈和幺奶奶一样，说话很大声而且很喜欢让我罚跪。但是相比较我更喜欢幺奶奶，因为她只是骂我和罚跪，而姨妈骂完我就开始不停地扇耳光，有时候走过来就是几耳光，什么都不会和你说，太开心时也是用力一个耳光赏给你。这个也导致我形成了现在能动手绝对不动口的性格。话说，我有一位堂姐，与我年纪相仿，只大我几个月。她父母都遗弃她，是我们的亲大爹收养了她，在我看来大爹一家人比较柔和，也许遇事就讲道理不会动手，堂姐现在的性格挺柔和的，凡事就轻言细语地耐心讲理。有一次，我在烧煤块的四方北京铁炉旁边跪了很长时间，感觉汹涌的便意越来越强烈，多次忍不住开口求饶："让我去个厕所吧，肚子痛得憋不住了，我会回来继续跪着的。"但是，一旁织毛衣的姨妈却尖声指责我："别以为我不知道你在想什么鬼主意！老实跪着吧！"越发难受的感觉令我感觉胸闷气短，姨妈他们也只是充耳不闻。最终，这场漫长的罚跪最终因为我被便意撑昏过去而结束。

其实，姨妈对我挺有感情的。她虽然打我骂我，却也经常在深夜为了我流泪，可怜我。不过那已经是在我成年后了，她怜悯我的无依无靠，焦虑我的未来，可怜我的无人问津。

长大之后我也常常想，如果我是一个男孩，姥爷会不会对我改变看法？我也会像哥哥和弟弟那样，得到他的宠爱与认可吗？但是，这是一个永远无法得到答案的问题。当然，我长大一些后姥爷和姨妈对我的态度有一丁点的改变，不会天天打骂了，我也偶尔反思，也许幺奶奶和姨妈的罚跪、责骂是因为儿时的我确实太过顽皮，也许大爹他们对我是真的疼爱，只是不够细心和耐心……幺奶奶老了，她变了，她好慈祥，整天笑嘻嘻的，说话音量还是很高但语气已经柔和了很多，大概耳边不再有孩子叽叽喳喳和不停地犯错来惹怒她，所以她变得心情平缓，嘴边的两个梨涡非常好看。我姨妈嘴边也有两个梨涡，不过她还是那么怒气冲天和暴躁。她们俩都胖胖的，高高的，凶凶的。现在我有了孩子我也能理解为什么屋子总散不去的是老母亲的喊声。

母亲把我接到姥爷家时，安排我在附近小学上学，距离祖祖家的路程是三公里左右。每天我放学都会走到奶奶家，晚上奶奶又把我送回去，我就给我奶奶说不想去姥爷家，指着电杆说奶奶你看我写的打倒姥爷。当时的我认为阻碍我回到祖祖身边的人就是姥爷，愚蠢的以为写几个字就能回到从前，当然，住在姥爷家的那段时间也有不少快乐，院子里的小孩特别多，我们一起打闹一起钻黑洞、爬树、跑电门、写王字等等。当然，这一系列玩下来屁股当然也少不了拐棍痛打和各种体罚，我常常因为思念祖祖而无法入睡，坐在院子里看月亮。月亮那么圆，那么亮，仿佛能够照亮我内心的黑暗。祖祖也在想我吗？

回忆起童年我最爱最快乐的就是和祖祖他们一起生活的时光。跟着祖祖，不用做任何家务，哪怕是极凶的幺奶奶也没有吆喝着要我做过家务，没有因为任何事情而打我，更不会砍我，犯错也只是罚跪。此时更是思念祖祖。为什么大人们把我挪来挪去都不问一下我的感受呢？前不久我和母亲争吵的时候，我有提到过"为什么把我送去姨妈家，不让我就在祖祖身边？"她说她问过我，是我主动要去的。真的是张口就来，永远都是满嘴跑火车，她和我朋友聊天说道："希望在我死了以后她能照顾她弟弟的下半生……"

的确，我从没有拒绝过他们的无尽索取，也是因为这样母亲认为我就应该把我所有的都给她。疫情的时候，朋友打电话来说有个寿险非常不错，我就跟母亲随口一说："我买个保险，如果我死了你就拿到一百万好不好？"母亲眉飞色舞地说："太好啦，谢谢，由衷地感谢你！"那笑容真的是比花还灿烂，我亲妈在谢我……谢我的同时大概希望我买定后立马就死。这时联想起很多年前，因为工作需要我经常坐飞机，有次她看见机票里没有买意外险把我臭骂一通："你怎么一点良心都没有？坐飞机不买意外险，飞机那么容易出意外，你居然不买意外险？有没有想过你买了保险，如果你死了能留钱给我，养你那么大至少有点回报撒……"这话让我陷入沉思，如果你真的觉得坐飞机那么危险，为什么不直接劝我不要坐，反而是让我去买意外保险呢？加上太多生活中她对我挑剔的细小琐事以及漠视，所以有次我喝多之后割了自己的手腕，想着把命还他们算了，不要再折磨我，利用我了！可，祖祖保佑我，愿我一生平安。

小学时代的我数学非常不好，虽然现在还是背不好乘法口诀，那时候也没少被数学老师把耳朵揪破皮的那类学生，每次揪耳朵的时候用力拧到我整个表情都扭曲了，感觉她力气生得再大点就一定保证能成功地揪下来，挺狠，不见血她就不甘心。母亲给我买了很多童话故事书，我喜欢看故事书，少时还曾经梦想成为一个作家。写作文的时候经常叙述里面的故事，有时候写得太细致就被同学告老师说我抄书。但是长大后不知道从什么时候开始不喜欢看书，看见字稍微多几个就头晕目眩。不过我们语文老师还是挺喜欢我的，她是我们班主任。说她喜欢我倒也不至于，她只是不讨厌我。看我在班上算是高个子就选我去跑1500米，平时也没有让我去专门练习过就让我跑，结果四百米的时候我就已经是累得用走的了，最后拿了第一名，不过是倒数，哈哈，能走完也是厉害的。不过，比赛结束后被班主任劈头盖脸地一顿骂，从此我讨厌运动，能躺着绝对不会坐着。

后来和朋友一起去贵阳艺校玩，见识到艺校的女孩们能歌善舞又能演，心里又种下了个演员梦。她们的舞姿如精灵般灵动，歌声宛如天籁般悦耳，字字句句都飘进我心窝，敲击着那个梦。话说我也是学过舞蹈的拥有舞蹈功底，小学时期母亲曾经让我学过两天的舞蹈，是的，共计两天的时间。可惜，就在这宝贵的两天里，母亲看我没什么进展，认定我不是跳舞的料，摇着头说："啧啧，哎……没天赋。"所以这件事就没有下文了。

14岁已经辍学的我被我母亲送到大爹开的汽车修理厂去学习，不知什么给了她灵感让她认为我会成为一个出色的修车工，又或者我不小心在某个时候展露出有修车的天赋。长期和一帮修车工人厮混在一起，喝酒抽烟，更加无心学习，就是这时我开启了我的抽烟史，性格也越来越"男性化"，加上淡定而自然眺望着远方的眼神，抽烟的姿势倒是越来越帅。

那时生父条件挺不错的，小日子过得挺悠哉，他某天突然想起了我，也不怪他想起我，因为修车厂是他大姐的，他总在那边进进出出看见我，见我穿得土说，要带我去省城玩几天买几套衣服，"丢他脸了？"我很不情愿地去了，穿着姨妈给我织的绿白格子的新毛衣、老妈买的黑白格子新鞋子去了。可能那一年流行格子吧。他的女人带我去逛街买衣服，不停地问我要不要这个要不要那个。抱歉，我其实和你们俩都不熟悉甚至很陌生，所以总是摇摇头。对于陌生人突然的热情任何人都不会爽快地接受吧。可是他发疯了一样地辱骂我："你这个脓包、草包、土包子，给你打扮都不懂，就算给你穿起龙袍也不像人样……"最终，他的女人虽然翻着白眼还是选了一套牛仔衣给我，衣服很收身，挺显身材的，回到家后身边所有的人都夸我换了套衣服后好漂亮、洋气。这可以说是用尊严换取的一身漂亮衣服，虽然不是我情愿换取的。他说带我去玩几天，其实打心眼里就没接受过我，还是那么嫌弃和挤兑。的确不可否认省城的人眼光就是不一样，给我挑的一套衣服穿起来非常好看，没有格子，但是我觉得那一套格子穿得更自在。此后我再没见过他。

　　时间跳转到体育彩票风靡的那个年代，他和他的二姐也是我的幺爹，家里人在幺爹家摆了一桌宴席。当时他说了很多感人的话，如何如何的对不起我、亏欠我。那些话语像温暖的阳光一样照进我心窝让我感受到前所未有的爱，刹那间找回了父爱，我终于有"爸爸"了，竟然被甜言蜜语灌得心软，内心深处的花朵仿佛也被这甜蜜的话语唤醒，全部绽放开来，包围了整个心房。我决定原谅他，立马把以前的不愉快抛之脑后，我第一次叫了他一声"爸爸"。结果他画风突变又露出很多年前那狰狞的笑和我说："我已经计算过体育彩票的中奖概率了，你给我2万元人民币，我就能中奖。我中了五百万就会分你一百万……"面对他的话锋一转和荒谬不切实际的屁话，我感到震惊和愤怒，完全无法理解他怎么会在这个场景下提出这样的要求。一直都懂反击的我，怒砸桌子，扯破喉咙用尽全力喊出了我的愤怒和不满："滚你的，你给我一万，我中了五百万都给你好吧！"摔门而出的我心里怒吼着："以后也不见这王八！呸……"花也枯萎了。

　　某次我在社交平台上看过一篇报道，讲了一个女孩子和她父母之间的矛盾。父母对她管教十分严厉，只关注她的学习，她没有任何属于自己的时间更别说是娱乐时间。在选择大学时,女孩选择了自己心仪的大学,也被父母修改志愿,另选了离家更近的学校。后来女孩鼓动父母让她出国,她极力描绘出国的好处,最终得以实现。

当然,出国之后的生活并不像女孩描述得那样轻松,她一直半工半读,实在困难时打电话向父母求助。电话接通后,另一端传来不停的辱骂,她的父母指责她:"如果不是因为要钱,你都不会打电话回来!……"哪怕他们已经准备好了给女孩的钱,还是要对女孩频加指责。这让女孩十分寒心,一气之下与家人断绝了联系。在与家人断绝联系的17年里,她不仅通过自己的努力获得了德国的博士学位,还组建了自己的家庭,有了孩子。当她的父母通过电视台联系到她时,她却拒绝了与家人相见。尽管知道父母即将离世,她仍然坚持自己的决定,不愿在他们临终前相见。

一个是处处被束缚、被苛求的人生,一个是置之不理、漠不关心的人生。我很羡慕她的勇气,可以勇敢斩断一切牵挂,勇敢为自己而活。

还有我堂姐,她曾经被她的亲生父亲拿斧头追着砍,头破血流,当我听到消息赶到她家时她刚好从急诊室包扎好回来。

尽管经历了如此多的伤痛和被忽视,现在她却选择了原谅。我很佩服堂姐的勇气和宽容,可以原谅生活中的伤痛,原谅伤害过自己的人。

我也曾试图理解生父、母亲的立场,或许他们有自己的苦衷,或许他们只是不懂得如何表达情感……我很多次试图打开心结,放下那些怨恨。但每每这种时候,我又会想到他们过去对我的冷漠和忽视,想到他们对我的无尽索取。他们看到我现在过得还不错,肯定后面又有接二连三的事情等着我处理,还是不要给自己找麻烦了。

我只能用自己的方式和解,不再纠结于他们的所作所为,不再让自己活在怨恨中。但是也不会再和他们有过多交集。这样的决定或许有些自欺欺人,或许不够完美,但是这是我现阶段能做出的最好的选择。我会继续努力地生活,用自己的方式寻找真正的幸福和满足。现在的我每天忙碌着工作和两个孩子身心的成长,不想再有一些负面的事物来扰乱我平静幸福的生活。

第二章　困兽笼中

抑郁症来得悄无声息，如同夜色中的阴影，慢慢笼罩了我原本还算平静的生活。它不仅侵蚀我的身体，更蚕食我的心灵，将我囚禁在绝望的深渊。我成了一只困兽，被无形的锁链束缚，四周是冰冷的铁栏，头顶是沉重的天空。我挣扎，我咆哮，却似乎找不到出路，每一次挣扎都只能让自己更加疲惫。

但是，即使在最黑暗的时刻，内心深处也总有一丝不甘和反抗的火花在闪烁。我不愿意就这样屈服于命运的安排，不愿意让疾病定义我的人生。于是，我开始了与病魔的较量，踏上了漫长而艰辛的治疗之路。

1. 病重

大概是 20 岁多一点的时候，我开始意识到自己的身体出现了问题。

最初，我只是感到有些不开心和情绪低落，但并没有特别在意，以为是正常的情绪波动，也可能是脾气天生暴躁、没有耐心。但随着时间的推移，这种情况变得越来越严重，我开始感到持续的悲伤、焦虑和紧张，以及恐惧，无法控制自己的情绪，逐渐失去了对生活的兴趣，对社交、工作甚至日常活动都觉得无趣和厌烦。同时，我也开始出现一些躯体和精神上的症状。比如，我出现了睡眠问题，总是难以入睡或早醒。还持续地感到疲劳和缺乏活力，即便有足够的睡眠时间，也仍然感到疲惫不堪，因为噩梦连连，每晚都是盗汗至全身湿透。就连注意力和记忆力也开始出现问题，无法集中精力去做事情，记不住任何事情。食欲也有变化，有时会暴饮暴食，但无论吃多少不到半小时就会出现饥饿感，有时又几乎没有食欲。还有身体上的疼痛，极度疼痛。整个后背尤其是上背和脖子，僵硬像石头。我必须去按摩才稍微缓解这种疼痛感，而且通常都是找男性盲人按摩，因为他们力气大。所有给我按摩过的人都说，从来没有遇到过像我的肩颈一样这么硬的，比肌肉男的还硬。现在才知道，那是神经绷紧导致经络紧张没有得到及时放松的原因。

如此多的症状，让我仿佛置身于一片混沌之中。我听不得任何冷言冷语，吵闹的声音更是让我感到烦躁不安，无法保持冷静。见到人群拥挤的地方，我总是会不自觉地颤抖，不愿意与人交谈，沉浸在自己无名的悲哀和焦虑中。我也曾经尝试着集中注意力去做一件事，但是每次都以失败告终。无论我多么努力地尝试，我的思绪总是会飘移，无法集中精力。这种感觉真的让我非常沮丧，我开始不断怀疑自己的能力。每一天，我都在努力寻找一个出口，一个能让我逃离这种痛苦的出口。但是，无论我走到哪里，都找不到一个安宁的地方。即使是在深夜，我也无法安然入睡，哪怕昏沉进入梦乡，也会有可怖的梦魇如影随形，纠缠不休。那血淋淋的梦境里总是在厮杀又或者被杀，再不然就是追杀，偶尔还会出现电影里的恐怖场景和邪灵。每当这时，我总是会从噩梦中惊醒，汗流浃背。此时的我害怕恐怖片，连恐怖片的宣传页都不敢看，对红色尤其敏感，每次看见红色都感觉莫名的冲动和兴奋，越来越不喜欢红色。

在这片混沌中，我仿佛成了一个旁观者，看着周围的世界，却无法融入、参与其中，感觉自己就像一片飘浮的落叶，无法找到归宿。这样孤立无援的日子，似乎永无止境。

最恐怖的事是，我感觉自己随时随地都会疯掉。脑海里总不受控制地回忆起童年时代见过的一个疯女人，她全身赤裸裸地在大街上奔跑，毫无羞耻地放声狂笑。她眼中只有纯粹的快乐，而没有其他任何的束缚和限制。我怕有一天自己也会像她这样，精神分裂之后失去自我控制，做出一些可怕的事情，例如赤裸地出现在大街上，又或者是伤害了身边的人等等。但偶尔又会觉得也许疯了对当时的我来说应该更好，起码不再被精神折磨，疯了就快乐了。

第二章　困兽笼中

其实，原本我也没有那么害怕自己会精神分裂。有次，有人告诉母亲，说省城的一个精神病专科看了保证能好，她带着我去了所说的那个专科。专科医生对我说："你的病就这样了，只能吃药控制……"更可怕的是她后面的话："抑郁症和精神分裂就在一线之隔，说不定下一秒你就会变成精神分裂。""下一秒……"脑子里不停地重复这三个字——下一秒！这样一番如今觉得不负责任的危言耸听的言论，在当时无疑是给我脆弱的精神上再架起个油锅煎熬我那吹弹可破的灵魂……对于一个精神极度脆弱的人来说，这是多么大的重击啊！一瞬间，天旋地转，我真的要疯了！空气凝重到停滞，我已经不能呼吸。自那以后，那个医生的话像是一个巨大的阴影，笼罩在我的头顶，让我无处逃脱，恐惧每一个下一秒。那时我的母亲也听进去了医生的话，"就这样了"，所以她不再理会我的病情。

当时我对自己的病症的了解确实非常有限，认为治疗就是医生的事，即便我了解了也是只能听医生的，"自救"这个词自始至终都没浮现于我脑中，从来没正视过这个问题，没有想过自己是不是应该去了解一下病症、病理以及康复手段，更不懂什么是自省，只单纯地认为医生说的就是对的，盲目地听从所有医生说的，寻医途中换了许多家医院和不同的科室，希望能够找到一个有效的治疗方法。然而，每个医生都给我开不同的药物，这些药物又基本带有极强的副作用。我清楚地记得，那些药物让我出现了恶心、呕吐、腹泻、皮肤红疹、晕厥、全身抽搐，还有酒瘾以及狂躁等一系列身体上的不适，还有那硬得发痛的脖子和锁骨处绷得紧紧的筋络都让我无比痛苦。同时，我的情绪也变得异常波动，时而兴奋，时而低落，仿佛在一座情感的过山车上无法自控。很多人都说我喜怒无常。

活着好累！难道就我一个人会这样吗？

当时我几乎每天都在无数次重复这句话。我开始担忧自己不会再有未来，不知道自己将如何面对这个世界，不知道是世界抛弃了我，还是我想逃离这个世界。

于是，我将自己与外界隔绝，连家人也不联系，当然他们也想不起来我。我把自己封闭在简陋的出租屋里，停掉了那些让我极度难受却对病情毫无帮助的药物，依靠电脑和酒精度日，一整件（12瓶，一瓶650ml）啤酒在天亮时分饮尽。白天也就吃一碗方便面，也有时候什么都不吃下，过着黑白颠倒的日子，很多时候两三天不睡，或者一天睡三四个小时就噩梦中惊醒。日复一日，如此反复。在这个一房一厅一卫的出租屋中，只有一张床、一台电脑、一个烧水壶，还有一个堕落的我。房间简陋无比，没有装修，墙面仍然是毛坯，月租仅需200元人民币。还记得那时候玩的是一款三国题材的网游，我充了不少钱在游戏里，看着角色成长、斗殴。游戏中的角色似乎映射了我的内心，我整天沉浸在游戏的群战中，每一次的战斗都会给我带来无尽的满足和快感。我似乎找到了一个可以发泄自己内心愤怒、狂躁和暴力倾向的出口。沉浸在虚拟之中，借助酒精和网游貌似忘却了自己情绪上的病态。

说到这里，我必须承认，自己真的是一个非常容易冲动且暴力的一个人。每个人都会幻想，而我的幻想常常沉浸在血腥和暴力的场景中，充斥着打斗、斗殴和流血的画面。我不太喜欢和人沟通，一旦意见不合，我就会选择沉默，拒绝与对方交流，大有一种老死不相往来的节奏。且每当有分歧的时候，我往往会采取极端的方式做个了断，只希望通过一次性的了断来解决问题，而不是通过理性的沟通来达成共识。我情绪上头时甚至会和人大打出手，因此赔了不少医药费，被警察带到公安局的事情也发生过很多次，已经严重影响了我的正常生活。

看到尖锐的物体，我就会产生一种强烈的冲动，想要拿它们扎人或者自己撞向它们，而且眼前还会出现撞上或者扎下去后血淋淋的画面；站在高处时，我甚至会有跳下去的冲动。这些思绪经常在脑中飘着，让我不知所措。为了避免这些冲动行为的发生，我会刻意避免去任何高处，甚至连二楼都不敢上；也不敢接触尖锐的物品，如剪刀、钉子或三角形的木条甚至于牙签等。

另外，当旁人大声说话时，我会变得非常烦躁。即便是亲人大声说话又或者是说太多，我也会无法忍受，想要对他们发脾气或采取暴力行为。有时候，我甚至会产生想要砸东西、打架的冲动，仿佛只有这样才能释放内心的压抑和愤怒，胸中总是有团怒火无处发泄，随时要燃爆似的，无论怎样都开心不起来。这或许和小时候的经历有关，大人们总是用训斥和体罚来镇压我的不听话。这种经历导致我认为武力可以解决一切问题，而沟通则显得多余，就是多余。

2. 治疗初期

一个朋友不忍看我再受折磨，他带着我去南京脑科医院，几乎看遍了每一个科室的每一个医生。我灰心了，可他坚持说还有几个专家心理医生，号不好挂但是已经网上排队买到了，一周后就可以问诊。这时候的我身边必须有值得信任的人，害怕独处，害怕陌生人，完全没有安全感，无论到哪里都要死死地拽着朋友的衣角，怕和他走散了我就会被陌生的一切吞噬。

在朋友的劝说下，我没有抱任何希望去了这位医生的诊室。第一次看诊时，医生以温和的语气引导我，让我逐渐敞开心扉，没有隐瞒地诉说出自己前些年经历，包括生活上的不良习惯以及曾经是个瘾君子，还有现在身体症状和精神上带来的痛苦。然而，随着谈话的深入，我好像没有什么痛苦，但是又非常痛苦，聊着聊着医生的语气让我不爽，带着敌意和嘲讽，这些言辞刺激到我。我努力压抑着情绪，试图保持理智，但最终还是没能控制住，情绪失控，拍桌而起，大声怒吼。令我没想到的是，这次并没有发生像以前那样的冲突。医生反而柔声向我道歉并解释，安抚我的情绪："我没有恶意。刚刚只是想看看你的容忍度到什么程度。"听到这样的解释，我感到震惊，同时也意识到，医生是在用一种特殊的方式帮助我面对自己的问题。漫长的问诊结束之后，我被确诊为双向情感障碍、中度抑郁和重度焦虑。医生为我开了四五种药物，并要求我一周复查一次。这次问诊是我寻医多年来第一次长时间对话，把生活上的点点滴滴问了个遍，之前的医生都是寥寥几句三五分钟问了症状就没多言语地给开了一堆药。

这次的治疗与以往的经历截然不同，虽然前三天刚刚服药的副作用让我非常难受，难受到心里说着"明天再这样我不会再吃药了"。但随着服药和复查的进行，医生每次都会给我打鸡血般的鼓励，加强我对康复的信心，我明显感觉到自己在逐渐好转。我的情绪逐渐稳定下来。原本持续的沮丧、无助和绝望感开始减少，取而代之的是一种平静和安心的感觉。两个月之后，我有了笑容，开始慢慢回归到正常的生活轨道中。虽然偶尔到人多的地方还是会紧张、冒冷汗，但是整个人的状态已经明显好转。医生告诉我，我可以逐渐减少药物的剂量和种类了。

听到这个消息的我是十分焦虑的。我害怕离开药物后又会回到之前的混乱无章中，那种痛苦和无助的感觉让我心有余悸。医生耐心地解释说，逐渐停药是治疗过程中的一个正常步骤，只要我继续积极配合治疗，注意自我管理和调整，就能够顺利度过这个阶段。他鼓励我要相信自己，相信治疗的效果。我很清楚地记得他说："你可以做到的。你是我所有病人里最不一样的，你很坚强。"这句话真的激励到了我，让我重新燃起了信心。于是，在医生的指导下，我开始慢慢地减少药物的剂量和种类。

停药的过程是十分艰难的，戒断反应带来的一系列如头痛、心慌、呕吐、腹泻、出汗、颤抖的副作用让我格外痛苦。也不排除这些反应是惊恐发作我不自知，医生说那个药里有冰毒成分，所以我必须靠自己的意志停下来，每当这时候，我就会想起医生的话，你可以做到的。你是我所有病人里最不一样的。我真的是不一样的吗？是的，我就是！肯定是！

三个月后，我已经只剩下最后一种药物，就是有上瘾成分的那个药。即将失去这个重要的辅助，我又开始隐隐担心。医生叮嘱我，最后的这个药物也要慢慢减少剂量，他建议我把每次的用药量分成很多份，每次逐渐减少一份。这时是2014年初，恰逢我的工作安排出差，需要出国。于是，我带着仅剩的一点药物和忐忑不安的心情来到了美国。我的第一次有效治疗暂告一段落。

3. 反复阶段

在出国之前，我一直在担心自己是否能够适应新的环境和生活方式。毕竟，离开熟悉的环境和亲朋好友，来到一个陌生的国度且语言不通，对于任何人来说都是一个挑战。我完全不会英文，读书的时候从来没有认真地学习过这一课，当然，别的科目也没认真学过。更何况，我还要面对抑郁症和焦虑症的困扰，担心自己在新的环境中无法应对挑战和压力。

值得庆幸的是，离开熟悉的环境，来到全新的世界，这种转变刺激着多巴胺的分泌，让我有机会从新的角度审视自己和周围的世界，主动或被动地认识新的朋友，尝试着与周围的人建立联系。他们来自不同的背景和文化，这让我可以试着了解和接纳不同的观点和价值观。另外，有限的社交活动，促使我把更多精力投入工作中。工作的顺利开展更是让我感到前所未有的充实和成就感。这些变化让我似乎忘记了过去的阴霾，忘记了曾经困扰我的抑郁症和焦虑症，整个人变得更加柔和和自信。

因为事业的顺利发展和病情的良好控制，我决定长居美国。也是在这段时间，我认识了我孩子的父亲，并在2015年迎来了我们的第一个孩子，我的大女儿。这个时期的我可谓是家庭事业双丰收，就在此时医生说我有产后抑郁症，可我没有觉得哪里不对，所以没有放在心上，"春风得意马蹄疾"，我开始飘飘然，觉得天都没有我大，眼里容不下任何人，一副地球少了我就不会转动的姿态。随之而来的是，我在感情里心胸狭窄，控制欲极强。我过于在意伴侣的一举一动，试图通过控制对方的行为和决策来确保自己的地位和安全。这种状态不仅让我的感情变得紧张而沉重，也让我深感疲惫和空虚。也许童年时生父给我留下的恶心的一面，导致我对所有男人都不信任。

获得绿卡后，我开始频繁地往返于国内和国外。生活似乎又回到了过去那种放纵和迷失的状态。酗酒、玩乐，这些曾经让我沉沦的事情再次占据了我的生活。这一阶段，我的病情再次突然复发，变得极度依赖孩子的父亲，几乎寸步不离地跟着他，甚至不允许他离开我的视线。任何一点微小的声音都会让我感到烦躁不安，对孩子也变得无心过问，雇佣两个保姆陪伴她玩耍就是，刷牙、睡觉翻身这些细微的声音都会让我大发雷霆、情绪失控。我会觉得任何人的笑容都是在嘲笑我，也会冒出"我不开心别人也不能开心"的情绪。暴力、狂躁的情绪又开始占据我的大脑，时常想拿一把刀，跟世界一起毁灭。

这时候的我就像一个被打破的瓷器，尖锐的碎片割伤了我自己的同时也刺向周围的人。

孩子父亲不忍心看我继续痛苦，带我去看西雅图专科医院的医生。到了医院后，医院的工作人员让我们先填一个单子，单子上的每个问题下都有几个选项。孩子父亲却在看完要填写的单子内容后，脸色逐渐变得苍白、神色紧张，紧紧拉着我的手用力到让我觉得疼，慌张地把我带出了大厅。我问他怎么了，他的声音带着无法掩饰的颤抖："如果你满足那张调查单上的其中任何两项，你就会被强制隔离治疗。我们不能继续待在这里了。我需要你，我们的孩子也需要你……"听着这话，我的大脑有一瞬间的空白，呆呆地看着诊室里带枪的警卫，庆幸孩子父亲把我带离了那里。同时也在想他为什么会带离我。

回家后，我们通过各种渠道找到了出国前治好我的那位南京医生，并回到国内接受治疗。然而，这次的治疗效果并不理想。因为怀孕，我的体质发生了非常大的变化，以前的药物失去了疗效，反倒是产生的副作用更加严重，导致我整个人发软、休克，整个人处于半瘫状态。

怀孕前，我从来没有过任何过敏反应。生完孩子后，我的身体似乎变得异常敏感，出现过敏原。还记得生产的时候，我在医院打点滴，我的接产医生急匆匆地跑过来，神情紧张地问我："你感觉怎么样？哪里不舒服？"我微微一愣，有些诧异地回答："我很好啊……"还没"啊"完，感觉到呼吸困难，眼前的景象瞬间模糊不清，立刻失去了意识。迷迷糊糊中知道自己被围在了一圈医生和护士中间，不知道过了多久，清醒过来，医护人员们微笑着对我说："没事了，放轻松。"原来，我刚刚整个脸都肿成了猪头，眼睛也肿成一条线，幸好医生及时在监控里发现了异常。这次与死神擦肩的经历一直让我心有余悸，不敢轻易尝试新东西，每次尝试一种新食物或药物时，我都会做漫长的心理准备，也是这次开始我对青霉素和芒果以及菠萝过敏，从此随身带着过敏药和肾上腺素注射剂，以备不时之需。

无奈之余，我们在国内找了新的医生，开始服用新的药物，并定期回中国做理疗。住院一个月的时候，我感觉自己又有了明显好转，药物和仪器理疗的效果非常显著，我每天都很开心，但是不知为什么，伴随着治疗的进行，我开始酗酒，从每天晚上半瓶红酒再到一瓶红酒、两瓶红酒、三瓶红酒……一种酒已经不够劲了，要混着烈酒喝。酒瘾越来越严重，甚至到了无法自控的程度。

时间来到2019年，也是我怀上小宝宝的一年，老家那一片的土地有了新的规划，政府要求迁移附近所有的墓地，其中就包括祖祖的。

祖祖的坟在山上，走上去要很久，上去之后还要穿过一片幽黑的墓地。没出国之前的那些年，我常常喝到凌晨三四点跑上去，坐在祖祖的墓碑前抽烟、喝酒，跟祖祖碎碎念地说话，将我所有的痛苦、悲伤、愤怒都倾诉给她。有时也会情绪失控，大声哭诉，质问祖祖为什么早早地离开我，责怪她为什么不把我一起带走，有时候期待坟墓裂开一个口子可以让我进去躺在她旁边，好让我彻底摆脱这个世界的痛苦和烦恼。然而，无论我怎么哭诉和责怪，那圆圆的坟墓始终沉默无声。只有那个月亮高悬，月光洒在墓碑上，也照亮我的脸庞，像是在安慰我，告诉我，她一直在那里，一直陪伴着我。

我们家是一个大家族，家族成员众多，但在迁坟的问题上，幺爷爷提出来后，没有几个人愿意掏钱。有人说："我又不跟老祖宗姓！"甚至有人说："老祖宗又没有保佑我发财，我凭什么拿钱给老祖宗迁坟？"得知这件事之后，我愤怒他们的凉薄，以为是迁坟的费用太高，他们无力承担。无论多少金额，我决定自己承担所有费用，打电话给幺爷爷询问具体的情况。然而，幺爷爷却告诉我，只需要四万多点。我愣住了，感到更加无语，只要四万块而已，这些人就不认老祖宗了。你们一人几百块钱心意也是能凑上的吧？还记得祖祖去世时，他们连祖祖的几床被子、几个枕头甚至碗筷都要瓜分掉，现在却说这样没有良心的话，做这样没有良心的事。

最终我全部承担了迁坟的费用，但因为各种原因无法抽身回国，我到现在还没去过祖祖的新墓地。不过，幺爷爷和三爹每年都会帮忙我祭拜爱我的祖祖。如果祖祖知道我现在已经为人妻、为人母，她肯定会为我的成长和幸福感到自豪，她会像曾经宠爱我一样，宠爱我的孩子们。老家的族谱上还留下了我女儿的名字，这让我很是欣慰。这族谱成了祖祖同我和我女儿之间唯一的联系纽带，给了我极大的安慰。无论时间如何流逝，无论生活如何变迁，这份独属于我们的情感都将永远存在。

自那以后，我一直保持着跟幺爷爷、幺奶奶他们的联系。不过他们逢年过节从不收我红包，总叫我照顾好自己和孩子，叫我不要担心惦记他们，他们一切都好，只是奶奶的身体大不如前，爷爷每天都照顾奶奶吃药和生活中的一切。这份亲情的温暖与坚韧，总能在某一些时刻像一束阳光温暖我的心房。

2020年，在疫情最严重的时候，我又生个宝宝了。孕期为了宝宝的健康，我停掉了所有治疗的药物，也强行戒掉了酒瘾，不过一天两三包的烟还是继续着。虽然这些药物在过去对我有一定的帮助，但在怀孕期间，我必须非常谨慎。咨询医生后，了解到我服用的药里有一种药物对胎儿不会造成不良影响，于是我决定暂时停止使用其他药，只服用一种。当然，随之而来的就是情绪的反扑，焦躁不安和恐惧又淹没了我。

有一次，我去做美容项目，操作时，我与医生闲聊。在听说我的状况后，他建议我可以通过运动和旅游来转移情绪，也可以尝试一下心理催眠。这位医生是ICU医生，有自己的美容工作室，对于职业医生的建议我相当上心。

回到家后，我就开始在网络上查西雅图的心理医生和催眠师，网上搜寻了很久终于让我发现了一位持证的中文心理催眠师。我抱着试试看的态度到了这位医生的诊所。诊所的氛围十分温馨简约舒适，可灯光对我来说太过于明亮。当我走进诊室时，医生微笑着迎接我。她看起来三十多岁，身材高挑，满脸笑容，眼神坚定。坚定到每次四目相对的时候她都想分个胜负，她的笑容让我感到亲切和放松。我们开始聊起天来，医生询问了我的一些基本情况，包括我的生活、工作和家庭等方面。但是接下来的两次就诊，让我感到有些失望。我们始终没有进入催眠的正题，医生只是简单地同我谈心，她总是说："下次就可以开始催眠了。"这两次问诊并没有对我造成太大的影响，我开始怀疑这个医生是不是徒有其名，也许她不懂催眠，犹豫治疗还要不要进行下去。

第三次治疗时，如果没有得到想要的催眠我就准备就不再看她了，无论催眠有没有效果，我就想要催眠。我们聊到了我生完孩子后体质改变导致的过敏问题。我告诉医生，我原本从未对芒果或青霉素过敏，但生完孩子后却出现了过敏反应。这让我在尝试新食物时总是感到极度焦虑，过度紧张时还会导致惊恐发作，甚至需要提前准备过敏药物以防万一。每次尝试新食物时都会感到极度焦虑，甚至需要提前准备过敏药物以防万一。医生解释说，这种过敏反应并不一定意味着我身体上的缺陷，而是身体的一种过度反应。她建议我保持积极的心态，逐渐适应新的体质变化，并寻找合适的方法来缓解过敏症状。而且过敏不会立马致死，之前打点滴青霉素过敏，严重呼吸困难以及肿胀是因为过敏原直接输入进血液，平时接触的食物量都不会太大，不会致死。而且世界上有很多人有过敏症，他们比我严重多了，但是也是健康地活着。过敏了大不了就吃个过敏药，很多人都靠每天吃过敏药来避免身体的过敏症状。

随着谈话的深入，我们话题逐渐转向了那个时时刻刻笼罩在我头顶的阴霾："抑郁症和精神分裂就在一线之隔……"医生还没听我说完，她双手一拍，皱着眉头说："哎呀，真会误人，知道你已经很脆弱了还吓唬你，太不专业了。"这举动让我憋了很多年的大气稍稍敢面对"下一秒"了。医生为我详细解释了抑郁症和精神分裂两者之间的关联与区别，她告诉我，它们之间虽然存在一定的相似性，但它们是两种不同的疾病，在症状、病因和治疗方法上都有很大的区别。这是我第一次真正接触到抑郁症的"真相"，也是这次才有了想去了解这个病症的念头。

这次问诊结束后，我关于过敏和精神分裂的心结终于被解开，对这位心理医生也建立起了信任。可是催眠还是没有进行，催眠已经在我心里萌芽，我要催眠。

有次高速堵车特别严重，只能以 3mile 时速挪动。突然"哐当"一下车被后面的车撞了。幸好车速非常慢，撞击并不严重。我回头问女儿有没有受伤或者哪里疼，她说没事，OK 的。我停车下去看了一下车尾，没有擦痕和损坏，那个撞我的人没有下车，只是挥手示意不好意思，此时本就拥堵的高速上被我挡住路的车喇叭按个不停。不会英文的我想着，人和车都没事就算了吧，免得麻烦，就上车继续拥堵着前行。可是随着时间的推移我开始恐惧开车，不知道是不是这次事件对我的影响，后来我根本无法开车，非常惧怕开车。孩子父亲开车带孩子一起陪我去心理医生的诊所，到达后我自己上楼就诊。跟医生诉说惧怕开车但是不确定原因，唯一能联系到导致不敢开车的原因只有这次。她和我梳理了一下事情所有经过，找到有可能导致我害怕的那个点，我配合她进行了催眠，问诊结束后，我下楼来到车前打开驾驶室的车门对孩子父亲说："下车！"他笑着半信半疑地问："你确定？"我点头确定，一脚油门踩下去打着方向盘，好像什么都没发生一样开车回家了。她又帮助我克服了新的恐惧。催眠真好，谢谢你，Lala！

秋冬交替之际，天气越来越冷，我开车送女儿上学。车内的暖气缓缓散出，却无法驱散我心中的烦躁。我感到一种莫名的压抑，女儿那些童言趣语现在听来就像喋喋不休的"紧箍咒"。情绪忽然就崩溃了，我大声喝止女儿："从现在开始不要再说话了！一句话都不要说！"女儿被我突如其来的严厉吓得愣住了，那双晶莹剔透的眼睛里充满了错愕和不解，她点了点头轻声问为什么，我发狂地大叫："你不要说话！"她"嗯"了一声安静了。抵达学校后，我赶紧把女儿送进去，给孩子父亲打去了电话，一通怒吼发泄。电话那头的他只是默默听着，偶尔安抚几句，却也莫名地让我慢慢平静了下来。

挂断电话后，我心中十分愧疚，女儿只是一个无辜的孩子，我作为母亲，却让她承受了我情绪的波动。想起女儿那张因我的大吼而泛起惊恐的小脸，我仿佛看到童年时的自己。这种内疚和痛苦点醒了我，催促着我去催眠师那里寻求帮助。

催眠师耐心地听我讲完发病的过程，安慰我之后，为我推荐了一位专业的精神科医生。

在美国看医生的经历确实与国内有所不同。这里的医生在开具处方前，会花费大量时间详细解释药物的副作用、作用机制以及我需要注意的事项。他们让我全面了解药性药理，甚至适当给我自己选择药物的权利。相比之下，我过去在国内看医生时，很少会得到这么详尽的解释。也是通过医生的讲解，我终于知道了我反复酗酒的原因——这也是药物的副作用，有一种药在治疗病情的同时也会让我产生强烈的酒瘾。这次治疗经历让我深刻体会到了药物的威力，也让我开始真正了解自己的病情。这次仍然要吃那会导致酒瘾的药，不过药量减半，而且只能偶尔难受的时候也是突发的时候应急吃。

在医生的指导下，我逐渐学会了如何选择合适自己的药物，并意识到不能一直依赖药物来维持情绪稳定。当我的状态逐渐稳定下来后，医生开始指导我逐步减少药量，直至最终停药。这个过程漫长且充满挑战，医生总是在我产生自我怀疑的时候给予我鼓励："你觉得自己有哪里不好呢？你明明很好！"最终，在医生的悉心指导和家人的陪伴下，我成功停药了。

4. "亦师亦友"的马医生

2022年，我有幸结识了一位80岁的老中医，马医生。朋友说，她因为焦虑导致的身体紧张不舒服，在马医生那里做了两次针灸就彻底好了，我听说之后，立刻决定去试一试，因为我很迫切地想要缓解病情导致的肌肉紧张，只要听说有任何能帮助康复的机会都会去尝试。

经过漫长的预约时间终于等来第一次问诊，他耐心地询问了我近半个小时的病症，最后并没有立刻为我进行针灸，而是给我开出了温胆汤的处方，并嘱咐我每天早饭后服用一剂，两个星期之后再来找他。我内心其实对药物有些抵触，更希望通过针灸得到直接的缓解，让自己紧张的身体放松下来。所以第二次看诊，马医生又让我吃两个星期温胆汤时，我有些不满了，出言不逊地挑衅道："马医生，你根本都不敢给我扎针，只会让我吃药！"马医生当时低头在写病例，没有做出任何回应。

服用温胆汤一个多月之后，马医生终于给我针灸了。但扎完，我还是紧绷着，感觉并没有任何作用。后续几次也还是这样，每次都有点怀疑，真的有用吗？回想一下刚到马医生这里问诊的时候和现在比较的的确确好转了一些，继续抱着半信半疑的状态继续针灸。

我每年有做定期的全身体检，那年的结果出来之后，医生跟我说："你的血小板有一点偏少，但是结合往年的数据来看，没有什么太大浮动。另外，你的胆囊有一些发炎，需要注意。"这个体检结果让我心里有了新的疑问，胆囊的问题是温胆汤引起的吗，还是马医生发现了症状才给我开的温胆汤？

转机总在不经意间，连续服用四个月之后，胆囊的问题有所好转了，马医生也给我更换了服用的药，换成了马医生自己研发的保健品——Peaceful，具镇定安神的作用。而且针灸进行到第三个月时，我惊喜地发现原本困扰我的经络疼痛逐渐减轻，月经也恢复了正常，颜色由深黑转为鲜红。在前期一年的针灸过程里我还是会有点紧张，听到隔壁病人的呼噜声还觉得很羡慕。现在我彻底放松了，能在扎针的时候进入睡眠状态。

2022年圣诞节，西雅图连续下了好几天大雪，交通受到了影响。而且圣诞节期间，诊所都已经放假了。面对突如其来的大雪，我没有提前规划拿够充足的药，导致中间有十来天停药。这些天，我的情绪波动很明显，也逐渐意识到Peaceful的作用了。

真的，身体有自己的节奏和力量，面对疾病与困扰，我们需要有耐心，有信心，有毅力。我的高敏感体质让我受尽了苦头，可是现在回头看还挺庆幸自己的高敏感。

记得刚在马老那问诊没多久的时候，我问他，这个病能不能治好，能不能根治？他很坚定地点头："能，肯定能治得好，只是需要时间来调理，你会逐渐康复的。"的确，在马医生那调理了一段时间以后，我身上的疼痛确实有所缓解。他每周为我进行一次针灸治疗，并配以药物调理，每次为我把脉时都会根据病情调整药方，效果逐渐显现。只是中医的疗效毕竟需要时间，不能立竿见影。

在例假前几天，我的情绪总是不太稳定，有时会闪过一些极端的念头，出现想抹脖子一了百了的想法，这让我十分震惊。我会开始自问自答：不是已经好了吗？几个月没有出现这样的思绪了？难道我会走上终结自己的路？我为什么会走上这条路？我的生活是绝大部分人都羡慕的，而我却想了结自己？我为什么要让自己被这些一闪而过的思绪扰乱？我需要整理一下自己的情绪，需要回顾一下是不是最近有什么事情刺激了自己。经过整理，我的思

第二章 困兽笼中

绪清晰了很多。这些念头曾经天天在我脑海里浮现，它们曾经如同顽固的藤蔓，日复一日地缠绕着我，试图在驾驭我脆弱的灵魂。但那只是过去，已是曾经。现在，我只是经前的正常情绪波动加上饥饿感所致，所以我需要吃点东西稳定一下血糖，拿出紫薯赶快大口大口地啃起来，没过一会果然没有那些乱七八糟的想法了。于是，我会随身准备一些小饼干和零食，确保自己不会饿肚子。因为我知道，饥饿感会让我情绪变得非常不稳定，想怒吼，会发狂般地愤怒，甚至出现过想吃人的念头，这种情况在经期前会更强烈。

逐步停止服用最后的那种西药时，我的家庭医生曾经劝阻过我，她有说到一句话："你怎么来对抗这个冬天呢？冬天就是会让人变得抑郁，你如果不吃药的话，我觉得你是无法跟这个冬天对抗的。"到现在我已经不太记得那个冬天有多难了，只隐约记得马医生给我进行了针灸治疗，有吃马医生自己研发的保健品能帮助平缓心情。那段时间我就是坚持加强运动，并在马医生的悉心调理下进行治疗。我内心坚信，运动能够带来改善，同时也深信马医生有能力彻底治愈我，让我摆脱对那些药物的依赖。马医生也建议我如果要断药，需要逐步减量，比如先减到十分之一的量，再慢慢停掉。就这样，我按照他的指导，一步步地、慢慢地度过了春天，最终彻底告别了那种药物。到现在，我已经有两年没有服用那种药了。

整个过程中，我相信自己，相信身体的潜能，也坚信马医生的专业与经验。正是这份坚定的信念，让我在断药的过程中没有轻易放弃，即使遇到困难和不适，也始终保持着积极的心态。信念不仅仅是一种心理支撑，更是一种实实在在的力量，它能激发我们内在的潜能，帮助我们克服一切困难。如今，我已经完全摆脱了药物的依赖，这不仅仅是因为马医生的精湛医术，更是因为我内心深处那份坚定不移的信念。

后来我感染了幽门螺杆菌，治疗的药物带来了严重的副作用，让我呕吐不止，无论吃什么都会立刻呕吐出来。短短两周内，我体重骤减了20磅，身体迅速消瘦。由于这种剧烈的呕吐症状，我去了好几次急诊室。医生开了止吐的西药，让我在睡前5小时内不能进食，甚至尽量连水都不要喝。尽管我严格遵守了这些医嘱，但一周过去了，呕吐的症状依旧没有得到有效缓解。

最终还是马医生通过针灸和中药为我调理，一周后我的胃开始好转，慢慢地开始吃一些比较清淡的食物。

这段时间我情绪很低落，因为吃药期间根本没有力气做任何的运动，稍微动一下就气喘吁吁，上楼都非常费力。康复之后，我逐渐恢复运动，逐渐加强运动强度，每天消耗大量能量，这也让我的情绪变得越来越好。有时我会想，如果小时候有人注意到我的体育精神，也许我会走上运动员的道路，用运动来抵抗那些不良的思绪。

在多次治疗中，我和马医生成了忘年交。虽然我们的年龄相差甚远，但他的医术和人格魅力让我深感敬佩。

问诊时，马医生会用简单易懂的语言给我科普医学常识。比如，提倡一日三餐不能过饱（马医生饮食很简单，但每天早上会吃一个煮鸡蛋）；还针对我的阴虚体质给了一些的饮食建议，例如可以多吃甲鱼、黑豆、鲍鱼等具有滋阴作用的食物，而人参、虾、红枣这些性温滋补的就要少吃。除了医学方面的指导，马医生分享的一些人生感悟也总能让我对生活有新的理解和感悟，坚定我治疗的信念。不过他话不多，总是短短一两句话。

在马医生那里看病大概半年时，我主动提起当初对马医生的挑衅，表达歉意。马医生只是温和地笑笑，不知道是已经忘记了还是压根就不在乎。他的宽容温和不仅让我感到敬佩，也让我对自己当初的行为感到羞愧。我意识到，自己的挑衅不仅无助于解决问题，反而会让自己更加固执和狭隘。遇到问题时，多像马医生一样，以开放和包容的心态去倾听和了解，也许会有不一样的效果。从那以后，我更加尊重和信任马医生。

写这段文字时，我突然意识到一件有趣的事情：近两年的问诊里，我竟然从来没有见过马医生的真面目！因为每次见面都是在诊所，马医生都戴着口罩。这件事倒是很符合我印象中的马医生的性格。他人很内敛，不多言不多语，讲话总是一针见血，直击问题核心。谈及自己的专业领域时，马医生曾说过，医生要有自己的判断，不能被患者的陈述带着走，因为患者往往只强调自己认为重要的信息，反而会影响医生的诊断；关于医患关系，他还说，患者愿意给医生聊一些他们不告诉他人的私事，这说明患者信任你；在面对生活和工作时，马医生强调效率，认为做事要快，不能拖拉，这样才会有时间做更多的事情。他就像一位深藏不露的武林高手，让人不禁想起武侠小说中的隐世高人。

马医生已经80岁了，眼也不花，耳也不聋，对病人亲和又有耐心。在美国，看病通常需要提前预约，但马医生为我破例了。那段时间我情绪特别不好，时好时坏的，他特意叮嘱我说："你的情况比较特殊，如果有什么突发事件，可以不用预约，直接过来就行。"

他老婆姓李，医术也很高明。而且李医生人很友善，对我的问题都会耐心解答，详细科普。他们相继在西雅图和贝尔维尤都开了诊所，两个人分别负责。最近几年，马医生已经进入半退休状态了，本来决定以后只在贝尔维尤坐诊周六一天，但是西雅图的老病人们有意见："你不能有了新病人，就不管老病人了呀！"面对这一番真诚的诉求，马医生觉得，不能因为自己的退休计划而忽视了那些一直以来信任和支持他的老病人，每周二继续在西雅图诊所坐诊。

我曾经在候诊的时候和李医生闲聊，谈到她的专长时，李医生表示她更擅长妇科和消化内科方面。等到扎针的时候，我就好奇地问马医生："李医生说她擅长妇科和消化内科，您呢？您对哪一科比较精通？"马医生的回答出乎我的意料，他带着一丝傲娇地说："每一个中医都是'万金油'，我每科都很厉害！"哈哈！这是我第一次见到如此孩子气的马医生，他对自己的专业充满自信。事实也是如此。

在我向马医生透露了自己要写书的想法。他听后非常支持我，鼓励我说："我是很赞同的，把你的经历和感受写下来，给更多和你一样的人看到，如果能帮到他们走出困境，这是一件好事。"马医生的话给了我很大的动力和信心，让我下定决心要写好这本书。

看医生、服药、催眠——我经历了一段漫长而艰难的治疗之路。从最初的迷茫和恐惧，到后来的接受和坚持，每一步都充满了挑战和不易。我也开始明白，治疗的过程并非总是直线前进，它充满了曲折和反复。有时候，我会因为药物的副作用而感到沮丧，有时候，我会因为治疗的进展缓慢而感到焦虑。但正是这些起起伏伏，让我学会了耐心，学会了在等待中寻找力量。

现在，当我回望这段治疗的旅程，我心中涌起深深的感激。感激那些在我生命中出现的专业医生，他们的专业知识和关怀给了我希望；感激那些陪伴我渡过难关的家人和朋友，他们的支持和鼓励给了我力量。

"困兽笼中"，相信这不仅仅是我个人的经历，更是每一个被疾病侵袭的灵魂所共同体验的挣扎与抗争。我愿意将我的经历分享给每一个正在经历类似困境的人。愿你从我的故事中获得一些启示，找到自己的力量和勇气。记住，无论多么艰难的治疗过程，都只是生命旅程中的一部分。我们有能力，也有权利，去追求健康和幸福。

第三章　心理的轮廓

焦虑和抑郁就像隐藏在暗处的影子，悄悄地影响着我们的生活。它们的存在，并非显而易见，却能深刻地改变一个人的感受、思维和行为。了解并认识这两位"不速之客"，是我们战胜它们的第一步。

在这一章，我将带您走进心理疾病的世界，揭开它们的神秘面纱。更重要的是，我将分享一些实用的小技巧，帮助缓解这些症状。这不仅仅是一个科普的过程，更是一次心灵的对话。在这里，我们不设限、不评判，只为了更深入地理解自己，更真诚地面对内心的感受。让我们一起踏上这段旅程，去绘制出心理的轮廓，去发现那些隐藏在日常生活中的心灵密码。

1. 抑郁和焦虑的真相

算下来，我与抑郁症、焦虑症对抗已经有近二十年了。日子最黑暗的时候，我感觉自己像是被困在一个没有光的隧道里，长时间地悲伤、焦虑、暴躁和失眠，几乎忘记了生活中的美好。康复过程中，我重新发现了那些被忽略的细微乐趣。品尝一杯咖啡的香醇，感受阳光洒在皮肤上的温暖。康复是一场心灵的旅程，饱含艰辛但也充满希望。在漫长的治疗过程中，我了解到了抑郁症和焦虑症的真相，也找到了一些缓解症状的小技巧，有从医生那里学来的，也有我自己摸索到的。在这里分享给大家，希望能为那些正在经历低谷、需要一线光明的人们提供一点帮助和慰藉。

当我们谈论抑郁症时，许多人常常误以为这只是暂时的情绪低落，却忽视了它背后复杂的生物学和社会心理学原理。事实上，抑郁症是一种严重的心理疾病，像一块巨大的暗影，笼罩在无数人的心头。抑郁症并非简单的"坏心情"，而是由生物、心理和社会多重因素交织影响而成的情感性精神障碍疾病。生物学因素包括遗传倾向、神经递质不平衡和慢性疾病等；心理因素涉及自尊心、应对策略和童年经历等；社会因素则包括人际关系、生活压力和重大生活事件等。这些因素相互作用，导致抑郁症的发生。患者常常表现为无精打采、疲乏无力、失眠多梦、食欲减退等症状，并且在独处时可能出现明显的情绪低落、兴趣丧失、压抑等情绪。而焦虑症属于神经症，主要特征是广泛性和持续性的焦虑或反复发作的惊恐不安，常常伴有自主神经功能紊乱、肌肉紧张与运动不安等症状。

尽管焦虑症和抑郁症在症状上有所不同，但它们在某些方面也存在联系。两者可能会相互伴随出现，也就是在一个人身上同时或先后出现，我就是这样一个例子。另外，它们在治疗手法上也有一定的相似性。

面对抑郁症和焦虑症，我们需要调整心态，以一种更为理性和接纳的态度来面对。首先，要意识到这是常见的疾病，而非简单的情绪波动。它不是软弱的代名词，也不是个人意志力的失败。你抑郁了并不是你的错，不是你矫情，不是你脆弱，不是你不够坚强。你只是生病了，就像天冷天热的时候人会感冒一样，就像人吃五谷会生病一样。抑郁也不过是一场精神上的感冒而已，它需要的是专业医生的专业治疗和管理。我们无须为之感到羞耻。

我和马医生曾经就抑郁症的话题聊过。马医生跟我讲，他很痛心现在的小孩子。很多家长在教育孩子的过程中，会对孩子施加各种学业、行为规范、未来规划等的要求，过于严厉的教育方式可能会让孩子承受巨大的压力。有些家长甚至误解孩子的情感表达，把他们的负面情绪视为矫情或者无病呻吟，不理解孩子痛苦和困境。这些情绪如果得不到及时的排解和疏导，逐渐累积肯定会对孩子造成负面影响。还有很多家庭不能接受孩子患上抑郁症的事实，认为这是一件羞于启齿的事情。无论是轻视还是以之为耻，家长的不理解和不支持都会让孩子感到孤立无援。家长们应当努力去了解抑郁症的相关知识，也许在抑郁症刚刚出现苗头的时候就能将其扼杀在摇篮里。

正确认识这两种病症并接受它们是第一步，及时寻求专业医生的帮助和建议是第二步。

2. 与自我和解

除了接受药物治疗，我还有一个定期的心理辅导，每周我们都会讨论一些不同的话题。例如，在经期的前几天，我的脑海中经常会一闪而过地出现抹脖子的画面。跟心理咨询师打电话时，她说她偶尔也会有这样的想法。一个专业的心理咨询师也会出现这样消极的念头，那敏感脆弱的我们又怎么能躲得过呢？所以我们要接受负面情绪的出现，并及时化解它们，学会定期释放心理压力，找一个亲近的、值得信任的家人朋友倾诉或找专业的心理辅导敞开心扉聊一聊。把一些最近发生的事情和期待的事情都整理出来聊上一聊，聊完后会发现那些压在肩头让我们喘不过气的事物其实并不是不能解决，有很多方式可以选择，极有可能是我们看事情的角度不一样，局限了最终的选择。

比起与认识的人倾诉我更倾向于和心理辅导倾诉，因为他们的专业知识能引导我们偏激的思想回归正轨，审视压力来源。仔细思考导致压力的原因，是工作压力还是人际关系压力？是健康问题还是其他因素？了解问题的根源后更有助于制定解决问题的方案。即便不能彻底解决，也可以找到一种能接纳的方式去和解。在制定可行的解决方案时，可以将问题分解成小步骤并逐一解决，可能更容易应对。

还有很重要的一点，我们要学会接纳自己，不要过于苛责自己且追求完美。尤其是在这个信息爆炸、美颜滤镜充斥的时代，人们对美的定义变得模糊而扭曲，容貌焦虑、身材焦虑等问题层出不穷。也有人沉迷在美颜后的自己不能自拔，导致无法接受现实中的自己。像我自己，就不是很能接受衰老这件事。在马拉松比赛结束后，我收到了官方邮寄的纪念照片，跟手机里几年前拍的照片对比明显憔悴了很多，身材也变得臃肿，这让我很焦虑。但有时候看看那些明星的路透生图，他们40多岁时脸上也是布满了细纹，皮肤状态也不是很好，脸部肌肉也是松弛的。这时心里就能得到一点安慰，觉得驻颜有术的明星都逃不过，那我只是一个普通人，又怎么抵挡得过呢？

我女儿画室同学的妈妈Jenny，是个美貌与智慧并重的女性。每次见到她，我都会被她优雅的气质吸引，尤其是她保持得极好的身材，长腿细腰。然而，让我颇感意外的是，一次闲聊中我得知她竟然有很严重的体重焦虑症。她每天都会盯着磅秤看，体重一旦略有上升就会非常不安。就连如此优秀的女性也难以逃脱对身材的焦虑，可见这种压力在社会中的普遍程度。

在学英语的时候，有一个问题关于出生年月日。和我同组的一位老太太，大概75岁，非常抗拒回答这个问题，她不停地发脾气大吼，很明显能够感觉到她对自己年龄的回避。我跟她说："你可以说你18岁，每天都是18岁。"她笑了，嘎嘎大笑。这样的逃避其实也未尝不可。老太太虽然年事已高，但对学习的热情却丝毫不输于年轻人。虽然岁月已经在她的脸上留下了痕迹，但她的内心依然保持着年轻和活力。75还是18，还有那么重要吗？

不管是服老还是不服老，我们都需要学会接纳自己。年龄只是一个数字，它并不能决定我们的价值和魅力。真正让我们与众不同的，是我们的心态和态度；真正让我们美丽的是内心的平静与自信，是对生活的热爱和积极态度。马拉松照片中的我虽然多了一些皱纹和憔悴，肉肉也不再紧实，但是眼中闪烁的坚韧和毅力让我看起来还是一样的光彩照人，别有一番岁月沉淀和经历累积后的美丽。我开始欣赏自己坚韧不拔的精神，欣赏自己为了目标而努力的模样，逐渐放下对"永葆青春"的执念。

缓解焦虑、处理压力是一个循序渐进的过程，需要耐心和时间。勇敢寻求专业的帮助，有助于更有效地应对病情。还有一点非常重要，就是不要完全听信任何人说的话，自己要学会思考、分析。帮助我解决过很多心理问题的心理医生就对我说过这样的话，无论任何人都不能过度依赖。

3. 缓解失眠

　　失眠是我每天晚上都要面临的难题，也是最让我沮丧的症状。明明已经很累了，一整天经历了很多事情，比如工作一整天还跑了五公里，明明应该倒头就睡的情况，我的大脑却异常清醒。数羊、深呼吸、想象平静的画面……各种助眠方法试完一圈，还是很难入睡。哪怕睡着了，也是疲惫不堪。睡着之后的我仿佛分裂成了两个不同的自我。一个陷入无休止的梦魇，另一个则飘浮在半空冷眼旁观，看着自己在噩梦中挣扎。始终不能进入深度睡眠，这一晚上完全不能缓解我身体上的疲惫，反而又造成精神上的焦虑。

　　在解决睡眠问题的时候，我发现了一种成功率比较高的方法：不要再过度关注入睡的过程，不要设定任何关于睡眠的期望。比如要求自己一定要在十一点之前睡着，这样只会让自己更加焦虑。关上灯，轻松自在躺在床上休息，放一个定时关闭的轻音乐或者催眠引导（我听一个催眠引导三年了，现在只要一播放我就能在很短的时间内睡着），眼睛自然睁开或者半睁半闭，可以胡思乱想，可以翻来覆去，选择自己最舒服的状态就好。不要再焦虑地追求睡眠，也不要再急于求成。当我们这样平静地躺在床上，我们就已经进入了休息的状态，这本身就是一种睡眠的形式。当然，保证房间足够黑暗，不要再去看手机，不要再做会让大脑高度兴奋的事情。如果在这样的放松中不经意间进入了梦乡，那就让它发生；如果依然清醒，也无需担忧。实在睡不着，就干脆就坐起来，做一点安静且会让自己放松的事情，完全不动脑子地随便拿着笔乱画一些东西，或者是写一点字，漫无目的地去写或记录一些东西。又或者闭着眼睛在这份宁静里寻找那些细微的声响，然后去想象那些声响的源头和场景，这也是冥想的一种。比如，听到水龙头没关好的滴水声，我们可以想象一下那个情景。水滴滴落下来散开时的样子，第二滴水又会在什么时候落下……慢慢地，你会发现在这个过程中整个人放松了，继续去脑补场景的时候在不知不觉中就进入睡眠状态了。

你的目标只是享受这份宁静的休息时光。如果半夜醒来，也不用懊恼，不要看手机计算自己的睡眠时间。保持安静且黑暗的环境，让自己继续享受休息状态就好。尽管醒着，也可以继续享受放松的感觉，不受外界干扰。闭上眼，放松身体，让自己逐渐沉浸在宁静的氛围中，或许你会再次进入梦乡，继续拥有宝贵的休息时间。这样，你不仅不会因为醒来而感到困扰，反而能够更好地保持放松和宁静。

在这个过程中还可以辅以深呼吸。深呼吸，不仅仅是一种生理上的调节，更是一种心灵的抚慰。当我们深深吸入空气时，胸腔扩张，氧气充盈肺部，随着血液流动至全身，也带走了紧张和焦虑。许多人发现，将深呼吸纳入睡前例行程序，不仅可以帮助更快地进入梦乡，还能提高了睡眠质量。实践深呼吸并不复杂。躺在床上，闭上眼睛，将一只手放在腹部，另一只手放在胸口。慢慢地，深深地吸气，感受腹部的隆起，然后缓缓地呼气，让腹部回落。重复这样一个简单的过程，让心随着呼吸的起伏平静下来。现在，每当我感到焦虑或难以入睡时，我都会进行深呼吸练习，它已经成为我生活中不可或缺的一部分。

4. 饮食疗法

当我们的情绪波动幅度比较大时，保持规律的饮食习惯显得尤为关键。

想象一下，当你感到饥饿时，身体内部的化学平衡可能会被打乱，血糖水平可能会下降，这可能导致你的大脑释放压力激素，如皮质醇。这些激素的释放会使你感到紧张、易怒和焦虑，让你误以为自己被消极情绪完全控制，仿佛永远都无法摆脱这种困境。其实这是一种非常正常的生理反应，即使是身体健康、心态平和的人，在饥饿时也会更加易怒。

因此，保持规律的饮食习惯对于控制情绪波动至关重要。只有规律地摄取足够能量，身体维持正常的血糖水平，大脑才有力气应对情绪的波动。为了建立健康的饮食习惯，我们可以制定一个合理的饮食计划，比如，每天定时定量吃三餐，设定固定的用餐时间，并尽量保持每餐摄入的量相对一致，有助于身体适应并做好消化食物的准备；均衡饮食，在食物选择上，确保包含足够的蛋白质、健康脂肪、纤维、维生素和复合碳水化合物，如瘦肉、鱼类、豆类、新鲜蔬菜和水果等；尽量避免高糖食物，高糖食品虽然能短暂提升血糖，但随后可能导致血糖急剧下降，从而引发情绪波动；保持充足水分，因为脱水也会影响情绪和认知功能。

记住，情绪波动是生活的一部分，而通过保持规律的饮食和采取积极的自我管理策略，可以更好地进一步控制这些波动，减少它们对我们生活的影响。不要害怕寻求帮助，也不要忽视自己的感受，有很多小技巧可以帮助我们逐步建立起更健康、更稳定的情绪状态，让我们更加平静、自信地面对生活的挑战。

5. 公园效应

在和抑郁症斗争时，我还发现了一个简单却强大的自愈方法——"公园效应"。科学研究已经证明，自然环境对人类心理健康有着积极的影响。项由芬兰于韦斯屈莱大学进行的研究发现，即使是在自然环境中短暂停留，也能显著降低人体的压力激素水平，并振奋心情。我的"公园效应"正是基于这样的发现。无论日程多么繁忙，每隔一段时间我都会尽量抽出 20 分钟，在公园进行简单的散步或只是坐在长椅上，享受周围的自然美景。这 20 分钟的自然沐浴带来的转变是很显著的，一开始我可能会因为过于安静而感到焦虑或沮丧，但在这 20 分钟里，我放慢脚步深呼吸，让自然的气息充满我的肺部，让自然的景象占据我的感官。随着时间的推移，焦虑和沮丧的情绪开始慢慢退去，取而代之的是内心的平静和安宁。自然环境为我提供了一种"恢复性体验"，身处其中，我感觉自己在被一点点"修复"。

除了心理层面的慰藉，生理方面的复苏也格外明显。阳光是身体产生维生素 D 的主要途径。维生素 D 在大脑功能中扮演着重要角色，特别是在情绪稳定和认知能力的维护上。研究显示，维生素 D 的缺乏与抑郁症、焦虑症等情绪障碍的风险上升之间存在密切关联。所以多晒晒太阳，有助于预防维生素 D 缺乏，更能有效地维护我们的心理健康。阳光还对调节我们的生物钟至关重要。生物钟，也被称为昼夜节律，是我们身体内部的时间管理系统，它影响着睡眠、醒来、饮食、激素释放等多个生理过程。适量的阳光照射有助于设定和维持正常的生物钟，从而改善睡眠质量，减少昼夜节律紊乱的风险，这对于抑郁症患者尤其重要，因为睡眠问题常常与抑郁情绪相关联。此外，自然环境中的新鲜空气富含负氧离子，这些离子能够促进新陈代谢的活跃，进而增强免疫系统的功能。

我鼓励每一位抑郁症患者都尝试"公园效应"。不需要特别的计划或长时间的徒步旅行，哪怕只是在公园里静静地坐着，也足以让你感受到自然的美好。记住，这 20 分钟是属于你的，让自己沉浸在自然之中，感受它的疗愈力量。

6. 漂浮疗法

漂浮疗法又叫感觉剥夺疗法。通常会在一个隔音、光线昏暗的漂浮舱或漂浮池里进行。漂浮舱里会注入大约 20 厘米的温水，温度与人体皮肤温度相近，以确保舒适感。水中溶解了大量的泻盐（硫酸镁），让水的密度大大增加，足以让人轻松漂浮在水面上。

完全摆脱重力的束缚，让自己在一片温暖、安静的环境中漂浮，这听起来像是某本科幻小说中的情节，但实际上这正是漂浮疗法带给我的独特体验。

我第一次接触漂浮疗法时，心中既充满好奇也带着些许紧张。随着液体的逐渐升高，浮力也逐渐变大，仿佛整个身体都被温柔地托起，漂浮在无垠的宇宙中。我闭上眼睛，耳边只有轻微的水声和自己的呼吸声，任由自己漂浮，感受着每一个细胞都在水中自由地舞动，很快进入"放空"状态。身体在逐渐放松，心灵也在逐渐平静。我能够清晰地感知到自己的每一个感受，从轻微的触摸感,到温暖的包裹感,再到宁静的心灵状态,一切都清晰而又真实。

漂浮还让我的肌肉得到了前所未有的放松。足够的浮力让我有机会摆脱重力的束缚,从最小的手指到整个脊柱,都能得到彻底的深层次的放松;我的肌肉不需要支撑自身的重量,也不需要再抵抗地心引力,这种体验是日常生活中难以感受到的。它为我提供了一种非药物的疼痛缓解方法。而且,肌肉的深度放松也有利于改善睡眠质量。

当漂浮结束后,我整个人都焕然一新,仿佛刚刚经历了一场深度的睡眠。在让我体验到身体的放松的同时,也给了我一个机会,让我能够短暂地离开日常生活的喧嚣,与内心深处的自己对话。我开始意识到,生活中的许多压力,其实都是我们自己给自己的负担。

7. 运动疗法

情绪波动、焦躁不安的时候还可以尝试通过几种疗法进行缓解。

五感法就是字面上的意思,视觉、听觉、嗅觉、味觉和触觉。抑郁和焦虑往往会让我们陷入负面情绪的循环中,通过五感法,我们可以将注意力从负面的思维中转移出来,专注于感官的体验。每个感官都可以成为一种放松和舒缓的方式。例如,可以仔细观察周围的景物和人物,尤其注意他们的细节和特点。又比如,最近不停地下雨,让我心情很不好。我就会闭上眼睛去感受外面的雨,去脑补窗外的画面,看那个雨滴声是从哪里来的,哪里的雨滴声最大。时不时会有飞机飞过的声音,然后我也会同样地闭上眼睛,仔细听飞机声,我就会辨别它是从哪个方向飞向哪一边。然后脑补到飞机灯的样子、整个飞机的造型以及它随着声音渐行渐远的画面。将听觉无限放大,那么那些原本令人恼怒的声音,也许就变成了一组气势宏大的交响乐。我喜欢咖啡和巧克力,遇到情绪不能自控的时候,我就会有意识地在脑海中想象咖啡、巧克力的香气和口感。还可以触摸一些柔软的物品,如手边的毛绒玩具、柔软的布料等，感受它们的触感和温度。五感法的魅力在于，它教会我们在情绪波动，或者无法控制地焦虑时，如何抓住当下空间中最明显的感受，并将其无限放大。这种转移注意力的方法，能够很有效地帮助我们逃离当下负面情绪的困扰。

另外一种有效的缓解技巧是呼吸法，深呼吸能放松身体，放松紧绷的神经。其中瑜伽呼吸法有很多种练习方式，包括腹式呼吸、胸式呼吸、腹胸式完全呼吸和单鼻孔清理经络呼吸等。但最基本的呼吸练习可以分为循环阶段：吸气、憋气、呼气，再憋气，一直循环。我会找一个安静的地方坐下或者躺下，闭上眼睛，慢慢地深吸气，心里从一数到四，然后憋气，再慢慢地呼气，感受气息在身体中流动的感觉。每个阶段都保持四个数的时间，这个过程其实很漫长，呼吸的同时会一直期待下一个四的到来。随着练习的进行，学会控制自己的呼吸后，我们还可以适当增加每个阶段的时间，从四到五，到六……就这样，在一吐一吸中，注意力完全从焦躁的心境转移到呼吸上，重新找回平静和松弛感。

除此之外，还可以尝试一些简单的身体运动来缓解焦虑，释放紧张感。

首先，坐在椅子上，把双腿放松放在地板上。然后，慢慢地摇动双腿，让脚尖轻轻触碰地面。感受腿部肌肉的放松和自然地运动，并逐渐加大摇晃的幅度。同时，保持呼吸的顺畅，将注意力集中在腿部的摇晃上，让心情随着摇摆而逐渐平静。

你也可以尝试手臂轻拍。将手臂伸展开来，然后用另一只手轻轻地拍打或轻拍手臂。从手腕开始，逐渐向上拍打到肩膀，然后再返回。注意放松手臂肌肉，避免用力过猛。让拍打的感觉渗透进你的肌肤，带走手臂的紧张感，给你带来一丝舒适。

尝试转动你的头部和颈部。慢慢地从一侧转向另一侧，然后再回到中间位置。接着，将头部轻轻倾斜到一侧，感受颈部的伸展，然后再换到另一侧。进行这些动作时，记得保持呼吸平稳，让头部和颈部自然转动，不必过于用力。

还有深蹲和舒展。站立时，确保双脚与肩同宽。然后，缓慢地弯曲膝盖，进行深蹲，再慢慢站起。重复这个动作，注意感受腿部和背部肌肉的变化。多做几次之后还可以增加动作的难度，例如抬起脚跟，只让脚尖着地保持支撑。还加入一些简单的伸展动作，如举手、弯腰等，让身体更加舒展。

即便是不能有大幅动作的场合，你也可以通过伸展和弯曲手指来帮助放松手部的肌肉。逐渐转动手腕，提高手指和手腕的灵活性，也可以尝试轻轻握拳，然后逐渐打开手指，这样也有助于缓解手部的紧张感。

这几个简单的运动不需要太多的准备和技巧，大家不妨在紧张焦虑的时候试一试。但是，在运动时要注意感觉和呼吸。这些运动应当是轻柔而舒适的，我们的目的是放松身体而不是引发过度劳累或者身体上的疼痛。个人的舒适度和健康状况始终是第一位的。

以上就是我在多年患病中总结出的经验和技巧，分享给正在看书的你，希望能够让更多人认识到心理健康的重要性，鼓励大家在面对心理困扰时，勇敢地寻求帮助，积极地采取行动，希望能给到你或你的家人朋友帮助。

现在，虽然我仍然偶尔会有焦虑和抑郁的时候，但我已经不再害怕它们。我知道如何与它们共处，如何从中找到力量。通过学会接纳自己、寻找支持、培养积极思维、品味生活乐趣和设定小目标，我逐渐找回了自己。不再被过去的伤痛所困扰。我逐渐明白，每个人都有不完美之处，而这并不是我必须隐藏的秘密。接纳自己，让我更加真实地面对内心的挣扎，康复并不是终点，而是一个重新定义生活、迎接新可能性的起点。

而且，看待事物的角度也很重要。曾经，每当我驾车出行，遇到有人在路上疾驰超车，甚至不惜逆行，我的第一反应总是满心的抱怨与不解，心想：这人怎么这么不顾自身安危，如此讨厌？然而，有一次，当我再次遭遇这样的情景，旁边的阿姨却以一种截然不同的视角看待此事，她轻声说："或许人家真的有急事，才不得已而为之。"那一刻，我心中不禁一震，恍然大悟：为何我总是习惯性地往消极的方向想，只看到他人行为中负面的部分，而忽视了背后可能隐藏的正当理由或紧急情况？如今，我也开始学着转变思维，学会了从积极的角度去理解他人的行为，不再武断地轻易下结论。

康复是一个循序渐进的过程，给自己一些时间和空间去适应和改变。在这个过程中，保持耐心、保持对自己的善意至关重要。当然，抑郁症是一种复杂的心理疾病，每个人的状况都不尽相同，需要综合考虑多种因素来制定治疗方案。如果需要治疗，我们还是要以医生的建议为准。

第四章　汗水的折光

在这一章，我们将探索一个充满力量和活力的主题——运动。对于每一位热爱运动的人来说，它是一种生活方式，一种自我表达，一种与世界连接的方式；而对于那些尚未体验过运动魅力的人，这将是一次全新的发现之旅。

1. 爱上运动

生完儿子半年后，我应朋友之邀开始尝试运动。

在瑜伽馆运动时，我觉得音乐好吵，不懂为什么开那么大声。但是那一次的经历让我感受到运动后的轻松，仿佛身体内的疲惫都被清除了。虽然第二天往往肌肉酸痛，浑身疲惫。

在那家瑜伽馆，所有的人都讲中文，这让我打心底觉得放松。坚持瑜伽锻炼半年后，我发现我原来僵硬的左手可以轻松抬起，驼背的情况也得到了缓解。更令我惊喜的是，通过这半年的运动，我惊恐发作的次数明显减少了，对声音也不再那么敏感，只有偶尔的时候才会觉得音乐太吵。

但是当时我还没意识到这是运动的功劳。直到 2022 年夏天，因为一些原因，我离开了常去的瑜伽馆，暂时停止运动。恰逢孩子们放暑假，我们一家人去了夏威夷度假。那是一个充满阳光和海风的假期，我们尽情地享受着海滩、美食和当地的文化，虽然刚到夏威夷的第二天，我因为时差状态极度不好。一场愉快的旅行让我完全放松下来。而且我一直觉得运动一定要在健身房，因为胆怯说英文没有去找健身房，就没有像之前那样保持运动。旅行结束后，我发现自己的情绪开始变得有些低落。尽管我尝试调整自己的心态，但始终无法摆脱那种莫名的烦躁和不安。

　　为了寻找释放情绪的途径，我开始在网上搜索合适的瑜伽馆。幸运的是，我找到了一家说中文的教练授课的瑜伽馆。我立刻预约了课程，希望通过瑜伽来调整自己的状态。第一节课的前半程，我心里总觉得憋着一股无名火，教练和其他学员的说话声也让我感到烦躁。尤其是旁边的那个女人，总发出嘲笑的声音，每当我提问教练一些问题教练回答的时候，她在旁边一直发出"哼，哼，哼"的声音，不可一世的样子不知道在哼什么。但随着课程的进行，身体逐渐进入了一种熟悉而舒适的状态，我开始专注于身体的每一个动作，感受着肌肉的拉伸和呼吸的流动。每一次深呼吸，都带走了我心中的一丝烦躁，为我注入了平静的力量。随着汗水的分泌，怒气也似乎在一点一点地消散，我的心情开始变得轻松愉悦，突然扑哧笑出声。

　　从这开始，我意识到了运动的重要性。随着时间的推移，我开始跟随健身博主进行举铁训练，尝试在综合健身房中挥洒汗水。那个健身房挺大，设备齐全，从力量训练器械到有氧运动器材一应俱全。在那里还有各种教练定时上免费课程，我接触到了许多以前从未尝试过的运动方式：壁球、游泳、尊巴舞、动感单车……每一种都带给我不同的体验和挑战，我享受着它们带来的快感。当然，随之而来的肌肉酸痛让我必须时不时就得去按摩放松。

　　也不知是针灸疏通了经脉的原因，还是因为长期跑步跟各种运动的原因。我一年四季都冰冷的手脚，现在也不冰冷了。

2. 运动中的思考

　　我找了一对一私教，教练是前职业篮球运动员。她为我制定的训练计划涵盖了背部、手臂、核心肌群等多个部位，持续一个半小时，全程无休的超级组训练。稍有健身经验的人都知道，这运动量非同小可。每组动作，她提供难、易两种版本，并设定 8 至 10 个数量供我选择。为了加大运动量也为了提升运动效果，我总是选择难的、数量多的。做到核心动作的时候我状态很好，一口气完成了 15 个，实际上我可以做更多，因为是无休锻炼接下来还有别的动作所以我才停下。

当运动到中途时，实在是热得慌，我便脱去了上衣，仅剩下运动背心，不经意间展露了我的腹肌。这时，教练上下打量的眼神让我有些不自在，语气也阴阳怪气起来，她冷冷地嘲讽道："作为专业运动员，我拥有自我驱动的精神。你一个普通人，这股毅力是从哪儿冒出来的？怎么也会有自驱力激励自己呢？"她话语中的讥讽让我感到极度不适。这时，另一个工作人员从旁边经过，她说经过的那个也是这里的教练，以前是瑜伽教练。我说，我也有瑜伽教练证（以前在国内学习的）。对方却用冷哼回应我，强调："人家可是很专业的，有二十几年经验了。"这种似乎在刻意打压我的态度让我极度不爽。健身房大概有规定，要经常给客户发消息，关心会员是否有运动，发饮食和运动计划。这件事之后，教练再也没有给我发过消息。当然，我也不屑她的任何提醒和计划，因为她的训练方法并没有给我带来预期的效果，只是消耗了一丢丢体力。反倒恰好给了我一个机会摆脱她对我的消极影响。我来健身房是为了释放情绪、提升自己，倘若因为别人莫名其妙的打压而灰心丧气，岂不是因小失大？去找其他教练不就好了？说不定会有更适合我的训练方法和计划呢。因为别人的过错而惩罚自己就太过愚蠢啦！

总之，各种运动慢慢地成了我生活的一部分，成了我调节自身状态的最有效途径。为了确保每天都能得到足够的运动量，我甚至会偶尔定早上五点的闹钟，起床参加高温瑜伽的课程。有氧运动带给我一种独特的愉悦感，比如说跑着跑着就会傻笑，瑜伽做到一半就开始微笑，举铁举到全身热乎乎的时候就很开心大笑……逐渐，我不再仅仅满足于单纯的运动带来的快乐，更渴望了解每一个动作背后的原理和意义。为何这个动作能达到这样的效果？为何我们需要避免某些错误的动作？这些错误的动作会导致什么样的后果？对身体有哪些潜在的损伤？

可以说，我对有兴趣的事物产生了好奇感，重新点燃了对生活的激情。当然了，运动的过程中也不总是开心的，难免会有一些不愉快的事情发生。

练习了近一年的普拉提后，我对普拉提的兴趣不减反增。为了更深入地了解普拉提的相关知识，也为了能更准确地指导自我练习，我决定考取普拉提教练证。虽然参加普拉提课程有一年，对动作比较熟悉，可是语言不通根本不能领会要领，这也是我想考教练证的原因，让我身体感受到普拉提带来的最大益处。但在全英文的理论课程和考试环境下，这依然是一次挑战。

是的，来美国这么多年，我始终没有掌握英语。可能是错过了语言学习的最佳年龄，也可能是压根没有语言天赋，甚至我也怀疑过自己是不是有语言障碍。反正，学习英文对我来说不仅很困难，还很排斥，哪怕我一天内把200个单词背一遍，第二天还是一个都想不起来。大概是自尊心和自卑在作祟，为了避免有尴尬的情况发生，我就直接从根本上杜绝，比如，我只去中国人开的超市；有时想吃西餐了，我宁愿花费更多的钱在网上订购，也不愿意去餐厅和人面对面用英文交流。

经过深思熟虑，我还是愿意为了普拉提这份热爱去努力、去挑战，鼓起勇气，通过常去练习的普拉提工作室报名了教练培训。

参加培训的第一天感觉非常不错，很开心。但是，当天6小时的培训时间快要结束的时候，我随机分配到的搭档突然和教练说："她不会英文，只能由我来指导她做动作，但她不能反过来教我，我也想得到她来指导做动作。"教练说："你考教练证不就是要教人吗？你教她不就好了？""好吧。"队友不太开心地答应了。

第二天，工作室的经理给我发消息，让我和另一个中国人组队，这样的话她可以帮我翻译。说到另一个中国人，我们是在同一家普拉提认识的，每周都见三次以上，见多了她就和我打招呼，还留下了我的联系方式。后来，我向工作室的教练咨询教练证的相关问题，她也在旁边，表现出很感兴趣的样子。了解后，她说："我陪你一起学吧，这样还能帮你翻译。"当时我就说不要："你这样会让我觉得亏欠你的，如果你自己想培训那就参加，不要因为想陪我帮忙我翻译才去，"之后我还重复了几次，和她说明自己的态度。

我们回到培训的第二天，自尊心极强的我犹豫了很久终于还是发了信息给她，因为我没有更好的办法，害怕别的同学不愿和我搭档，也怕再发生昨天被嫌弃的场面。开心的是，她很爽快地答应和我组队，而且说她会迟到，

第四章　汗水的折光

让我找个位置等她。很巧，那天因为堵车我发消息告诉她，我也要迟到几分钟。她说："好的，我会找个位置等你。"约定好一切的我开开心心地到了培训室，走到她旁边刚要打招呼，她却说："我已经有队友了，你去找那个韩国女孩吧。"我一下子愣在原地，没回过神来。工作室经理就在旁边，说没关系，让我留在这里。我指了一下旁边的她的队友，示意自己可以去找那个韩国女孩。经理说："你就留在这里，你们三个人一个队伍。""好吧。"经理已经这样说了，我只好硬着头皮留下来。此时，我已经察觉到同是中国人的她脸色非常不好，拉垮着脸，显然对我的加入感到不满。

由于培训室的空间有限，教练做动作时往往每组只能有一个学员跟做，然后再由这个学员指导组内的另一个成员。同为中国人的搭档跟教练做完后，经理叫我做一下轮的动作，同时，她叫另外一个搭档来做，经理直接过来拉我坐在垫子上，她直接无视我又再一次叫另外一个搭档来做。另外一个搭档也很尴尬，客气地说："让她做吧，我的腹部好像有点不舒服，正好需要休息一下。"

坐在垫子上的我手足无措，满脑子都是她说过的话："我陪你一起学，我给你做翻译……我给你做翻译，我陪你一起学……""好的，我找好位置等你……我找好位置等你……"我的天，我脑子怎么了，为什么停不下来一直在回想这些话？我感觉自己要疯了，真的，为什么会这样呢？她为什么转眼间就判若两人？其实我从始至终都没有期待过她的翻译，为什么经理一定要我和她组队？我深呼吸，安慰自己，专心学习，心率上来之后就好了，就会忽略刚才发生的事情，那只是一件小事而已。我尽力将注意力集中在动作上，想要让自己感到疲劳。可是不行，根本不行！我要疯了！我觉得教室里的所有人都在看着我，他们可能在内心嘲笑我。这种想法让我感到无法忍受，我迫切地想要逃离这个现场，真的是一分钟都待不下去了。泪管被眼泪涨得酸痛，我拼命压制着，不让眼泪流出来。明明很久没有哭过了，甚至曾经以为自己忘记了如何哭泣。然而，此刻我无比难过，这样莫名被嫌弃甚至让我怀疑是不是自己做错了。我明明一开始就没有想过要依靠她的翻译，也没想过要和她组队。真的是太委屈了！脑子很晕，很晕，感觉整个房间都在转，我是不是快不能呼吸了？不行，我不能继续这样，我必须分散注意力，要不然就赶快离开这里。

我起身直奔那个孤身一人的韩国女孩，挤出我生硬的英语问她："你好，我不会英文，可以和你搭档吗？"她微笑着回应："当然，我的英文也不好。"她的笑容让我稍稍放松了一些。教学还在继续，韩国女孩让我先学。这次的动作有点难度，我很快就累了，紧张的精神状态终于得到了缓解。随着心率的逐渐上升，刚才那些症状已经消失得差不多了。这个韩国女孩有点内向，但很有礼貌。我们之间交流虽然有些困难，有时不得不借助肢体语言和表情来表达自己的意思，但是有说有笑，总体来说还是很愉快的。

大概三个小时结束，到了休息时间。一起报名的女人去门口透气的时候经过我旁边，我微笑着向她点头。没想到，她竟然斜眼看我一眼，把头抬高，径直走了过去。什么鬼？哪来的优越感？我去门口透气，特意微笑着走到她身旁去想缓和一下刚才的尴尬。此时她又头一甩，大声用英文和另外一个同工作室的学员说话，绕过我走开了。一瞬间，眼泪几乎要夺眶而出。发生了什么？怎么能有人如此人前人后两副面孔？我做了什么要让人这样排挤和嫌弃？内心不停地自我询问让我几乎崩溃。好想回家，好想离开这里，此刻的我如此脆弱，又或者是太在意别人对我的看法导致。

这时刚好孩子爹打电话来，电话接起时他温柔的声音传来："怎么样啦？是不是很累啊？好几个小时了，有没有带够吃的呢？辛苦啦！"我哽咽着哭泣起来。他慌乱地问我怎么了，诉说完后他说："回家吧，没必要坚持，不值得。"跟他讲完之后情绪稍稍得到缓解，而且课程已经进行一半了，再有三小时就完成了今天的培训，我说："再看看吧，已经完成一半了，就这样离开下次还是要重复这次培训。"后半程的三小时培训时间过得太快了，因为太过于专注而且都是我在做动作。

回到家后我情绪不太稳定，为这个事情不开心，我的焦虑加重了，培训后的第三天一天之内出现了五六次惊恐症状。此时我意识到脆弱的神经受创不能再让自己陷入之前那种环境中学习，我要改变方式，于是我聘请了翻译，和教练沟通以后她赞成我带翻译一起去学习，找了好几个翻译，说真……这个现象不是我一个人会遇到的，尤其是在国外，中国人真的喜欢忽悠中国人，第一个翻译真的可以用"什么玩意"来形容，完全不专业，更不要把"敬业"两个字和他联系在一起了。看视频翻译内容，他看完十几分钟视频后就讲了一句话："这个就是说关于我们的皮肤细胞。"我期待地看着他，等着他接下来的内容，他却说："没了。"我问他，细节内容呢？他说："这个都不是解剖学，我去抽根烟。"啥？抽根烟？看了十几分钟只得出一句简短的14个字的总结，紧接着就要去抽烟？我以为找了翻译就可以解决问题，现在这个"翻译"本身就是问题。

每周我有普拉提私教课，我的普拉提私教是一个美丽的白人，她性格和善，蓝绿色的眼睛特别漂亮。她在了解到我和那个中国人之间发生了什么之后，她开解我，让我心胸宽广点，也许她没有这样排挤我的意思等等。但显然这个翻译对我提供的工作机会并不上心。我继续在广告平台发着找翻译的广告，没过多久就收到信息，给我发了两个时间段和她家地址。我回复她说："我一周需要五天翻译，这些时间都不太合适，一周就只有两个时间段可以选择而且还要开车单程近半小时去你家，太远了。"她说："你知道我在公司一小时时薪是70吗？给了你时间，你不能来，我想帮你也没法了。"脾气火爆的我气不打一处来，立马回怼："广告上明确地写了40美金一小时，这个是支付翻译的费用，别用'帮'这词，高尚得好像自己在做义工，拿着70而已的时薪还惦记零碎的40，哪来的勇气让你口出狂言？"

后来我的心理辅导给我介绍了一个刚毕业的女孩，陪我一起到现场学习，一起看视频然后翻译。上课时，她很认真，很喜欢学习，比我还认真。如果有不懂的专业术语，她就查到懂为止，看明白之后记录下来再翻译给我听。后面索性她直接做我的课程搭档了，每节课都是全程开心。她陪我完成了所有需要培训的课程，之后我也再也没在培训室见过她。

记录这段经历，是想告诉大家，也再次提醒我自己：人生犹如潮起潮落，有时我们会遇到一些小挫折，这些挫折可能会影响我们的情绪和生活。但是，不能让这些挫折击败我们，我们要勇敢去面对和解决问题。遇到消极、占便宜或打击我们的人时，我们要勇敢地回击他们，不要让他们的话左右我们的情绪，不要憋在心里不说，这样只会让我们的情绪更加压抑。哪怕只是一句简单回怼的话，也可以让心情舒畅。当然，如果你能自己消化情绪，不一定必须回怼。而对于我来说，选择适当地回怼，反而能让我的情绪更快地消散，这纯粹是我个性使然，不吐不快。

英文是一座大山，关于理论考试，我只能买些中文的相关理论书籍，努力学习。但是每个品牌工作室的规定都是不一样的，我还是无法清楚了解一些动作上的禁忌。

我自己通过翻译器在网上做期末笔试，151道题，正确率在80%以上才可以通过。我完全依靠翻译器完成了考试，正确率只有57%。考试结束后，普拉提导师发邮件告诉我需要补习哪些方面，会再申请一次考试机会给我，而且还叮嘱我一定不要用翻译器来辅助考试。的确，翻译器并不能完全准确地翻译考试内容，导致我不能正解题意，很多最基本的题目做错了，这也是为什么我第一场考试分数那么低。补习时，一直陪同我学习普拉提的那个小女孩翻译陪着我，我们一起在现场学习，她翻译给我听。这时，很多内容我才真正地理解了，并不是翻译器胡乱翻译的东西。

经过了一顿恶补学习，教练也给我申请了再一次考试的机会。考试时，她通过视频给我翻译试题内容做笔试，经过两小时的测试，最终正确率92.22%，我通过了笔试考试！记录这段文字时，我已进行了最终考试，拿到了普拉提教练证，全项通过。我们都加油吧！为了热爱的运动！为了激情的生活！

3. 马拉松的新奇体验

我儿子的校长非常励志。有次我们俩吃饭的时候，她和我提起她女儿鼓励她去参加马拉松，大概一周后她又和我说，她试了一下跑了4mile。当时我挺震惊的，好厉害，体力真好！我一直保持锻炼，天天不间断地运动，可是只能跑2.5mile。以前我也尝试过跑步，但是跑步时无法呼吸的窒息感让我恐惧，怕自己会因为跑步，致死最终没能坚持下来。每次都试图通过张大嘴巴增加摄氧量，反倒打乱了呼吸的节奏。那天听校长说完，我暗暗下决心要超越自己的局限。半个月后，我已经跑了好几次 4 个 mile。

再次和校长交谈的时候，她又说她已经报名马拉松了。真是个有勇气又了不起的女人，马上 50 岁了，从未有过跑步经验，竟然能有勇气参加马拉松。这次谈话之后，我几乎不做别的运动，每天都在练习跑步，告诉自己每天多一点点，就一点点。直到有一天跑了 6.8mile 都没感觉到疲惫。第二天经过校长办公室的时候，我神采奕奕地问校长："你的马拉松准备得怎么样了啊？"校长说："周五刚跑了个半马距离！"羞愧和不知名的感觉瞬间涌起，我本想来炫耀一下自己努力跑了 6.8mile，结果……好吧，忽略了我推动自己向前的时候，别人也在进步而且可能是更大的一步。人家都跑了 13.1mile 的半马距离了，我才 6.8mile，就跑来和她"炫耀"。

回家后，我找了特别空闲的一天，早上八点多就出门开跑，一直跑，一直跑，跑了没多久就开始岔气，右下腹痛得无法快速跑，看了一下手表速度是在 14 分一个 mile，大脑一直喊着"加油，没有到目标呢还早，不能停"。大概在 8mile 的时候，感觉脚趾周边有些疼痛，后来越跑越痛，痛得有些发麻，心里想着：噢！原来超过 10mile 是这样的感觉呀！脚指头会痛，好吧，加油！还有 3 个多 mile 就胜利了！不能白痛，一定要完成，就能突破自己参加半马了，此时下起了小雨。跑呀，跑呀，脚趾痛得越来越发麻，我的步子越来越小，快要筋疲力尽了。而且口好渴，本来有带一瓶放了能量饮料的水，因为太重中途倒掉了一大半导致后半段没水喝，多想这时有个亲友团能递过来一杯水啊！最好再有掌声以示鼓励！也可以来个啦啦队激励下！哈哈！经历了 3 小时多奔跑终于跑到 13.22mile，立马拍照记录，发给校长给我也报名半马。内心的喜悦感、满足感爆棚！自己超越了自己的感觉真好！感觉好是好，回家后无法走路了，两只脚磨出非常大的血泡。回想在完成一个人的半马之前真的太焦虑了，准备了很多东西，还去买了专门的能量补充剂，害怕中途脱水，又可能低血糖，一切都是看短视频学习经验的时候反倒被吓到，某些人为博眼球胡乱说一通，还没跑就开始不是焦虑就是纠结买哪个能量饮，要不要穿压缩袜等等，跑完后也就大气一喘，不就如此，合脚的鞋袜，适当喝一点点水就足够对付半马了，哈哈。

　　经历了一周终于比赛的日子终于要到了。直到比赛的前一天，也就是周六的白天，我还在争斗要不要参加，看着其中一只水泡还没好的脚，想想周六的早上看医生，医生说我肝胆区域轻微发炎，虽不足以用药，但是已经引起情绪变化，建议不要跑步。可我不想第一次参加比赛就放弃，我的人生中从未有过我主动想参加的任何竞赛，而且举办方在邮件里说得很清楚，沿途都是专业的救护人员以及救护车，很安全。即便这样，容易陷入焦虑的我仍然一夜没睡好，临睡前还在幻想孩子们在比赛终点等待我的场景，梦里一直在奔跑都是关于比赛的画面。周日早上非常不想起床，自我争斗了好一会，还是起来参加活动，但心里的抵触情绪一直浮动，吃了早餐后心情才慢慢变得平缓。

　　叫了一辆Uber出门了。内心稍微有点恐惧：今天的气温只有-2°，到处都结霜了；上次跑半马时磨出了两个大大的水泡，距离今天已经整整一周了，锃亮锃亮的两个大水泡还没有完全恢复。今天才是第二次跑半马，能行吗……我一直告诉自己，会害怕还是因为做太少又或者是没有做过，对自己的不信任，经常做的事情熟悉了就不再害怕。快到活动场地的时候，出门前明明刚去过洗手间的我非常内急，感觉要憋不住了。"只是紧张！"我不停地对自己说。

　　早上七点，天还没亮，大雾围绕的市中心好朦胧。我给校长发信息，她给我带来了我的比赛号码——6869。很不错的号码嘛！校长的号码是6868，不仅"牛"而且"发"。我俩在靠近赛道口的位置拍了张合影，背景是一排醒目的移动厕所。哈哈！真是足够独特的背景。我内心既激动又紧张，这是我第一次参加比赛，很怕自己不能完成或者速度太慢，毕竟上次跑完半马距离用了3小时15分，而现场举牌的时间最多也是2小时50分钟。现场喇叭里有人在唱国歌，参赛者们有的在拉伸，有的在和同伴击掌，热情高涨，准备迎接挑战。结冰的地面还滑倒了一大片选手……我仿佛置身于一场盛大的庆典中，好像在看热闹。校长微笑着对我说："你确定你的脚可以吗？"我眨眨眼笑着说："没事。"

　　出发指令响起，参赛者们像离弦的箭一样飞奔而出，激情与荷尔蒙瞬间点燃了整个赛道。校长和我说了一声"前面等你哈"也飞奔出发。我也不敢怠慢，看着手表控制速度和心跳尽量保持同一个频率，紧随其后。然而，刚刚起跑几分钟，鞋带突然松了。好吧，原本就处于紧张状态的我，顿时变得更加慌张。人潮拥挤，我心乱如麻。为什么有这么多人？我会不会因为人多而晕倒？我的抑郁症会不会因此发作而疯了呢？看着他们一个个超过我，我感觉自己像是倒着跑一样，不断后退。内心开始崩溃，觉得自己好糟糕，恐惧和焦虑几乎让我无法承受。这一刻，原本以为已经康复的我才意识到康复不是一蹴而就的，而是需要每天成长一点点、再一点点的过程，让自己变得更强大、更有抗压能力。加油，你是最棒的！你要成为自己喜欢的模样！什么都不要想，不要乱想，把精神集中在步伐上，来，让我看看怎么才能步伐更大些、速度更快些。我看着从后居上的参赛者们，告诫自己要控制好心率和速度，保持均衡。就这样，我自己和自己对话着，自我鼓励着。

　　路边，热情的呐喊声此起彼伏，参赛者的名字被高声呼喊，阵阵鼓励和助威的声音分散了我的注意力，赶走了我的恐惧和焦虑。随着 1mile 标志的接近，我看见路边的补给点了，志愿者在为参赛者倒水，他们准备了矿泉水和能量饮料。每隔大约 1mile，就有志愿者和参赛者家属为选手们呐喊加油。整个城市被雾霾笼罩，朦胧的高楼、熙熙攘攘的街道，大家都在全力奔跑，快乐地跑着、笑着。此时此刻，我心中的恐惧和顾虑已经完全消失，取而代之的是无比的快乐和兴奋。志愿者的加油呐喊仿佛为我注入了能量，让我的步伐比平时迈得更大。每当感觉筋疲力尽的时候，就会有志愿者出现在路边大喊加油，让我重新振作精神。

　　跑过一段距离后，一个染着黄色头发的男孩引起了我的注意。他在跑道外围，身体倾斜着伸出一只手与跑者们击掌，同时大声地喊着："你是最棒的！你一定能做到！"起初，我并未太在意，只当是志愿者独特的鼓励方式。太阳出来了，透过建筑和树木照射在身上，有点热了。这时，我又看到了刚刚被我甩在身后、染黄头发的男孩。他在转角处依然倾斜着身体，伸出手与每一位跑者击掌，口中不断地说着鼓励的话语。瞬间，我被他的坚持和热情打动了，他仿佛理解每一位跑者的艰辛和喜悦，用他的方式给予我们力量。我不知道他何时跑到了我们前面，也不知道他在前面等了多久，但他无疑为所有参赛者提供了奔跑的动力。很可惜，我因为在外圈，没能够和他击掌。

在漫长的赛程中，我逐渐感到体力透支，身后的跑者一个个超过了我。心想不能这样，要定个目标才行。前方有个红色衣服、黑色裤子的小姐姐，她的衣服湿了一大半，步子也迈得很小，看起来很累的样子。而我还没怎么出汗，就她了，应该是个软柿子，我肯定能追上她！于是，我提速跑到她身后。令我吃惊的是，还与她没肩并肩，她就突然加速，哧溜一下跑前面去了。吓！她不是已经很累了吗？竟然还有爆发力一下子甩开我好不容易追上来的距离。好吧，我调整呼吸和心率，稳住阵脚，不让现在的差距拉得更远。

好渴，还有些饿，早上就吃了一片面包和一小碗麦片。虽然沿途经过了很多补给站，但是也不能一次性喝太多水。因为运动时，血流主要集中在工作的肌肉上，而不是消化系统，大量饮水可能导致胃部不适，甚至引发恶心、呕吐等不良反应。过度饮水还会导致血液中的电解质被稀释，尤其是钠含量。这种状况被称作低钠血症，症状包括头晕、恶心、抽搐甚至昏迷。因此，跑马拉松的运动员通常采用小口喝水的方式，逐步补充体内流失的水分。此外，一些运动饮料含有电解质，有助于维持身体内的电解质平衡。话说，运动让我学会了不少东西。虽然读书的时候，我是那种常被老师训斥、责罚的学生，总是出现在校长和班主任的办公室门口。现在反而通过运动爱上了学习（当然是除英文以外的学习），不仅提升了体质，还学到了许多常识和小知识，甚至对健康养生也稍有领悟。口渴又饥饿的 6869 号有些迈不动脚步了，但这时我还在奔跑，还在追逐那个被我定下的目标红衣服的小姐姐。

哇！补水站！我停下脚步，拿了一杯水，在路边，拉伸着刚刚一直在抽筋的腿。几次原地拉伸，怕拉伸时间不够很快又抽筋，又怕拉伸时间太久被人远远地甩在后面。大概两分钟后，我起身更大步地追上去，试图补回刚刚消耗的时间。也许是因为步伐太大，不到五分钟又开始抽筋了，甚至比先前更痛。脚趾头也开始痛，很有可能是上周自我练习磨出的水泡被磨破了。即

第四章 汗水的折光

使是这样,我仍然没有看见红衣服小姐姐的背影,更别说追上那个光一样的校长了。

说起校长,她在我眼中是光一样的女人。这不只是形容她跑步的速度,更是她的柔韧和果敢。有次我们聊天,提及她创办幼儿园的经历。疫情给很多幼儿园带来了巨大的冲击,面对重重困境,她承受了巨大的精神压力和经济压力,毕竟还有老师的工资要支付。那段时间她非常焦虑,甚至患上了抑郁症,需要服用医生开出的治疗药物。然而,随着疫情的好转,她凭借着顽强的意志和聪慧的头脑,成功摆脱了幼儿园运营危机和抑郁症的困扰,不再需要依赖药物。每天早晨都会起床游泳,锻炼身体。我也吃抑郁症的药,所以我知道那些药的后遗症和副作用有多么可怕。有些药根本没办法停下来,需要很长时间的减量过程。我现在还在吃一个西药,已经是一粒药的30分之一了,每次减量都会让我痛苦至少半个月,当然不排除绝大部分是因为心理作用,要知道这一粒药不过才25毫克。我知道,有些必要的药物是为了控制一些病情,服用是不可避免的。但药物依赖的危害性又是另一方面的问题。逐渐减药是身体适应的过程,是避免断药后出现戒断反应的必经之路。这从科学的角度来讲,是完全有必要的。这也是为什么我逐渐减量的原因。对于她能如此迅速地摆脱药物,我内心充满了敬佩。每次和她吃饭、聊天的时候,我都有收获。尽管我们聊的大多都是闲话家常,但她的每一句话里都是正能量。这样一位如同光的女人怎么能不让人想要亲近呢?

离终点站还有1mile,我迈着大步奔跑着,尽量不去想小腿的抽筋和脚趾的疼痛。看到市中心的斜坡时,我有点绝望,感觉自己没办法跑上那个陡峭的斜坡。就在这个时候,她出现了!噢!红衣服小姐姐出现了!我心中瞬间充满了力量,开始全力奔跑。这次我真的迈开了大步,与小姐姐的距离越来越近。就在我要追上她的时候,她已经开始提速了。因为我们5分钟后就会完成这次的比赛,现在是证明超越自己的时刻开始倒计时了。猜猜这个时候我又看见了谁?是的,黄头发男孩!这次因为快要到终点了,我提前跑在内圈,快接近他的时候,我跳起来和他击掌庆祝,大喊:"谢谢你!"我笑得很开心,跑得飞快,超过了一个又一个,感觉自己像是风一般的女人,嗖嗖地就飞过去了。喇叭中不断传来通过终点的参赛者的名字……飞奔中我听到了自己的名字，激动得差点停下来，虽然我一直厌恶生父起的这个名字。过于兴奋的我以为自己已经冲过终点线了，看到前面的横幅才反应过来还有几步。

加油啊！要微笑迎接胜利！跨过了终点线，我拿到了这次比赛的纪念章。时间定格在2小时33分。这氛围真的太振奋人心了，比我一个人跑快了42分钟！我的天！进步得太快了！虽然两个大脚趾都带着上周磨出的水泡，但是我的心率和速度都非常均衡。我征服了自己，超越自我的感觉真的很好。焦虑和抑郁似乎已经远离了我。我发现它们很怕我，怕我成长、怕我内心变得强大。当内心逐渐变得坚强时，我们或许会发现曾经的焦虑和抑郁不再像过去那样让人畏惧。它们变成了生命中的一部分，虽然仍然存在，但不再是无法逾越的障碍。成长和坚强让我学会接纳自己的不完美，就如同这场马拉松，校长用时2小时23分，比我快了10分钟。下一次，期待下一次和她一起奔跑，我要加油追上这个曾经被抑郁症折磨得靠吃药才能稳定思绪的女人。

以前看见有人雨天跑步、马路边跑步、公园跑步我就觉得，他们真是吃饱了没事干也不嫌累得慌，为什么要这么折腾自己？现在我明白了，不是累，不是吃饱了撑的，是磨炼。磨炼我们的意志，让我们接纳焦虑以及抑郁。抑郁只是一种情绪，我们要学会接纳它，然后逐渐淡化它，不要让它在心中生根发芽。内心的成长并非摆脱一切痛苦，而是学会与之共舞，那些曾经令人生畏到非常的情绪，变成了内在力量的一部分，甚至是大部分。正是这些经历让我们更深刻地理解生命的意义。在坚强的过程中，我们逐渐找到对自己的理解，接纳自己的过去，并迈向更充实、自信的未来。所以，不要害怕内心的焦虑和抑郁，它们或许正是促使你成长为更坚强的关键因素。相信自己的力量，勇敢地迎接挑战，你会发现一个更强大的自己。

身体的冰冷感、手心的冷汗以及瑟瑟发抖的身体，这些都提醒着我需要锻炼。是的，是时候走出舒适圈，做一些从未尝试过的事情。即便最终没有取得什么伟大的成就，但只要能驱使自己踏入陌生的环境并完成一些从未完成的事情，就已经非常难能可贵了。这就是康复的起点。我开始迈出步伐奔跑，去人多的地方逛街、吃饭，并向公园里慈眉善目的老人打招呼、问好。

关心身边的人，关心他们的同时也在温暖自己；当我对他们微笑时，他们也会温柔地回应我，那笑容能治愈一切烦恼和焦虑。渐渐地，我们会被这些笑容包围。嘿，当你对别人微笑时，就像是给他们一个心情小礼物。笑容是不需要言语的善意表达，当别人回应你的笑脸时，你们之间仿佛建立了一种默契和互相懂得的感觉，大家一起创造了一个充满温馨和理解的小天地，相互治愈。当然，关心也要有个度。过分的关心可能会给对方造成压力甚至不适。每个人的接受程度都不同，有些人可能更喜欢享受自己的世界，不太喜欢别人过多的关心。所以，我们在关心他人的时候，要灵活一些，留意对方的反应。如果对方显露出紧张或者不太愿意接受关心时，就可能需要适度收敛一下。总的来说，展现关心不仅需要深入理解和尊重对方的感受，同时也要尊重他们的独立性和个人空间。这样，关心才能够发挥最好的作用，成为一种积极的、令人愉悦的体验。

我的故事，或许只是千千万万个通过运动找到自我救赎之路中的一个。如果你是运动爱好者，这一章可能为你提供了新的视角，让你意识到运动不仅仅是一种身体锻炼，更是一种心灵的疗愈。无论您是在跑道上，还是在瑜伽垫上，或是在游泳池中，都请记得，每一次的努力，都是向着更健康、更快乐的自己迈进的一步。以不同的心态去体验熟悉的运动，一起去发现运动的新意义吧！如果你在这之前完全没有接触过运动，希望我的分享能点燃你探索运动世界的好奇心。从轻松的散步开始，迈出第一步，一起来体验运动带来的身心变化吧！

第五章　孤岛之外

在茫茫人海中，我们每个人或许都曾感觉自己是一座孤岛。特别是在抑郁症的阴影下，这种感觉越发强烈。在病得很重的时候，我感觉到了前所未有的孤独，被隔绝，被误解，仿佛与世隔绝，孤立无援。没有人能完全理解我的感受，没有人能体会我的疼痛，更没有人能在精神上给予我真挚的支持。那段时间，我渴望能找到一个理解我的朋友，能感同身受地了解我的痛苦的朋友，能在精神上给予我真挚支持的朋友，但是没有。

当我们在谈论朋友对于抑郁症患者重要性的时候，其实是在谈论一种无形的力量。这种力量恰似一座桥梁，跨过心灵的鸿沟，将一座孤岛与另一座孤岛连接起来。这种力量，它虽无形，却强大到足以在患者心灵深处点燃希望的火花，激发出与病魔抗争的勇气和力量。

1. 识于微时的老友

通过一位共同的朋友，我结识了彼此有很多共同点的李清，我们都是性格率真、大大咧咧的人，很快就成了无话不谈的好友。

我俩喜欢在一起喝酒吹牛皮发神经，哪怕是在路边的小豆腐摊，一边吃小豆腐吹着啤酒瓶也能瞎聊到天明，经常聊到激动处唾沫星子横飞，我俩看着横飞的唾沫示意豆腐摊上的豆腐……相视，同时捂住嘴哈哈大笑起来。

李小清是个极度花痴的颜控，看到帅哥就走不动路，好色程度满级。

我们都喜欢打麻将，只可惜她技术太差，摸牌、出牌总是看半天，逢"赌"必输，偏偏自己还觉得打得很好，总想叫着朋友们打一会，可以说是

"又菜又爱玩"。这已经是很多年前的事情了,说不定她现在已经成了一名棋牌高手,也未可知。

李小清大学是英语专业的,每次喝多了就站起来手指着一个方向叽里呱啦地讲英文。

她还有点神经大条,总是记不住人名,但尤其喜欢在酒桌上叫着别人喝酒。人家明明姓刘,她招呼着"李姐,喝一个",过一会又成了"王姐";别人的隐形眼镜掉地上了,她帮人家捡起来吹一吹,让人家再戴上,说她吹了就等于是消毒;喝多之后非要让别人喝牛奶泡干贝,说可以解酒;在九寨沟的时候,明明已经高反了,还在"嘻唰唰"地和朋友喝着青稞酒划拳……但是,她人格外爽朗又热情,周围的朋友都很喜欢她,没人介意她这点的粗线条。

我俩也会有争执,我脾气急,偶尔冲她发火,她总是包容我,嘿嘿一笑,然后哄哄我:"你不要生气了。"生病之前,李清邀我在她那里住了几天,天天抽烟喝酒吹牛皮是肯定的,她像伺候大爷一样照顾我。经常是她妈妈煮好面端过来,我俩吃完美味的面条,二郎腿翘起,优哉游哉地点燃一根饭后烟,再等着她帮我倒杯水。收拾碗筷也是她的事情,完全体现出她优质伴侣的一面。那几年我每天睡到下午两三点自然醒,然后就出去吃饭喝酒,再去酒吧,如果还觉得不过瘾就接着去 ktv 唱歌或者蹦迪,总之夜生活丰富,常常到天亮才回家休息。每次我叫李清晚上出去玩,她总是说有事,很少跟我一起去。那时候我不明白她哪里来的那么多事要忙,人活着不就是吃喝玩乐嘛。现在我才理解,工作、家庭、梦想……总是有很多事情在牵扯着。

李清从事旅游行业,出国之前她总是喜欢带我到处去玩,体验了各种新鲜事物。有段时间,我姨妈想出去旅游,李清正好开发了一条新的旅游线路,就在我老家附近的高过河。我们一拍即合,李清为我们提供只收成本的旅游服务,我们帮李清测试新的线路。于是,姨妈一家以及我和李清一行人去了高过河。当天晚上,除了姨妈、姨父,我们几个年轻人结伴去看夜景。五个人喝了 12 斤米酒,都有些醉了。我素来看不惯表哥的女朋友,她性格强硬,总是对大表哥颐指气使,语气里命令意味十足。借着酒意,我俩起了冲突。

打闹的过程中，我和她推拉起来，越推越用力，扑通一声，我俩双双落河。

"幺儿，我来救你！"别看李清喝多了，反应快得很，大喊着直接跳进了河里。

不会游泳的大表哥看到我俩落水，惊慌地喊："快救我妹，她不会游泳。"同是不会游泳的表弟也大声呼喊，寻找能救援的工具。水很深，表哥的女朋友一直踩我的身体，好让自己往上蹿出水面，我根本无法露出水面。这时候，李清游到我旁边大喊："你不要踩她了，我推你上去！"紧接着又对我说："幺儿你不要乱扳，我拖住你的下巴往岸边游。"幸好，用我垫脚的那个女的很快被我哥拉上去了，一番折腾，大家都有惊无险地上了岸。看着湿漉漉的李小清，我真是又恨又爱，恨她不顾自己的安危，爱她对我的真挚情谊。让我想起有一次我们喝多了跟隔壁桌客人起了冲突，李小清也是这样，和隔壁桌大打出手，人家援手拿出刀来，她第一反应是让我"赶快跑"。挺聪明的，打不过就跑。第二天，酒意未散的我们无精打采的，一大早起来去漂流。没过多一会她看见帅哥立马精神百倍地和路人打水仗，竟然漂了9小时，天都黑了。

李清真是我见过的最可爱、最勇敢、最善良的酒疯子！

还有一次，我们一堆人去西江苗寨玩，为了更好地了解苗寨，李清还给我们找了一个当地导游。晚餐的饭桌上，陆美丽、庆哥、李清和我被当地的苗族姑娘不停地唱歌敬酒，喝得晕头转向。他们那有个习俗，敬酒给别人的时候喝酒人不可以碰酒碗，不然要全部由这个人喝完。那些美丽的苗族女孩一碗又一碗的酒喂到我们嘴边，看着一桌子的美味菜肴吃不到。导游看我们玩得很嗨，也加入我们的酒宴中。差不多晚餐尾声时，导游和我们说他有另外一个团需要过去一下。晚餐结束，五个人醉醺醺去山顶看夜景，又喝了不少，前前后后加起来得有十几斤米酒，都喝迷糊了。尤其是陆美丽走路都要搀扶，她还执意必须只去男厕。

酒意催生尿意，陆美丽和李小清频繁尿急，但是距离山顶和山脚的卫生间都还很远。这时候，我们发现路边停着一辆大货车，很适合做遮挡物。陆美丽先蹲了下去，李清还特意脱下外套帮陆美丽遮挡。放水声刚刚响起，"嘟

第五章 孤岛之外

嘟嘟",那辆货车竟然缓缓启动,开走了!大概是我们都喝多了,谁都没有注意到驾驶室里有人,也没听见货车发动的声音。只留下陆美丽一人在风中凌乱!哈哈!

往山下走路过一处,风景不错,陆美丽张罗着大家拍全家福。这拍完全家福准备回住处,拐进通往民宿的小路,我们发现路边灌木丛里趴着一个人,是导游!他醉得迷迷糊糊,直接睡倒在路边了,身上的钱包和证件也不知道都丢到哪里去了。大家又"七手八脚"地把他抬回了民宿,还给他起了外号叫"喜(洗)羊羊"。回到住处,我们几个继续喝,李小清彻底醉了,一直喊着:"老板,麻烦煎个鸡蛋,我要吃单面的!我要吃6个!"第二天起来看那由陆美丽拍的全家福……只有一个不知是谁的脚尖,且模糊。

……

和李小清在一起的时候真的有太多美好、快乐的回忆了。

也是李清先发现了我的病情。当时在李清家聚会,大家都玩得很开心。李清说,那天我格外沉默,人声鼎沸的时候,我趴在窗户边抽烟,眼神没有焦点,直勾勾地发愣,叫了我好几声才有回应。她问我怎么了,我的反应也很迟钝,应付两句就又开始发呆。强颜欢笑的时候,嘴角还隐约有一点抽搐。

我到美国之后,因为国内外的时差和各自繁忙的工作我们的联系渐渐变少。而且我不喜欢向朋友单方面倾倒情绪垃圾,不想给她们增添负担,所以我们之间倾诉心事的机会也越来越少,联系远不如以前频繁。每次通电话,我们的话题总离不开美食。我们俩都很爱吃,不过李清喜欢自己动手做。我跟她提到什么吃的,她都能侃侃而谈,给我讲制作过程。她还喜欢借着时差在我临睡前给我发美食视频和恐怖音效,不是馋我就是吓我。

直到前几天打电话聊天,李清竟然说她因为抑郁症自杀过,后来为了遮挡伤口还在上面纹了身。我真是难以置信,在我心里她一直是个心胸开阔、乐观开朗的人。

下面是李清对这段经历的自述:

抑郁症,从来没有想过这个病会和我有关系。直到我会为了一张纸或者是任何一个发出的声音而暴躁、易怒,甚至每天起床想的就是死亡之类的事情。

毫不夸张地说，我每天早上起床，我家人的神经都是紧张起的，我会因为水不热大发脾气，会因为一句话扔杯子。

我就知道我心理出问题了，然后有一天，一件很小的事情发生了，我选择了自杀，当我用刀片割开自己的动脉，我觉得是一种解脱，我心里感觉到一种轻松。

闺蜜从死神那里把我解救了出来。去医院之后，医生说还有0.5毫米就麻烦了。闺蜜怕我再做任何傻事，那段时间她一直陪伴着我，开导着我。

我内心很感激她，但是开心不起来，我觉得很痛苦，内心在挣扎。

我决定回家，看见妈妈突然之间多了很多白头发。我开始思考自己为了什么事情变得这样的消极。

感情、工作、家庭，是每个人必须面对的问题。只是有些人活得通透，想明白了而已。

而我焦虑，让自己走进了一条死胡同里。

我得改变。我得自救。

于是我买了一只猫，我把每天我内心想说的话和它说。有人问，为什么不找人聊天，把心里的话说出来，至少朋友还可以开导你，和你说话？

一只猫能做什么？还治愈人，那是不可能的事。

我想表达的是，不是养一只猫那么简单的事。而是从养猫开始，我学会的是什么。我们是相互自愈的过程。我们人其实就是需要一个很好的聆听者。

但人是很奇怪的，以前爱出去和朋友一起聊天，说着有用没用的闲事，可是当大家都各自有了家庭、工作，大家都为了自己的家庭忙碌的时候，谁有空来听这些，就算是听了，各自的立场不一样，得到的信息就不一样，久而久之，你就不爱再去说。和家人说，更是不会有一样的共鸣。

而我和我的猫，我无话不说，虽然我在自言自语，但有它一直陪着我，只是默默地听，没有任何的意见。我得到了我内心的一种语言宣泄。

还有就是一种责任。当语言、情绪得到了宣泄，我内心就开始慢慢地开心起来，很多人不懂，我到现在才明白，很多的事情都是从缺爱开始。

父母的爱，是理所当然的爱，是一种会被我们忽略的爱。朋友之间的爱，是一种肝胆相照、患难之交的爱。爱人之间的爱，是我们渴望内心得到归属的爱。

不管从哪个层次出发，我们终结一生，都在追寻着这些爱，渴望着被爱，从而追寻的过程失去了自我，丢掉了自己的灵魂。

而我感谢身边家人、朋友们对我的关心，让我慢慢地好起来。

又加上疫情结束，我开始工作，去了很多城市，看到了很多很多好的事情。

我发现了生活从另外一个角度去体会，其实是很美好的。你得找到生活的正能量。

首先，得排除焦虑，控制好情绪。当情绪稳定，就不容易被一些外来的事情波动内心。

再好好地去工作。哪怕这个工作不是自己热爱的行业，也要保持好的心态去对待。

再就是好好爱自己。只有好好爱了自己，其他的任何事情才不会影响到你。而且你会发现，爱了自己，就找回了自信。拥有一个健康的身体，胜过一切。

定期地清除掉自己的垃圾情绪，可以去运动，可以去喝酒，可以去做任何你觉得可以发泄情绪的事情。

每年给自己制订出游的计划。去看看世界的美好，去发现美的事物。

我是这样去做的，慢慢地我不再抑郁，不再想着消极的事情，甚至不会再轻易地为了一点小事而暴怒。

反而我现在看待很多的问题，都是平稳的心态对待，你会发现，那个曾经开朗的我又回来了。我真心地为了以后的生活而更加地努力。

看到曾经最好的朋友和自己一样深陷抑郁症，我内心十分复杂。一方面，我深感同情和理解，因为我知道抑郁症带来的痛苦和无助。李清那样一个开朗明媚的女孩需要经历这样的苦难，这让我心中充满了痛惜。更加遗憾的是，在她最艰难、最需要支持的时期，我没能陪在她身边，没有给予她些许关怀和慰藉。这种缺失让我深感内疚。另一方面，我又为她能够坚强地走出困境感到由衷的开心。我知道，这背后需要极大的勇气和决心。她的成功，不仅是对她自己的肯定，也给了我们其他人巨大的鼓舞。

在李清的自述中，养猫的经历尤其引起了我的关注。这种与宠物的交流，虽然看似单向，但实际上对情绪的稳定和恢复有不可忽视的作用。猫咪虽然不会说话，但它们是极佳的倾听者，能为我们提供一个安全、无压力的环境，让我们能够自由地表达自己的情感和想法，而不用担心被评判或批评。对抑郁症患者来说，孤独感往往会加重病情，而一只可爱的猫咪能够成为我们生活中的良伴，给予我们极大的温暖和安慰。这种持续的陪伴感在康复过程中起着不可忽视的作用。而且猫咪的柔软毛发、温暖的身体，包括它们的亲近行为本身就是治愈的良器，能够帮助我们释放身体中的"幸福激素"，比如催产素和多巴胺。这些化学物质有助于缓解紧张情绪并提高心情。另外，养猫还增加了患者的运动量和活动量。照顾猫咪需要定期喂食、换水、为猫咪清洁身体、清理猫砂盆等，这些任务会让患者的日常生活更加充实，有助于建立更规律的生活习惯，同时也增加了他们的身体活动量，对身心健康都有积极的影响。

李清现在仍然在从事旅游行业，最近她经营的一家酒店式养老院就要开业了，把自己的事业、生活都打理得风生水起。她就是这样通过自我反省、自我调整和积极寻求帮助，最终走出了抑郁的阴影，这是一件非常了不起的事情。

希望李清的分享能够给那些正在与抑郁症抗争的人带来希望和勇气。

2. 初心不再的旧友

早些年确实有一个女孩子给过我很多生活中的细节的帮助。那段时间，我的抑郁症状很严重，我一直尽量避免出门，有时几个月都不出一次门。家里需要什么东西都是她帮我买，有什么需要亲自到场办理的也都是她陪我去

第五章 孤岛之外

做。我们两个的友谊也在这个过程中逐渐深厚。在美国，这样的友情显得尤为难得。在国内，我们的朋友大多是从小认识的，容易交心，但在这里，人们往往不会轻易透露自己的心里话，好像会被人拿去当作茶余饭后的笑谈。所以我很珍惜我们之间的情谊。

这个女孩年纪比我小，但是很懂事能干。她失业之后，询问我哪里能找到工作，我顺理成章地邀请她来我的公司工作。公司现有的股份她可以想投多少就投多少，可以直接参与公司的管理，也可以选择直接拿分成。

一开始，她工作非常努力，很多事情都处理得井井有条，也是这个原因让我更放心地把所有事情都交给她，让她做抉择。后来慢慢地，她有意无意地提了好几次希望让她老公也进入我们公司工作。我考虑再三，最终同意了。于是，她和她的老公都在我的公司工作。然而，过了一段时间，他们的工作态度逐渐变得懒散，引起了其他同事的不满和投诉。我查看监控录像发现，她的老公经常在工作时间坐在办公区域无所事事，玩一会儿就走了。

查看监控录像时，她就在旁边，陪我一起看，她脸红着不好意思地时不时瞄我一眼，看我表情是否有何不妥。看完之后，我非常委婉地提到公司开支过大，需要裁员。她也在视频里看到了她老公确实一直在偷懒，便主动提出让她老公辞职。谈话结束的当天，我和他们夫妻俩，还有其他人一起吃了顿饭。当然，吃饭的时候我们并没有提裁员的事，这件事只有我和她心知肚明。第二天她就开始传言，说在饭桌上她老公还不知道要被炒掉，如果她老公当时知道这个消息，不知道会作何反应，说不定会做出什么惊天动作，还说她自己在职期间一个人撑起了整个公司。

确实公司很多事情都是她说了算。每次她遇到需要抉择的问题来问我的时候，比如这个该怎么做，那个该如何处理，我通常都会先询问她的意见，在她表达自己的想法后，如果是正确的，我都会表示赞同并鼓励她大胆放手去做。那时候我的确病得很重，没有太多精力去处理公司事务，但是我没想到对她的鼓励和信任最后变成了她"一个人撑起了公司"，我差点就误以为是她创建了公司。

中途还发生过一件事情，让我心里非常不舒服。我自己还有一个工具店，公司需要什么工具都会直接从我的工具店购买。然后她找到了一家在加州销售我们所需工具的厂商，价格比我店里的便宜大约一块五。为了赚取中间差价，她就自己开车去加州买，每次买几万个。除了卖给公司，她还会卖给别人，按照我工具店里贵一块五的价格。有一天，她跟我讲她不能工作，要去加州。我问她去干什么，她说帮别人买工具，正好公司也缺，就去买一点。然后她就给我算了这笔账，说一趟下来她可以赚取两万多块钱的差价。

听完之后我心里非常不舒服，她这是在明目张胆地亏空公款。深思熟虑之后，我打电话跟她谈了这个问题。她回应说，她只是想购买更便宜的工具，为公司节省成本。我反驳，无论是在我这边买贵一点的工具，还是去加州买便宜的，最终赚取的利润都是我的。她这样做相当于从我的口袋里白白拿走了两万多块钱，还在我面前炫耀。我告诉她这是违法的行为，属于亏空公款。

她解释说，她的初衷是省下这笔钱后拿给我。我感到非常困惑，工具店本来就是我的，这笔钱本来也是属于我的，在她那里转一手的目的是什么呢？如果我想要便宜的工具，我可以自己去其他地方买。

在她所在公司的运营过程中，我把所有的现金流、财务、进账等核心事务都交给了她，对她可以说是百分百的信任度，没有留有任何防范之心。然而，这样的信任却在一瞬间崩塌，一下子什么都没有了。我所谓的"什么都没有了"，不仅指物质上的损失，更重要的是我们之间的信任、默契和友谊已经不复存在了。也许她早就有自立门户的打算了，曾多次背着我和我的客户们联系，不过客户们完全没有理会她，而是告诉我，我佯装不知而已。

我跟她说："刚认识你的时候，你那么懂事，那么可爱。而且我们都是彼此交心的朋友，我不明白你现在为什么变得这么计较，甚至连一分几角都算得清清楚楚。"她提高音量，瞪大着双眼回答："我原本就是这样的人。"

我们本是彼此信赖、无话不谈的好朋友。在我精神上最难挨的时候，她那些默默的关心和帮助都让我体会到了温暖。可惜，在利益面前，看似坚不可摧的友谊还是变得脆弱不堪。这并不是因为友谊本身不够坚固，而是因为在现实世界中，人性的复杂性往往超出了我们的预期。

我们总是习惯把人性简单地划分为黑与白，善与恶，好与坏。然而，在现实生活中，人性的表现往往更加复杂多变。有时候，一个人可能在某一刻展现出善良、无私的一面，当利益的诱惑出现时又暴露出贪婪、自私的一面。生活就是这样，它不会因为我们的期望和理想而改变。在这个复杂的世界中，我们唯一能做的就是学会面对现实，学会处理各种复杂的人际关系，以及学会如何在利益与友谊之间找到平衡点。这并不容易，因为其中涉及个人的价值观、道德观以及对于"成功"和"幸福"的定义。

在这个过程中，我们可能会遭遇背叛，感受到失望和痛苦。但最重要的是，我们不能因此而自责或是怀疑自己的价值。我们的感受和幸福是最重要的，它们不应该被外界的评价或是他人的行为所左右，不要因为别人的背叛而自责或者怀疑自己。我们值得被善待，值得被爱。

3. 朋友筛选法则

我承认，在面对朋友的背叛后，我确实经历了一段难以言说的悲伤、愤怒和失望。即便现在再次提起，依然让我心绪难平。但是人不能总是活在过去的阴影之下，不停地回望伤害对我们并没有好处。自我疗愈和重新选择朋友都是我要面对的重要的课题。

我开始反思，在这段友谊中，我扮演了什么角色，又是什么导致了这样的结局。我意识到，在未来的友谊中，我需要更加注重朋友之间的沟通和理解。我要学会真诚地交流彼此的想法和感受，避免误解和隔阂的产生。同样，我也要设立健康的界限，学会说"不"。我需要懂得拒绝，保护自己的利益和感受，不能再为了迎合他人而牺牲自我，这样的友谊才能建立在平等和尊重的基础之上，帮助自己避免潜在的伤害。

在选择新朋友时，我也变得更加谨慎。我会花时间去观察和了解他们的品性和价值观。不再急于求成，而是愿意用时间去检验一个人的真诚。虽然朋友的背叛让我痛苦，但这并不意味着所有的友谊都会如此。我相信，世界上还有很多真诚、善良的人，他们值得我去认识、去珍惜。我不会因为一次伤害，就关闭自己的心扉。我依然愿意勇敢地去爱，去信任。我相信，真诚的友谊，是人生中最宝贵的财富之一。

关于如何挑选朋友，我把它比喻为绘制一幅支持网络的图画的过程。首先，添加那些能够"听懂我"的人——他们知晓我的抑郁症，不仅不会对此评头论足，反而愿意在我需要的时候给予理解和关怀。而在这群人中，有一位朋友的故事特别值得一提——在前文中提到的陪我去南京看病的朋友。那段时间，他总是认真地倾听我的诉说，还会在我讲完之后立刻给予反馈。比如他会告诉我，我的某些症状他也曾有过，尽管他的情况没我那么严重；他会鼓励我："真的，我觉得你会好起来的。"也许他并不能完全体会到我内心的挣扎和痛苦，但他言语间透露出的真诚让我觉得自己不那么孤单，让我看到了一丝希望。

接着，我希望在这幅画上增添一些色彩，也就是那些和我有共同爱好或相同三观的人。他们可以是和我一起谈笑风生的伙伴，也可以是和我一起分享运动心得的朋友。和他们相处，让我的生活变得更加丰富多彩。以前年轻的时候，我经常幻想自己可以和有钱人成为朋友，天真地以为自己也能因此变得富有。但是随着年龄的增长和阅历的积累，我逐渐意识到，真正的财富并不是通过简单的社交关系就能轻易获得的。真正的有钱人往往都付出了艰辛的努力和长期的积累，才取得他们的成就。他们的成功背后也隐藏着无数的辛酸和付出，只是这些努力往往不被外界所看到。只有努力成为一个优秀的人才可能收获财富，否则接近有钱人并没有太大的意义。通过自身的努力和才华获得成功，我们的社交圈子自然而然地也会随之提升。

想明白这个逻辑之后，我对那些只追求名牌、奢侈品的人逐渐失去了兴趣，甚至和他们没有了共同语言。以前我们还会聚在一起聊最新款的手提包、流行的颜色和品牌，讨论着谁又入手了几个 Kelly，谁又配了几个 Birkin。然而，现在这些物质追求对我已经失去了吸引力。我已经很久很久没有走进爱马仕的店铺了，因为我发现那些并不是我真正渴望的。我现在更注重的是自己的舒适和内心的满足，而不是外界的评价和物质的堆砌。我穿的衣服可以是一万块一件，可以是一块钱一件，只要穿着舒服，自己喜欢，我完全不在意它的价格。

同样的，我现在更倾向于结交精神世界富足的朋友。有些人虽然物质上富裕，但精神上可能很贫乏。相反，有些人虽然物质条件一般，但精神饱满，与他们交流共事更能带给人内心的满足。

当然，这幅画还需要一些明亮的色调，代表那些积极向上、能给我带来正能量的人。我们能够感受到他身上散发出来的积极阳光的气息，仿佛环绕着一层耀眼的光环，有一种无形的感染力与带动性，让周围的人都不由自主地被他所吸引，感受到生活中的美好。我女儿画室同学的妈妈 Jenny 就是这样的人，她看待事物的角度总是那么积极向上，哪怕是一件看似消极的事情，也能发掘出其中积极的一面。偶尔有一些抱怨也只是在客观地分享糟糕的事情，而不是单纯地传递消极情绪："你看，还有这么糟糕的事情！"很快她又会展示出事情的另一面，让我们明白，即使生活中有糟糕的事情发生，我们依然可以活得很美好。她无疑是一位优质的朋友。

还有我的 ESL 课程老师，Jean。在这一章提及 Jean 似乎有一点跑题，因为她是我的老师；但也恰如其分，因为她的鼓励和支持给了我很大动力，在我心中她是最好的老师。回想我的学习历程，如果小时候我没有经历过耳朵被拧的痛苦，也许我就不会那么抗拒背诵乘法口诀；如果读书的时候我能遇到像 Jean 这样充满爱心的老师，我或许会对学习充满热情。

Jean 和我以前的老师都不一样，她很温柔，很耐心，总是笑容满面，耐心讲解。虽然我们大部分学生都在努力地想要表达，却半天说不出一个完整的单词，即便花费了好几分钟，也只能勉强挤出一个生硬的词汇。哪怕这个过程再艰难，她都会耐心地倾听，直到我们完成笨拙却坚定的尝试。她总是鼓励我们："我会帮助你""是这个词真的很难，所以你读起来才很费劲""不要怕，以后会好起来的"……我在美国先后参加过六次 ESL 课程，但每次都没有超过十天，我总是很快就感到无聊和抗拒，然后离开学校。但是在 Jean 的课堂上，我却找到了坚持的动力。这些温暖的话真的给了我很大鼓励，激励着我成为更好的自己。

也请注意，这幅画并不是无休止地添加元素，我们需要谨慎选择与我们产生交集的人和事。有些关系，初看好似能增添色彩，但长久相处却可能带来疲惫和压力，就像画中的杂乱线条，会破坏整体的和谐与美感。比如那些经常将负面情绪无休止地倾诉给我们，而很少或根本不考虑我们的感受和需求的朋友；比如围绕着物质享受和浅显的娱乐展开交流，而缺少真正感情连接的朋友；比如那些怀着目的接近并试图从我们身上得到一些利益、好处的朋友……

在绘制这幅画的过程中，也要记得给自己留出一些空白，代表我们的个人空间和隐私。毕竟，每个人都需要一些独处的时间来自我疗愈和反思。

最后，别忘了，这幅画只是生活中的一部分。虽然朋友的支持很重要，但专业的心理治疗或药物治疗也是不可或缺的。它们就像画框，能够保护和支持我们的这幅"支持网络图"。

所以，挑选朋友其实就是在细心地构建自己的社交图画，让它在我们的生活中发挥最大的作用，帮助我们更好地应对抑郁症带来的挑战。

4. 如何与抑郁症患者相处

在这个快节奏、高压力的社会中，抑郁症已成为一个不容忽视的心理健康问题。当我们身边的朋友或家人面临抑郁症的困扰时，我们该如何伸出援手，陪伴他们度过这段艰难的时光呢？

首先，我们需要明白，抑郁症并非简单的情绪低落，更不是无病呻吟，这是一种需要被理解和关注的疾病。设身处地地去理解他们的感受，而不是急于评判。也许我们无法完全感同身受他们内心的痛苦，但最好的支持就是倾听，去感知他们的需求。让他们知道自己的忧愁和快乐都值得被听见，也真的有人会听见。伸出你的手，让他们知道在这场战斗中，他们并不孤单。一句简单的"我在这里"，"我会陪着你"有时候比任何话语都有力量。所以，如果你身边正有人在经历这样的困境，不要犹豫，牵着他的手告诉他"我在这里"，愿意陪伴他们走过这段路。

除了倾听和陪伴，我们也要尽自己所能为他们提供实质性的帮助。比如，主动帮助他们寻找并联系专业的心理咨询师或精神科医生。抑郁症是一种需要专业治疗的疾病，而专业的医疗人员能够提供最准确的诊断和最有效的治疗方案，越早治疗越好。即便是小小的行动也可以带来巨大的改变。无论是陪他们去看医生，还是提醒他们吃药，又或者是做有氧运动。这些实际的帮助都能让他们感受到温暖和关怀。

同时，我们也要关注他们的情绪变化，给予他们足够的关心，经常用积极和鼓励的话语来支持他们，避免任何可能让他们感到更糟的负面语言。抑郁症患者往往会因为自卑或焦虑而避免社交活动，导致他们更加孤独和封闭。我们可以主动邀请他们参加一些社交活动，如聚餐、聚会或旅行等。

即便他们开始好转，也不要放松警惕。恢复需要时间，就像等待一朵花慢慢开放。保持耐心，相信他们的力量，陪伴他们一步步走向光明。

抑郁症，这个看似深不见底的漩涡，其实并非无懈可击。有了朋友的陪伴和支持，我们就好像得到了一面坚固的盾牌。他们不只是听你诉说，而是真正理解你、接纳你，在最无助、最黑暗的时刻，可以给你一束理解和支持的光。也希望身边有抑郁症患者朋友的读者们都能够更加理解、关注和支持他们。抑郁症并不是一种可耻的疾病，而是一种需要关爱和治疗的心理健康问题。你的陪伴、倾听和鼓励，对于患者来说是无比宝贵的。请不要忽视他们的感受，你的关心和理解，也许会改变一个人的命运，为他们带来新的人生可能。愿你在人生的旅途中，能够成为别人的灯塔，照亮他人的孤岛。

第六章　小手牵大手

生命中，总有一些人的存在如同熠熠生辉的礼物，光是想到就觉得心底忽而亮堂。对我来说，我的两个小朋友就是这样的存在。他们用小手牵起我们的大手，以一种纯真和信赖的力量引领我走出心灵的暗角，让我学会了如何去爱、如何去珍惜。他们的天真无邪和纯真情感让我重新审视自己的生活，让我意识到保持对生活的热情是多么重要。与其说我养育他们，不如说他们治愈了我。

1. 截然相反的姐弟俩

我女儿非常活泼，有一颗不受拘束的童心，为我带来了无尽的欢乐，但有时也让我感到有些无奈。

她患有轻微的小儿多动症，精力尤其旺盛，好奇心和求知欲更是令人惊讶，和我小时候既相似又不尽相同。她比我更加聪明，但也像我一样叛逆，说了不能碰的东西一定要碰，说了危险的东西一定要自己验证，有种不撞南墙不回头的决心。每当她惹恼我时，都会噘起那可爱的小嘴，示意我："嗯，嗯，嗯。"那意思再明显不过了，她想和我亲个嘴嘴。进入游泳队之后，她的多动症得到了改善，专注力和之前相比也有明显提升。她自己也很喜欢运动，常常主动要求去练习，我很担心她会超负荷。晚上九点，游泳队的练习已经结束了，她又叫我陪她打乒乓球，老母亲表示真的熬不动啊。

女儿在画室有一个小伙伴，小女孩的妈妈长得很漂亮，她就好奇人家的爸爸长什么样子，非要我开车带她去那个小伙伴家。巧的是，小女孩的爸爸就是给我做超光子并建议我寻求心理医生帮助的那位医生。为了满足女儿的好奇心，我真的带她去了小女孩父亲的工作室，和前台说我有个朋友要介绍给郭医生，前台微笑着去和他说明了我的来意。我带着女儿在会面室见到了郭医生，他看起来很友善，非常亲切地过来和我女儿打招呼问好。我到现在还记得女儿当时一边打量着郭医生一边若有所思的表情。孩子的世界真是充满了好奇和惊喜，一个小小的发现就能让他们快乐一整天。

女儿一直想在家里养鱼，我们就买了一些热带鱼放在楼下的客厅里。把鱼带回家以后，孩子爸爸说鱼不能放在普通的自来水里，需要用一种特殊的水。我和女儿表示怀疑，问他："你怎么知道？"孩子爸爸说："因为我有一个好父亲，他告诉我的……"这句话对我触动很大，他的父亲告诉了他这件事，而他又告诉了他的女儿。这样一个小小的经验传递不就是爱和温暖的传递吗？这种能感受幸福的小确幸让我非常满足。时间总是在不经意间流逝，如果我们不经常回想这些美好的瞬间，它们就会悄悄消失在记忆的长河里。久而久之，我们可能会忘记自己曾经拥有过这些幸福，觉得自己不幸福。那天，女儿非常积极地帮忙换水，换她爸爸所谓的特殊的水，足足在小鱼前待了两个小时，一会儿指着其中一条彩色的鱼，激动地喊："看，这条鱼多漂亮啊！"一会儿又满脸惊喜地看着几条小鱼在水里玩耍。她的小脸上都是兴奋，眼睛一直亮亮的。第二天早上，小姑娘一睡醒就"咚咚咚"地往楼下跑，要去看鱼。楼梯刚下到一半，就看到鱼缸里几条小鱼都翻起肚皮漂在水面一动不动。是的，她心爱的小鱼都死了。可怜的女儿号啕大哭。

以前，我也曾是一个好奇心爆棚的孩子，对周围的一切都充满了探索的欲望，就连别人杀黄鳝我都要凑过去看个究竟。可是随着年岁增长和病情反复，我最终还是成了"冷漠"的成年人，变得少言寡语，治疗时医生让我怎么做就怎么做，让我吃什么药就吃什么药，再不像少年时。相当一段时间我也很坦然地接受了这个变化，认为这是成长的必然过程，我们必须舍弃那些天真的好奇心，才能成为成熟稳重的成年人。

但是，女儿的童心和好奇心让我重新审视自己，让我意识到好奇心并不是孩子的专属，而是每个人都应该保持的一种心态。我希望在未来的日子里，能够和女儿一起探索这个美好的世界。在她的陪伴下，重新找回那个对世界充满好奇和期待的自己。同时也希望能够在她的成长过程中，我能成为她探索世界的伙伴和支持者。

最近，我家后院的风信子长出来了，特别好看，有深紫色，有淡紫色。我女儿早早地完成了作业，也练了钢琴，然后去后院摘了一朵淡紫色的风信子，特别香。我提议说："你可以把这朵散发着迷人香味的花送给你的老师，他一定能感受到你的心意。"女儿先是点头说好，过一会的发言却让我有些措手不及。她认真地说："妈妈，我想了一下，我不想送给老师。我想等你死了以后，把这朵花放到你面前。"一瞬间，我五味杂陈，心里的感受难以名状。是欣慰？是感动？还是一种难以言喻的崩溃？这朵花在她心中是美丽的，她想把最美好的东西留给我，我知道这是一份纯粹的不加任何修饰的爱。可为什么，她不能在我活着的时候，用这朵花来表达她的爱呢？尽管她患有多动症，我依旧耐心地引导她理解这个世界的道理，包括生老病死的自然规律。我付出了无数心血，努力教导她。这种教育的挫败让我短暂地崩溃了。也可能是她觉得美好的东西应该送给妈妈，奈何我从来没给自己过过生日，所以她才觉得唯一能送东西给妈妈的时候就是妈妈离开的那天，或者是那天比较特殊所以要送鲜花，也不排除是电视上看见送已故的人礼物就是鲜花等等，总之当时听见她童言童语的我是崩溃的。

我带她参加了一个体能训练班。刚开始去的时候，她面对着一个挑战：跳山羊。站在跳箱的一侧起跳，同时用手撑在跳箱上，像骑马一样跨过去。那个跳箱对她来说有点高，她尝试了很多次都跳不过去，总是直接骑在上面。但是，她一直没有放弃。大概上了四五次课后，我惊喜地发现她已经可以熟练地完成这个动作了。看到她的进步，我真是无比的欣慰和感动。为自己的付出感到值得的同时，也感慨孩子的坚韧和成长。

我就是在这些崩溃与治愈的交织中一路走来，每一次的挫折、每一次的困惑，都让我更深入地了解我的孩子，更细致地观察他们的需求和反应。教育并非一蹴而就的事情，需要时间，需要耐心，更需要不断地尝试和调整。希望在这个过程中，我和孩子能够共同成长，都能成为更好的自己。

儿子和女儿性格也完全不同，两个小孩的对比很明显。比如，不可以碰插孔这件事。跟我女儿强调之后，她一定会故意去碰，拿手指往里摸，摸不到就找个细小的物体往里插。而我儿子听我讲完之后，会反问我："既然这么危险，那你为什么不找东西把它塞起来？"他更倾向于通过逻辑和理性去理解世界，而不是通过冒险和挑战。

客厅的橱柜下面放了三箱矿泉水，为了不用弯腰拿，特意摞在一起。拉一下最上面一层剩下一半的水，里面剩下不多的矿泉水就会一直晃悠。儿子好像从中发现了新乐趣，站在旁边一直扯着玩。看着矿泉水晃晃悠悠的样子，担心掉下来砸到他的我，有意识地克制自己想要发脾气的急躁，深呼吸后耐心地跟他讲："你不要这样弄。一会矿泉水倒下来会砸到你的脚，很痛哦！"听着我夸张的语气，他想了想，往侧边移动两步，站在自认为安全的距离，用单手继续远远地够着拉，让矿泉水晃动起来。我说："你这样不行哦，因为你力度不够，不可能掉下来砸到你的脚，你要更用力一点才会掉下来。"他想了想走到矿泉水正前方双手用力把被晃得移位的矿泉水用力往里推回原来的位置。完事之后，拍拍手，一副很卖力且如释重负的样子："好了，这样就不会砸到大家了！"

他不仅很有安全意识，还懂点养生。因为我跟他讲过，天气不好比如下雨的时候就要穿不会渗水的小皮鞋，天气好的时候才能穿透气的鞋子，他就记住了。每次出门前都会问我："今天天气怎么样？"如果得到的答案是在下雨，他就会把他最喜欢的那双柔软透气的鞋子放起来。出门的时候，必须把帽子戴好，拉链拉好。而且，他只喝温水。这种一本正经的样子，真的很像一个养生小老头！

我偶尔会跟孩子们说"如果不学习就会变成废物"。他不想上幼儿园的时候就会跟我说："妈妈，我今天想当废物。"他的稚嫩声音真是让我既惊讶又好笑。如果被他逮到我短暂的偷懒时刻，他还会教育我："你是想要放弃吗？难道你想要当废物吗？"好吧，有个小可爱在背后"鞭策"我呢！

一个三岁小孩脑子挺灵光的。每个周四他姐姐要去画室一个半小时，他也想去，但是他太小了画室不收，我只能带着他和我朋友一起去普拉提馆，我和朋友做运动他看手机。某次我朋友有事就取消了我们的约会，他说："妈妈我想陪你去做运动。"因为我在做运动的时候他能看手机。我回答他："宝宝，运动那边预约是需要两个人才可以进去的哦。"他思考了一下："妈妈，我和你不是刚好两个人吗？再来一个就是三个了你知道吗？"瞬间让我觉得这娃可以往理科发展。

我给我女儿和儿子讲过一个懒鸟效应的故事：有两只小鸟，一只从小就勤奋，从不懈怠地练习飞行；另一只则非常懒惰，整天躺在床上，依赖勤奋的小鸟带来食物。过了很久很久，勤奋小鸟的飞行技术已经超强超厉害，懒惰的鸟依旧过着安逸的生活，等待着食物的到来。有一天森林着大火了，那个火焰飞得老高老高，蔓延得很快很快。面对火海，勤奋的小鸟凭借着强壮的翅膀飞了出去，成功逃生。然而，懒惰的小鸟却因为长时间缺乏锻炼，翅膀无力飞不起来，最后被烧死了。

故事讲完的时候，我儿子发挥超强的逻辑思维，说："妈妈，我们每天都有学习，我们每天都在成长，爸爸老是躺在床上看手机，那他是懒惰的鸟吗？"我笑着回答："对呀。"他语气坚定："那我要去消防局上班。我要当消防员，我要有消防员的车，我要有他们的工具，做一个真正的消防员，如果'爸爸鸟'被烧的话，我就要去救他。"瞬间，我心中的某一处仿佛被击中，瞬间化为一汪春水，温暖而柔软。为什么会这么有爱，为什么这么小的细节会那么暖心？忽然大脑不停地搜索起我自己年少的时候。不知道我那个时候有没有说过什么话去感动过我的家人，或者是我的家人有没有那么一瞬间捕捉到我的童心和爱意。

儿子太过于懂事了，他表现出的这种超乎年龄的成熟，有时候让我甚至忘记了他还是个孩子，把他当作一个大人来对待。和他相处时，我不会常常去哄他，也不会频繁地拥抱和亲吻他，包括对姐姐也是。也许是因为，我自己从小也没有经历过这样的亲昵举动和热烈的情感表达，不习惯这样做。我女儿有时会对我说："妈妈，我想抱抱"，"妈妈，我想亲亲"。每当这时，我都会积极地满足她，给她拥抱和亲吻。但有时当我情绪不好或她表现得调皮时，我可能会不自觉地拒绝她，这会让她伤心大哭。这是我需要改正的地方。

弟弟的成熟时常让我有种错觉，觉得再过两年，等他上小学之后，我可能就不用再为他操心了，他可以自己处理好一切事情。不知道这种信心从何而来。

虽说弟弟思维成熟，但是年龄摆着这里，他终究还是个小孩子，偶尔表现出的天真和孩子气十分可爱。

他很喜欢车，每次去超市都要"提"各种新车，经常模拟交通场景，奶声奶气地给汽车配音。还挑食得很，糖果和巧克力对他的吸引力是相当的强烈，每次吃饭时嘴里不停念叨着什么，要么就唱歌。

有一次，家里的阿姨休假，我又懒得出门，就决定在家为他们煮一碗面条。面条里加入了青菜、荷包蛋和肉片，看起来色香味俱全，十分诱人。然而，当我女儿尝了一口后，却突然发出了奇怪的声音，然后把面吐了出来。我儿子目睹了这一幕，他立刻一手捂住嘴巴，另一只手在空中摇摆，身体不自觉往后闪躲，表达出不要的意思。他观察着我，斟酌着措辞，生怕伤害到我："妈妈，我真的很爱你，但是我不敢吃，我好害怕，我可以不吃吗？"看他这副样子，我真是哭笑不得。

虽然在大多数情况下弟弟都是个很治愈的小孩，但难免也会有让我伤心的时刻。我在瑜伽馆做运动的时候，他刚好在上画画课。他的课程结束，我的运动还没做完，为了不让他乱跑，我在手机上找出了他最喜欢的《蜘蛛侠》。

然而，当我结束运动，准备离开时，他说："我再多看一会儿。"为了公平起见，我提议玩剪刀石头布："如果你输了，我们就不看了，就回家；如果你赢了，我们就多看一分钟。"他很爽快地答应了，但遗憾的是，他输了，但他不愿意接受这个结果，要求再玩一次。我坚定地拒绝了他的请求，毕竟已经八点多了，我们需要回家。可他却因此大哭大闹，甚至动手打我，我没理会他。

随后，我们一起去车上等女儿。她的老师带她出去吃饭并补习功课，然后会送她回来。女儿上车后，好奇地问弟弟为什么哭。我尽量平静地叙述了整个经过，但心中的委屈和疲惫却让我声音有点哽咽。我为了这两个小朋友每天都尽心尽力，帮他们安排各种想去学的课后活动，照顾他们的起居饮食，照顾他们的情绪。现在，儿子却因为不让看手机就动手打我。

女儿听出我声音里的委屈，也绷不住了，放声大哭，抓着我的胳膊说："妈妈，你可千万不要把它写到书里面，这以后我们看到会很伤心的。"

但是，作为记录生活点滴的习惯，我还是决定把这件事写在书里。我明白女儿的担忧，她知道弟弟这样做是不对的，也希望我们的家庭充满和谐与快乐。但我知道，儿子的举动只是小孩的下意识行为，并非对我有恶意。真实的记录能够让我们更好地回顾和反思，相信我和孩子们以后再看这段故事，一定能够看到我们彼此的成长和变化。

2. 孩子们教会我学习

我从小目睹的就是长辈们跷着二郎腿嘴里叼着烟在烟雾缭绕到睁不开眼的房间里打牌，打麻将、打纸牌的场景，抽烟、喝酒、熬夜是常态，貌似谁不会就脱离了社会，跟不上潮流似的，花钱大手大脚，从不把钱当回事。在这样的家庭环境的熏陶下，我也不负众望地学会了这些习惯，手指轻轻划过任何麻将牌没有摸不出来的，我和老妈同住一个屋檐下，经常各自忙着各自的牌局，酒局大概一两个月会碰见一次。也认为钱就是拿来用的，有钱就花反正都是赢来的。而且，我深信人生就应该要尽情享受，就是要去打牌、抽烟和喝酒。反而想不明白的是，为什么大人一定要叫我们去读书学习，抽烟喝酒也用不上乘法口诀吧？

那时候我不懂什么叫家庭责任感，什么叫家庭观。我从没有想过家庭和婚姻是要去维系的，也不曾觉得人与人之间是要沟通才能达成共识，只是单纯地觉得结婚就是领取一张结婚证，然后生孩子，生活在同一栋房子里。对于教养孩子更是没有概念，父母还需要陪伴孩子吗？还需要培养孩子吗？生了孩子，就是生了孩子。至于孩子要怎么样成长和发展，那就是孩子自己的事情了。这就是上一代的人给我留下的家庭观和育儿观。

直到女儿改变了我。

在我女儿三四岁的时候，我开始给她物色幼儿园，当时遇到了一个被极力推荐，说是很优秀的幼儿园。但是，因为那里的教职工全员使用英文，我没有办法跟他们沟通，最终只能放弃。现在再回头看，我意识到自己当时的决定似乎并非明智之举。毕竟，身处美国这样的英语环境中，早期为她打下坚实的英文基础是很重要的。现在，女儿在学习中显得吃力，主要原因就是她听不懂英文，理解起来很困难。

5岁时，她开始对跳舞、画画感兴趣，表现出强烈的想要学习的欲望。但是那个时候的我还沉浸在病态中走不出来，非常抗拒开车，更不用说用英文跟培训机构和老师沟通了。所以，我只能选择发广告，请讲中文的老师来家里教她唱歌跳舞。

她逐渐长大，看着身边的同学都掌握了很多技能，她自己就特别希望学会，求知欲越来越旺盛。我就是被她这种喜欢学习的心态感染了，她对所有事情都有一种渴求，让我意识到我必须为她创造更好的学习环境和条件，无论如何我都要为她或多或少地做一些事。然后看着她画的画一天比一天好看，看着她会写的字也一天比一天多，看着她掌握的知识一天比一天丰富，我就感觉人的确需要学习，要到一些环境，才可以真真正正地成长。

有次因为接下来的课连接得很近，我就提前了十分钟去学校接她。谁知道刚一出校门口，她就开始掉眼泪，非常委屈地说："为什么要这么早接我，还没有下课呢！"和朋友一起吃饭，朋友家有三个孩子，女儿特别喜欢和她们玩。午饭饭桌上，小朋友们兴高采烈地讨论着玩具，女儿跑到我朋友跟前，问了人家一道数学题，朋友说我："你别逼疯她了，她跑来问我她不会的数学题。"这真的不怪我，她已经不是第一次在吃饭的时候问别人数学题了，平时就喜欢玩手表里的计算机。还有画画，因为多动症，她打扰了画室的其他小朋友，画室不打算让她继续留下来。她得知后，眼里含着泪说："妈妈，我以后再也不会跑去和同学们说话了，也不会在画室里跑来跑去了。我想画画。"那无辜又渴望的眼神真是让我的心又酸又软。

看着女儿对学习的热情与日俱增，我不由得想到自己曾经的抗拒和抵触。

每次面对新技能的学习，我总是会很紧张，害怕自己学不会，害怕自己出现失误，害怕别人异样的目光和嘲笑。我从来不会一个人去洗车，因为洗车店的轨道我总是开不上去，后面的人会不停地按喇叭，而且我看不懂全英文的自动支付页面。另外，作为深度咖啡爱好者的我因为语言障碍也不敢去店里买咖啡，只好买了咖啡机自己在家做很难喝的咖啡。这些都是因为惧怕学习所造成的生活不便。

我觉得自己也应该去尝试着学一些新技能了。不仅是为了女儿，更是为了自己。随着接触运动的次数增多，我更加领悟到学习的重要性，开始尝试各种不同的运动项目。除了瑜伽，我还尝试了跑步、壁球、尊巴、游泳等，哪怕自己很怕水。原来这个世界上有那么多有趣的东西，难怪我女儿喜欢学。

最近，我还一直在思考一个问题。随着社会发展，电子化、智能化已经成为我们日常生活的一部分了。我们这一代人还算幸运，对电子设备和系统有一定的了解和接触。但是，对于比我年长的一些人来说，他们可能从没有接触过电脑，甚至不知道怎么开机和关机。当然，这并不意味着他们没有知识和文化，他们可能文化水平很高，某专业领域造诣深厚，但是他们对电脑一窍不通。这种对比让我不禁感慨，过去人们到了四五十岁可能就感觉自己步入老年的标志，开始走向人生的下半段。在如今这个信息爆炸的时代，年龄的增长已经不再代表什么，无论年龄多大，学习的步伐都不能停止。知识的更新换代是如此之快，以至于我们所学的东西可能很快就会过时。这就要求我们不断地学习新知识，提升自己的技能，以跟上时代的步伐。

年龄的增加不再意味着能力的下降或学习欲望的减退。相反，它应该成为我们继续探索和成长的动力。生活在这个快速变化的时代，我们需要终身学习，不断地更新自己的知识库，才能保持竞争力和适应力。

而且在看完《被讨厌的勇气》后，我坦然接受了自己不会英文这件事，每个人擅长的领域不一样罢了。世界上要学的东西太多太多了，我不会英文，你也未必会中文；我会打麻将，你还未必会呢。所以我开始尝试自己去洗车，哪怕后面的车因为我付款耗时太久而按喇叭示意不满；去店里买咖啡，用翻译器打出我想要的咖啡名称；去西餐厅，照着菜单上的图片找出自己喜欢吃的食物；去各种超市……我开始积极勇敢地拥抱生活。

我儿子观察到我和我女儿都在努力学习，特别是看到他姐姐画画时，他主动提出也要学习画画。当他看到姐姐上中文课时，他坚持要求我们也为他安排同样的课程。重点是，一个仅仅三岁的孩子，竟然能够在 iPad 前稳稳地坐上一小时，专心致志地跟着老师学习中文，老师提出来的所有问题他都能回答上。不论答案的对与错，他的学习热情和专注力都让我深感震惊。

家庭氛围对于孩子的成长有很大的影响，这是我现在才意识到的一个问题。如果孩子不是天生就非常自律的话，我们不去给他营造一个良好的学习环境，反而整天无所事事，跷着二郎腿，叼着烟搓麻将，我们又怎么期待孩子能够静下心来学习，甚至去成就一番事业呢？这是绝对不可能的。他们可能这一分钟还在努力学习，下一秒钟就已经在玩游戏了，完全无法正视自己的未来规划。

有时候我也在想，我给女儿安排这么多课，会不会让她都没时间玩了。但仔细想想，其实也不是我主动要给她排这么满的课，所有课程都是她感兴趣、主动要求学习的。甚至有时候晚上九点了，她还希望我能给她再安排点课。

很多人认为，孩子的童年就应该好好玩，尽情地玩。这话说得没错，但我看着她在上课、补习的时候那开心的笑容，我就在想，她在上课的时候是不是就已经在玩了呢？每当掌握一个知识点后，她脸上的笑容，那种满足感，真的就像是大丰收一样。也许学习和玩耍并不是互相排斥的，毕竟每个孩子都是独一无二的，他们有自己理解和体验世界的方式。只要我们给他们足够的爱和支持，他们自然会找到属于自己的路。

我曾经看见一个特别调皮的熊孩子，做了一件在我看来肯定会被大人狠狠教训的事情。我心里想，这孩子肯定惨了，等着看他父母怎么收拾他。然而，出乎我的意料，事情并没有像我想象的那样发展。他的父母并没有惩罚他，反而视若珍宝地和他交流沟通。我当时很疑惑，不明白怎么会有家长这样教育孩子。如果那个熊孩子所做的事情发生在小时候的我身上，我一定会受到惩罚，没准都有可能打死我，我的脑海中甚至已经再现小时候因为调皮被打的画面了。我女儿犯错误的时候,我心里时常在想:也只有我这个好妈妈才会原谅她、包容她。但是熊孩子这件事让我意识到,原来严厉的惩罚并不是一种普遍现象。

我反思自己为什么会有这种感觉,可能与我从小被打到大的经历有关。我以为这种对待方式是常态,每个人都应该经历。但现在我明白,我遭受的对待并不等同于常人所遭受的对待。每个家庭的教育方式都有所不同,挨打并不是每个家庭都会采取的方式。

我陪女儿参加过一个小男孩儿的生日聚会,现场氛围很愉快,孩子们玩耍得很开心,而妈妈们则聚在一起聊天,话题大多围绕着学校。到了切蛋糕的环节,孩子的母亲说了一些话,表达了对孩子的感谢,夸赞他懂事、会照顾弟弟等。这一幕让我很有感触,我最初的想法是,做妈妈就应该是这样的,用夸奖的方式让孩子知道一些事情并借此得到成长。

但是回家之后我又仔细想了想,觉得自己的理解可能有所偏差。教育是具有多样性的,每个家庭都有自己独特的教育方式。因为不同家庭的文化背景、教育观念、孩子性格以及成长环境等多种因素都是不同的。有的家庭可能更注重培养孩子的独立自主能力,鼓励他们积极参与各种活动和社交场合,锻炼他们的沟通和协作能力;有的家庭则可能更强调学术成绩和知识储备,为孩子提供丰富的学习资源和辅导;还有一些家庭可能更注重孩子的情感教育和心理健康,努力为他们营造一个温馨、和谐的家庭氛围。对于我的孩子来说,我更希望他们在现在的年纪可以更专注自己的快乐和成长,而不用过早地承担懂事的责任。当然并不是说不引导教育孩子,而是更应该关注的是孩子的内心需求,让他们在快乐的氛围中成长。比如我女儿的生日聚会,她最想要的是一个超级大蛋糕和一个全程跟拍的视频,希望整个派对都充满美人鱼的元素。我尽力满足她的愿望,摆放她平时难得一吃的棒棒糖,让她和她的朋友在欢乐的氛围里拥有最单纯的快乐。再比如,我本身是一个很容易焦虑的人,在培养孩子时,我自然希望他们学的东西就更多一点,懂的东西更广一点,将来能学以致用。同时,我也希望他们能有更多的社会见识,所谓的多见见世面。这是指,我希望他们能够接触更多元的人群和环境,了解社会的多样性和复杂性，将来就能更好地适应社会。每周三，女儿的家教老师 Ian 都会带她出去吃饭，无论是奢华的高级餐厅，还是日常的普通餐馆。我都希望她能在这个过程里见识到生活的不同面貌，让她明白，我们的家庭能够为她提供这样丰富多样的生活体验，让她尽情享受这些美好的时光。我的初衷并非只是让她体验物质的优越，更是希望她能够培养出独立、明智的价值观。我不希望她未来因为几顿高级餐厅的晚餐，或是朋友圈里一些看似光鲜的表象，就轻易地被别人迷惑。

教育方式的多样性给父母带来参考的同时，也带来了一些挑战和机遇。挑战在于如何找到最适合自己孩子的教育方式，既要避免过度溺爱，确保孩子们不会因此变得骄纵任性，又要保证他们能够深切地感受到来自家庭的温暖和爱意，从而建立起健康的情感基础；既要防止过度严厉的教育方式，以免给孩子的成长带来压抑和挫败感，还要确保他们品行正直，培养出既有纪律性又富有创造力的个性。

3. 平等的亲子关系

儿子的性格跟我很不像，总是希望别人跟他讲道理，每次跟他讲什么的时候，他就会两只眼睛盯着你，然后认真地听你在说什么，听完以后他会自己思考。思考以后，还会提出一些相关的问题以及反馈。有什么想法也都是直接表达。"我很生气""我很不开心""我不喜欢你这样做"……用现在流行的话来讲，就是从不内耗。经期之前，激素分泌旺盛，荷尔蒙完全不受控制，我偶尔会跟他发脾气。他也会大哭，双手抱在胸前："哼，我不理你了。"但是过一会儿又凑到我身边，"喵……我是一只小猫咪……"这是来"和解"了。这举动融化了我的心，很暖，谢谢他能在被骂后还化身小可爱来化解我的怒气。所以我在我儿子身上意识到了一个问题：并非所有问题都需要用暴力和大声的责备来解决。相反，只要我们用温和的语气耐心地解释，把问题的危害和重要性讲清楚，孩子就能够明白、理解。

虽然我明白这个道理，但是事情发生的时候，我真的很难理性地做到这一点。

比如，早上我儿子先醒了，过了一会又听到女儿在卧室说话的声音。我在楼下叫她快点刷牙洗脸，穿好校服一会送她去学校。那天刚好家里的阿姨休息，做完早饭之后，我还要准备女儿上学要带的午饭。一整个早上，我像个陀螺，忙得团团转。而且我很不喜欢做饭，一走进厨房就心烦意乱。

等我把所有东西都准备好之后，还没见女儿下楼。当我上楼看到她躺在床上"装睡"时，我内心的怒火瞬间被点燃。我忍着怒气拍拍她，试图叫醒她，但她仍然装睡，一动不动。"你真的没有听到我叫你吗？"我提高了分贝，语气严肃。她睁开惺忪的睡眼："妈妈，我真的没有听到，我刚醒了一下，又睡着了。"尽管她解释了，但我依旧很烦躁，催促她赶快抓紧时间洗漱。都已经走到楼梯口了，我又折返回去，指责女儿磨蹭，毫无时间观念。

下楼时，儿子打破了紧张的氛围："姐姐，你看妈妈今天好辛苦，有好多事情要做。"他凑到姐姐身边问："姐姐，你今天是很累吗？"有人一关心，女儿的情绪也绷不住了，湿了眼眶："我真的睡着了。"

看着她委屈的样子，我忽然于心不忍，觉得自己是不是对她太凶了，但我知道，我的性格就是很急躁，很难在气头上保持冷静。

吃完早饭之后，我女儿主动收拾碗筷。她知道今天阿姨不在，想为我分担一些家务，其实她已经是很懂事的小朋友了。

孩子毕竟是孩子，他们有着自己的天性和节奏，我们不能要求他们像成年人一样思考和行动。如果要让他们像大人一样自律，什么都能做到，这对他们未免太不公平了。

真正让我意识到问题的严重性是在一次女儿游完泳洗澡的时候。我看到她右后肩上有两个几乎重叠的紫红色牙印，一个比较浅，一个很深，已经咬得呈紫红了，一看就是很用力要下去的。我问女儿这是怎么回事，她说是同学咬的。"别人咬你，你为什么不制止呢？而且连续咬了两口！"我急切地问。女儿有点委屈："他们不跟我玩，但是后来我实在很痛，我叫他停下。我非常非常痛的时候，我才让他停下来。"听到这里，我心中五味杂陈，愤怒和心疼交织。她的意思是，她为了讨好其他小朋友，为了他们跟她一起玩，就去忍受这种疼痛。我不敢想象这个事情如果再严重下去会发生到什么程度。如果女儿到了青春期，有人以类似的方式要挟她，你要跟我玩可以，但是你要付出一定的东西，她会不会也委曲求全？

安慰完女儿，我和老师进行了沟通。在冷静下来后，我开始反思自己的教育方式，发现自己在对待孩子的问题上，深受童年时期的影响。我的童年是不幸的，充斥着大人们的愤怒和暴躁，他们总是用简单粗暴、缺乏耐心的方式和我沟通。现在我也依葫芦画瓢地成了我讨厌的那种人，虽然我时时刻刻提醒自己要用爱去养育他们，但我根本没有办法躲掉从小亲身体验过的点点滴滴。我在和孩子们的互动中过于强调规则和纪律，忽视了情感的传递。有时候可能会用命令式的语气与孩子交流，让他们感觉被压迫。

我必须及时改变自己和孩子的相处状态了，要用更加温和、耐心和理解的方式和孩子交流，尝试用更多的拥抱和鼓励，让她知道，无论她做什么，我都会在她身边支持她。有时候我就在想，我应该把自己也当成一个孩子，用平等的视角和孩子们相处，融入他们。要认真倾听他们的想法和观点，及时给予他们积极的反馈。即使他们的意见和我们的想法不同，也要尊重他们的权利，鼓励他们表达自己的看法。

这对我是个挑战，需要改变自己暴躁的脾气，需要戒掉从小耳濡目染的习惯，但是我希望能够建立一个更加健康、更加充满爱的家庭环境，让我的孩子们在一个支持和鼓励的氛围中成长。

半年前，我女儿主动跟我倾诉她的苦恼。她告诉我，她发现自己和别的孩子不一样，觉得自己很奇怪，甚至不喜欢这样的自己。听到这些话，我内心很乱，很诧异，也很难过，更是焦虑万分。我立刻对她表示了支持和鼓励，尽力向她传达了爱自己的重要性。我很庆幸自己因为上次女儿被咬的事情及时进行了自我反思，调整了和孩子们的相处方式，让女儿能够大胆和我分享她内心的想法，现在还有足够的时间把这种消极情绪扼杀在摇篮里。在这之后，我也和她的家教老师 Ian 讨论了这个问题。Ian 老师肯定也和她讲了这个问题，虽然我不完全清楚他们的具体谈话内容，但是我知道这些谈话和鼓励对她产生了积极的影响,我再次询问女儿是否喜欢自己,她回答:"喜欢,我们都是不同的个体,每个人都是不一样的,要接受自己的缺点,比如说我就是很磨叽很拖拉,可是这就是我,我仍然爱拖拖拉拉的自己。"等等!她说她拖拖拉拉!瞬间,刚放下的心又有了新的焦虑,女儿好像是在告诉我她知道自己有拖拖拉拉的习惯,也接纳了自己所有的缺点并不打算改正……好吧,她至少懂得爱自己了。

不久之后,她要参加一个画画比赛,现在正在构思阶段。我问她:"你可以跟我分享一下你的想法吗?"她回答:"每个人都是不完美的自己,每个人都是有缺陷的。但是,我们要爱自己。"我说:"那你准备怎么画呢?"她说:"我准备画一个小女孩不爱自己,很困惑,好像自己要掉到水潭里一样。然后等她想通了,她就会长出翅膀,变成彩色的,然后从困住她的水塘里飞出来。"接下来的话更让我震惊:"她是美丽的,无论她怎么样不完美,她都是她自己,她会接受她自己的不完美。"这幅画象征着她对自我的接纳,我为她的成长感到欣慰,她已经从一个困惑的孩子成长为一个懂得爱自己的勇敢女孩。一个人无论有多少缺陷和不足,他都是独一无二的,都值得被温柔相待,都值得被爱。

4. 孩子身上的我

我女儿经常说,有个可爱的弟弟就会有个搞笑的妈妈,有个搞笑的妈妈就会有个奇怪的女儿。从去年开始,她就动不动想结婚。和小区的一个只见过一两次的小男孩约定长大后就结婚。聊天时,跟她的老师说:"你该结婚了。"我问过她:"女儿,你为什么想结婚,是觉得结婚是很幸福的事情吗?"她说:"对呀,结婚就是很幸福的事情。以后我会对我的宝宝很好,他们如果想学画画,我就给他们安排课让他们去学画画,如果他们想游泳我就带他们去游泳。如果他们有任何想做的事情,我都会安排给他们做……"我继续问:"那你怎么赚钱呀?""这个时候已经赚钱了呀,我是一个餐馆的老板了!我会做很多很多好吃的菜，然后让我老公拿去餐馆卖，赚了很多的钱。我就可以把这些钱拿来给我的宝宝他们一起用，给他们上课，给他们买好吃的……"

看着她，那一瞬间我明白了，孩子就像一面镜子，反映出我们的模样，学习、复刻我们的行为和特质。在她的观念里，我们的家庭是幸福的，妈妈是爱学习的，妈妈是特别爱宝宝的，宝宝要做什么事妈妈都会带着他们去做。她感受到的是，妈妈做这一切都是很开心很幸福的，所以她憧憬的未来也是这样的。我很庆幸自己给孩子们营造了积极、幸福的家庭氛围，为孩子们提供了情感支持和安全感。当然，我心里还有稍许自责。女儿小时候，我还深陷病态没有走出来，错过了很多和她共度的重要时刻。同时，由于我自己对英语的抗拒，也遗憾地错过了为她打下坚实英语基础的幼儿时期。如今，看着眼前活泼可爱的儿子，我时常努力回忆女儿小时候是否也有如此可爱的一面，可是只有一丁点儿的画面感。我懊恼自己为什么要被一个看不见摸不着的病魔所困扰，以至于错失了女儿珍贵的幼年成长。遗憾无法弥补，但我深知要珍惜当下，全心全意地陪伴孩子们，不断创造新的共同回忆，不再缺席他们的成长。

各种技能和知识的学习也许超出了我的能力范围，只能为他们找专业的老师指导，但是，关于精神层面的塑造，这是家长的责任。需要我们做的不仅仅是口头鼓励或短暂的激励，而应该通过自身的行动来展示正确的价值观和积极的生活态度。孩子们会从我们的行为中学习，他们会观察我们如何面对挑战，如何处理困难，以及如何保持积极的心态。

2024年3月31日8:15，我陪我女儿完成了她人生的第一个5km户外跑。还没跑出小区的时候她就摔了一跤，膝盖磨破了皮，我问她能不能坚持，她哭着说："我没事的妈妈，我可以完成。"跑步结束后，她的苹果手表给了她5个运动奖章，她非常开心，小脸蛋上是满满的幸福，好像她征服了全世界一样。每次看见她脸上开花般的笑容时我的心变得很暖很柔软。

之后我还带女儿参加了一次马拉松比赛。这次的心态和我之前自己参加时的忐忑、犹豫截然不同。上一次，比赛的前一天，我心里各种担忧，翻来覆去没法入睡。甚至第二天起床时，还产生了抵触情绪，犹豫还要不要去。

但这次不一样，我特意提前一天开车一个多小时去取马拉松的号码牌，往返就两个多小时。第二天早上六点，我就起床准备好一切，开车带着女儿前往马拉松的出发点。整个过程，没有一丝的懈怠情绪，反而觉得这是一次难得的经历，可以和女儿一起感受马拉松的魅力和氛围。

我女儿还是很厉害的，第一次跟我一起跑步的时候，就一口气跑了六公里，让我不敢相信。弟弟现在虽然才4岁，但是也能跟着我跑一点。他还主动提出要跟我一起训练跑步，说："妈妈，你训练我跑步吧，长距离对我来说太难了，我跑短距离，我也想以后跟你去参加马拉松，我也想去比赛。"我很开心因为我的影响，孩子们能够从小如此热爱运动，并且拥有一个健康的身体。

当然，这种影响是双向的。我努力为孩子们做出正能量的榜样，引导他们走向积极的人生道路。同时，他们也在不断地激励我，让我更加坚定地朝着更美好的方向发展。我们相互影响，共同成长，形成了一种积极的互动和反馈。

"幸运的人一生都在被童年治愈，不幸的人一生都在治愈童年。"不幸的是，我属于后者；但幸运的是，我有两个可爱的小朋友——我的女儿和儿子。大手牵着小手，信任、依赖和爱就在这之间传递。在陪伴他们成长的过程中，我仿佛重新走过了自己的童年，重新养育了童年的自己。我总是被他们的纯真和童心打动，这是世界上为数不多的纯洁圣地。和他们在一起我仿佛置身于一个无瑕的世界，我可以卸下防御的盔甲，好好审视自己的内心，让一切焦虑和浮躁都归于平静。

第七章 自我的革命

我们总喜欢向光而行，但有时候，最强大的光芒并非来自外界，而是源于我们内心深处的自我革命。每一次自我挑战，每一次心态调整，都是我们自我救赎的一步，都是一场关于自我的革命。生活就像一场永无止境的修行，我在其中跌跌撞撞，却也在其中逐渐成熟与坚强。回首过去，曾经的那些困惑和迷茫，如今都变作宝贵的财富。

古装剧里，门派的少主被恶灵附身了。而这恶灵正是他父亲昔日的手下，意图借助少主的身躯增强自身力量，进而解救其被囚禁的主人——即少主的父亲。在关键时刻，一位来自天外天的神仙降临，施展神通把恶灵从少主体内驱逐了出去，让少主得以恢复神智。当少主与这位天外天的神仙对话良久时，他的脑海中突然又响起了另一个声音，令他头痛欲裂，内心挣扎不已。面对此景，天外天的神仙感慨道："看来，并非外界的力量试图入侵你的身体，控制你的意志。有时，是你自己无法驾驭内心的纷乱，导致自己与自己为敌。"

这番话让我深有感触。的确，人生中的许多困扰和挣扎，往往并非源于外界的压力或干扰，而是源于我们内心的恐惧、疑虑和不安。只有当我们学会掌控自己的内心，才能真正地走出困境，迎接更加美好的未来。

1. 做情绪的舵手

在日常生活中，我们经常会遇到各种触发情绪的事件，而愤怒是其中最为强烈和难以控制的一种。然而，学会如何正确处理愤怒和压力，是我们每一个人都必须面对的重要课题。不妨以我前段时间经历的一连串的琐事为例，讨论一下如何正确应对愤怒和压力。

我在国内买了一些家乡的土特产，并请朋友帮忙交给我筛选后的快递公司进行中转至我的目的地。这家快递公司货物丢失会照价赔付还退还运费，我也和她再三确认了是否赔付条款属实，前两次邮寄过程相对顺利，我都有惊无险地收到了包裹。然而，最后一个包裹却迟迟未到，也没有任何消息。我联系快递公司询问情况，他们坚称只寄出了两箱，而且我也只付了两箱的转运费。

朋友明明给我寄了3个包裹总重85斤，但是我只收到了两个，重量为30斤。面对我的再三追问，快递公司开始含糊其词。他们先是告诉我快递被卡在海关了，后面又说需要走另一个较慢的渠道寄送。但是，我对此完全不知情。当我再次询问时，他们开始避而不答。这种情况持续了整整半个月，我的耐心几乎被消磨殆尽，暂且不说物品本身的价值，我内心迫切想要快速拿到东西的心情，大几千昂贵的空运快递费用，以及由此产生的极度失望和愤怒，都已经达到了顶点。情绪上头的时候，我给对方发送了一段文字，内容直白地指出对方行为的不负责，连最基本的诚信都做不到。没想到，她反倒对我恶语相向，最后竟然还把我拉黑了。

我明白，他们之所以如此嚣张，无非是认为我身处国外，无法与他们面对面交涉。即使是在国内，又有几个人会为了一个快递而大动干戈，特地跑去当地面对面交涉呢？面对这种困境，我难道只能自己生闷气吗？

因为女儿上学的问题，我们搬家到了新的城市。在入住这个房子的前一天，房子的主人拉尔夫把每一个地方都做了仔细检查，并拍照记录下每一处损坏或存在的印记，以确保我退房时会还给他一个一模一样的。我明确告诉他，如果弄脏了我会负责将整个房子重新油漆，保证恢复原状，但是细心的拉尔夫还是坚持一一拍照。也许是我大大咧咧习惯了，对这种极其细致的做法感觉有点不太适应，觉得过于麻烦和不被信任。但是我也明白，每个人都有自己的生活方式和处事原则，拉尔夫可能只是习惯用这种方式来保护自己的财产，所以我还是选择尊重并尽量配合。

第七章 自我的革命

这个拉尔夫刚买完房子就租给了我，所以他自己也还没住过这个房子，对这儿挺陌生的。当然，相应的就是房子没有经过彻底的修整和维护，导致我不得不经常面对各种小问题。按照我们这里的租赁惯例，房屋出现任何问题，无论大小，皆由他负责修缮，而且签约的租房合同里也是如此写明了由拉尔夫修缮屋里屋外，租客只要爱惜房屋即可。眼看天气马上就要热了，我发现房子的纱窗拆下来还没有装，于是叫了装修的师傅。师傅说纱窗的把手坏了，网纱的部分也有破损，需要买新的来换。拉尔夫听了之后，说他自己来看看能不能搞定。他来查看之后，用胶布把破洞的地方都贴上了，也买了新的门锁部分准备自己换，但是新锁的尺寸和型号都不对。那天他自己弄了好几个小时也没弄好，只得先行回家，准备重新选购合适的门把手。

不久之后，他买到了新的、比较合适的门把手，问我："你会装吗？"我说："我不会装，我从来没做过这些事情，也不想做"他又问："那你家阿姨会装吗？"我说："阿姨70多岁了，你觉得她会装吗？"他说："这个很简单的，你叫她学一下就可以了。"我说："不好意思，阿姨要做饭、洗衣服，家里事务都是她一个人做，她已经很辛苦了，没有时间来学这个。"而且她已经70多岁了，我不觉得她有义务或者说能力去学习组装一个纱窗。

某天，一位水务局的工作人员忽然到访，对家里进行了细致的漏水检查。在确认所有水龙头都已紧闭无误后，工作人员表示水表仍在缓缓转动，这说明家里某个位置存在隐秘的漏水问题。经过一番仔细的搜寻与排查，我们终于找到了漏水的位置。有一个户外的水龙头坏了，虽然关紧了，但是一直在漏水。确认好漏水之后，拉尔夫立刻购买了一个定时器，他自己过来安装。安装的时候我不在家，所以后来要使用的时候，拉尔夫一边自己翻阅着说明书，一边通过视频通话的方式教我怎么使用定时器。但是，通过视频通过的指导并不是那么清晰有效，步骤烦琐又难以理解，需要先点击一个菜单，按住某个功能键五秒，再跳转到另一个选择键，紧接着还要把左边出水管的水龙头拧下来更换到右边的出水管使用……总之需要一系列操作才能完成顺利出水。等等，请注意一下这里，更换水龙头到另外一个出水口，这个定时器有两个出水口，能轻易拧动出水口的人我想应该少见吧。

对此，我是有些不满的，我们家中的家务都是由一位70多岁的阿姨负责，她连简单的电子产品都不会使用，甚至不会用微信发送视频，更不用说如此复杂的操作了。我很疑惑，为什么拉尔夫不能直接更换一个易于操作的水龙头，一拧就直接出水，又简单又实用的不好吗？但他说找不到等等，具体的原因我到现在也没能理解。现在这样一直漏水，那多出来的水费也要我承担吗？

总之，无奈之下我暂时同意使用定时器，至少先解决漏水的问题，避免水资源浪费和产生不必要的水费。我想着实在不行每次用这个水龙头之前都由我先操作打开，再让阿姨做浇花之类的后续内容，而且是手动浇花。按照法律来说租客只使用自动浇水系统，没有责任用手动浇花。谁知道第二天拉尔夫找来修水管的师傅也不会用这个定时器，他拆下来之后没有把它装回去，水龙头还是一直不停地漏水。我只能再次发消息询问拉尔夫解决办法，结果他的话语里说我对漏水事情抱怨，说我一直在抱怨。

我很好奇我的哪句话让他觉得我在不停地抱怨。毕竟水费是我在付，水龙头一直漏水我当然会烦恼，这个问题一直不解决，对我来说就是一个困扰，毕竟水费是由我支付，因为漏水，我两个缴纳了1000多美元的水费，要知道，正常来说2个月水费也就在200左右。

在沟通解决水龙头的过程中，我和拉尔夫还因为更换的费用产生了分歧。我询问维修师傅更换一个日常大众家庭都在使用的那种最简单的水龙头需要多少钱，对方表示人工加材料费共200美金，拉尔夫却说师傅跟他说的是100美金，而加装定时器只需要五六十，所以他才选择定时器而不是更换水龙头。我没办法确定装修师傅会跟他说100，因为以美国的人工价格来说，这是不可能的事情。后来我翻看和他的聊天记录里他清清楚楚的文字里说了换水龙头两个一共300美金，这件事让我想起我们搬进这个新家的第一天。当时我找了清洁公司对整个房屋做彻底清扫，包括中央空调的深层管道清洁、地毯清洗、各种管道清洗等各项内容。我一直都是找这家公司帮我清洁，前年我家清洁的时候花了700美金，然后今年这个房子他们告诉我需要1000，因为房子面积变大了，清洁工作比之前那边要很多，耗时和工量都要大很多。

第七章 自我的革命

清洁完的第二天，拉尔夫问我花了多少钱，我说1000。他表现得很诧异，他说怎么可能，他跟我说是650啊。当时我就蒙了，我心想我和清洁公司那家的老婆关系还挺好的，怎么可能跟你说650，跟我说1000呢？而且之前在我家那边打扫的时候还700，不可能反倒变便宜了吧？这两次价格的分歧，都好像我故意报高价格能从中牟利一样，话又说回来，清洁的钱是我自己出的与拉尔夫无关，可这金额差让我心里十分不舒服。

暂时解决了水龙头漏水，家里的门又出问题了，一扇门脱轨了。门是实木的，非常重，我和阿姨尝试了很长时间也没办法将其修复到位。最让我担心的是，这样重的门如果突然掉下来，不小心砸到孩子们该怎么办。我和拉尔夫沟通后他说没在本地，我也没问具体来修门的时间，过了几天另外一个门锁也坏了，无法打开，完全拧不动，我用东西撬松了锁用尽全力晃动那个锁很久才打开，告知拉尔夫后定好了维修时间，但因为网购的门锁迟迟没到，维修时间一再推迟。等门锁终于到了，却发现型号不对。另一扇脱轨的门也只是简单地将滑落的轨道重新推回去，却没有意识到轨道松动可能是因为长年累月的使用导致固定不牢，很容易因为门的重量而再次垮下。果然，我们一拉，门又掉了下来。考虑到门的重量和孩子们的安全，我建议拉尔夫找专业的维修人员来彻底解决问题。然而，他却反过来质问我，是否有正确使用门，孩子们是否在玩耍时用力拉门了？难道门的使用方法不就是拉开再关上吗？而孩子们的力气足以拉动一扇大人都觉得费力的实木门吗？拉尔夫开始数落我："我每个礼拜都要过去帮你修东西……你连最基本的把水龙头取下来换到另外一边都做不到，还需要别人来帮助你……"这些话真是让我啼笑皆非，反复上门维修难道不是因为房子过于老旧又没专业修整吗？难道不是反复买错配件吗？从纱窗、水龙头到现在的门锁，问题层出不穷。我都没有怨言这样反反复复的维修会占用我的时间，影响我们一家的正常生活。我每个月都按时支付租金，拉尔夫当然有责任确保房屋设施的正常运作。我为什么要因为你的房子出现问题就改变自己的生活方式呢？

之前，他还跟我家阿姨说过："你让她做吧，她还那么年轻。"这里的她指的是我，这样的话让我感觉非常冒犯和不适。先不说这是我的家事，他作为房屋主人本就没有立场来干涉；就算我真的愿意并且有能力去处理家务琐事，那我请保姆是为了什么呢？每个人的精力都是有限的，我既要照顾孩子，又要忙于工作，现在刚搬家又要修补屋子，我真的觉得自己有些力不从心，难以从容应对这一切。更何况，我还要时刻关注并照顾自己的情绪和身心健康，让生活达到平衡，可这些乱七八糟的事让我更加身心疲惫。

这明明不是什么无法调和的矛盾，只是一个态度的问题。如果拉尔夫在交付房屋之前，能够进行彻底的维护和检查，而不是花费大量时间拍照以方便后期划分责任，我相信我们之间的矛盾会大大减少。同样，如果在维修过程中，拉尔夫能够更加细心地选择配件，避免因选购错误而增加维修的难度和复杂性，我相信我并不是一个不通情达理的人。最简单不过的方法就是找专业人员来处理这些不是更好吗？很多租客遇到任何自然坏掉或者老化的配件，都会直接打电话让房东来处理。而我自己能动手做的事情，我都会尽量自己去做。我们刚搬进来的时候，有很多小地方都是坏的，我都自己叫了师傅来修。比如有一扇百叶窗需要换，拉尔夫说换吧，到时候再跟他一起算费用。我也没跟他计较，因为一个百叶窗加上更换的费用也就200左右，我觉得这种小问题没必要那么计较，包括之前烘衣机的管道脱落也是我付钱修好的，还有很多地方的修修补补。结果他现在却……我也有想过自己拿200把水龙头修好就算了，但是我不想再这样继续纵容他了。

提到态度问题，让我想起去接女儿下课的时候。女儿一上车，我们正打算离开，一辆车开过来准备在隔壁车位停车。位置很窄，我有预感这辆车一定会蹭到我的。准备提醒一下对方司机的时候，那个女司机却用仇视的眼神瞪了我两眼。好吧，我决定保持不动，等待她完成停车。结果不出所料，果然撞上了，她的倒车镜刮到了我的倒车镜，发出"哐当"一声被刮掉了一点漆。然而，她只是瞥了我一眼就打算离开，眼神里透露着仇视和轻蔑。这下轮到我纳闷了，你撞了我，不是应该道歉吗？打算甩个眼神"杀死"我就转头离开？等她停好车，我打开车窗，用生硬的英文问她："Do you know you just hit me?（你知道你刚才撞到我了吗？）"她回应说："是的，我撞到你了，但看起来并不严重，只是轻轻刮了一下。"我接着说："然后呢？你是不是应

第七章 自我的革命

该跟我道个歉？"她这才笑着说："哦，对不起。"我回应道："没关系，就这样吧。"然后我就离开了。

其实，事情的严重性往往取决于对方的态度。这位女士及时道歉，我瞬间觉得，即使她把我的倒车镜刮得很严重，也不是太大的问题，因为她的态度非常好。如果她继续用那种仇视的眼神看着我，不跟我道歉，我可能也会选择报警，哪怕把事情搞得复杂。只是为了内心的情绪有一个发泄的出口，并不是想得到什么实质性的赔偿。在反观和拉尔夫之间的数次摩擦，他不停地指责我，甚至试图支配我，不仅超出了其应有的界限，也无视了作为租户的我应有的尊重与权利。生活中，无论是小摩擦还是大冲突，以一颗平和、理解的心去对待，用积极的态度去沟通，往往能将问题化解于无形。而那些消极面对问题、试图逃避责任的人，只会让事态变得更加复杂。

随后几天我一直受拉尔夫的影响，心情不是很好。在接女儿回家的路上，也无法保证专心致志，脑海里全是他发来的信息："我本来是看你不容易，结果你却把别人对你的好当作是理所当然……我只是想不到你来美国这么多年还是抱着这种大小姐心态……想不到你不但不感激，反而变本加厉……"这些话分散了我的注意力。那条路限速25迈，但是我开到了30迈，然后就被路旁的警察拦截了，还闪了警灯。我停下车，警察下车时，我惊讶地发现他竟然是前几天来过我家的那位。那天，我朋友把车停在路边，没有停在我家门口，引起了邻居的误会，结果招来了两辆警车，而他就是其中一位。

我试图用轻松的语气打破尴尬，提起之前的事情，试图用蹩脚的英语介绍自己的身份和情况。警察听后笑了笑，也想起了那天的事情，他点头说："是的，我记得了。"我用蹩脚的英文问他："你是要给我开罚单吗？"他犹豫了一下，然后笑着说："这次就算了，但下次别再开这么快了。"

那一刻，我真的感受到了自己内心的成长。十年前，我也曾因超速被开罚单，还被告上法庭，被判七年间不能有任何的违章，要不然就会没收我的驾照。当时的我沉默不语，只是乖乖地把驾照交给警察。然而现在，我敢于用我那不甚流利的英语去沟通，去争取自己的权益。尽管在回忆那天的事情时，我只能用蹩脚的英语挤出几个单词："my home the car park……no no good."但重要的是，我已经不再害怕用英语去沟通了。这不仅仅是语言上的进步，更是我内心成长的标志。这次的经历让我深刻体会到，内心的强大比任何外在的力量都要重要。它让我在面对困难和挑战时，能够保持冷静，勇敢地表达自己。

虽然这次勇敢的表达让我颇有成就感，但是和拉尔夫的矛盾多少还是影响到了我。就在第二天，我又一次无法集中注意力，开车时根本就没有注意到时速限制是多少，结果又超速了，被开了217美金的罚单。

权力差异真的可以改变一个人对自己的认知。回想起他一开始对我输出的讯息，言语中强调着他对我的帮助和善意。这不是一种寻常的提醒，而是间接的暗示着我是需要被照顾、帮助的一方，是脆弱、有缺陷或不足的。反之，他便在这关系中占据了强者的地位和人设。在这样不平等的关系中，我也逐渐相信了他对我的评价和定义，从而不自觉地认为他的观点和输出都是正确的，甚至被迫对他的行为产生了极度的感激，虽然事实上，他只是在履行合约规定的义务。想起他对我说过的一些话，例如："你不但没有感恩之心，还得寸进尺……"我心里感受到的极度愧疚，是我至今也无法弄明白的。我常在想，我是不是不知足，不讲理，很过分等等。但细想起我跟他沟通的诉求，如修理掉落的门框和（其他的例子），其实都是我和家人的居住安全和基本需求。这样矛盾的情绪，我想是他作为关系中的"强者"让我对他充满歉意并报以感恩之心，以此来操控我的想法和情绪吧。比如，每次我礼貌性地回复"谢谢"之后，他都会紧跟着发来一些长篇的消息，强调我理应对他表示感激，似乎我欠了他一份极大的人情。这一系列的行为让我对他产生了极度的恐惧和惧怕，以至于当他用侮辱和骚扰的言语攻击我时，我都不敢做出任何反击，生怕又是自己做得太过分，不够知足和感恩。

我也尝试过努力去改变我们之间的不良关系，但换来的似乎只有更可怕的情绪绑架。当我慢慢的意识到自己的情绪失控时，我尝试向他表明说他的行为已经给我造成了恐惧，甚至不敢再点开他的短信了。他的回复竟是："嗯，其实我也不敢点开你的短信，因为害怕是哪里又坏了。"这时的我强烈地感觉到我的表态不被承认，并且还被冠上了更严重的罪名。他采用这种逃

第七章 自我的革命

避责任的方式，企图让我产生内疚感，仿佛是我单方面造成了我们之间的问题。之后的沟通都是：我说这些困扰已经让我睡不着，他说他因为担心我他也睡不着，无论我说什么他都总以我的话来还击，这种行为真的让我觉得很无语也孤立。

总之，搬进新家的整个过程都不是很顺利，总是有这样那样的事情发生。但生活好像总是这样，给我们一些连绵不断、突如其来的变故，这些事情的发生往往让我们措手不及，还没反应过来状况，心情就已经被糟糕的事情影响。旧的问题尚未理清，新的问题又接踵而至。生活如同多米诺骨牌，一连串地倒塌，迅速堆积，让人感到无比压抑。那段时间，"郁结于心"几个字非常具象地体现在我的身上，那些未解的问题、堆积的困扰，像一块巨石堆积在心头，让我喘不过气来。它们如同无形的刺，不断刺激着我的情绪。

如果放在以前，面对压力和挫折，我肯定会选择逃避，试图将自己藏在安全的壳里，一个人生闷气。这种方式仿佛在惩罚自己，不仅无助于问题的解决，反而让心情更加沉重，让问题积重难返。

为了缓解内心的怒火与不满，我学会了适当地宣泄。运动成为我释放情绪的有效途径，比如跑步，每一步的迈出都像是把烦恼和压力踩在脚下，随着汗水的流出，那些负面情绪也在一点点排出体外；比如打壁球，用力地挥拍，球被一颗颗猛击到墙上，再猛地回弹。每一次挥拍和反弹，都在把心中的怒火与不满拍出体外，让它们随着球的轨迹消散在空气之中。当然，宣泄并不意味着放任自己沉溺在情绪中，在情绪得到释放之后，我们还是要冷静地面对问题，寻求解决之道。虽然山高水长，我没办法亲自解决和快递公司的纠纷，但是我可以借助朋友的力量，帮助我报警，提供所有相关证据和聊天记录，让他们帮我。尽管时隔大半年，快递公司仍未给我应得的退款，只给了点零碎补偿，但我已经从这场无耻的纷争中解脱出来。维权是一定要的，却不会再用愤怒惩罚自己。

问题解决了，心结自然就打开了。即使真的遇到了实在难以解决的问题，我们也一样可以寻求专业的心理疏导，切忌一个人生闷气。

而且，我发现控制情绪的关键，其实在于区分情绪作用下的主观认知和客观事实。

当愤怒来临时，我们的主观认知往往会被情绪的波涛裹挟，我们可能会觉得全世界都在与我们为敌，每个人都对我们不怀好意，这种主观认知的偏差会让我们做出错误的判断和决策。比如，我们可能会因为一时的气愤而说出伤人的话，或者做出冲动的行为，这些都会在冷静下来后让我们感到后悔。所以，控制情绪的首要任务就是学会在愤怒来临时保持冷静和理智，不被情绪所左右。面对忽然暴涨的情绪，我们可以通过深呼吸、暂时离开现场、冥想等方式来平复激动的心情，让自己有足够的时间和空间恢复平静。

同时，我们也需要培养一种客观看待问题的习惯。在愤怒过后，我们应该尝试从不同的角度去审视事件，了解事情的全貌和真相，避免被主观认知所误导。通过收集更多的信息和证据，我们可以更加客观地评估情况，然后做出更为明智和合理的决策。

在生活的旅途中，我们总是会遇到这样那样的困扰和挫折，或许来自快递的失误，或许来自对方的出尔反尔，但无论是什么，它们都是我们成长路上的磨砺。每一次的耐心沟通，每一次积极地寻求解决，都是我对生活的积极态度和对问题的勇敢面对。我相信，只有真正掌握了应对情绪的智慧，我们才能在生活中游刃有余，享受到更多的快乐和满足。

现在，我已经不会再在意任何人对我的看法，无论背后或者当面说我任何好话还是坏话，我都觉得那些是无关痛痒的，我的唯一追求是活出自己的快乐，而且我现在对各类聚会敬而远之，更享受一个人的时光——沉浸于品尝健康美味的佳肴，陪伴孩子嬉戏于他们的小小世界。我尽量避免给他人带去麻烦，同样也不喜欢别人来打扰我，尤其是那些繁琐的应酬，它们会扰乱我平静而简单的生活节奏。远离这些纷扰后，我发现内心前所未有的清澈，烦恼似乎也随之消散。曾经，即便是简单的出门散步或逛街，我也习惯于结伴而行；而今，我独自便能悠然自得。独自品尝海鲜大餐，独自享受涮火锅的乐趣，每一口都滋味醇厚，比与人共餐更加自在。我随心所欲，无需与任何人协商或妥协，时间全由自己支配。世人常畏孤独，而我，却在这份孤寂中找到了自我成长的沃土。孤独，对我而言，已化为一种深刻的自我探索与独立生活的艺术，一种无需依附、全然属于自我的存在方式，我已在独处中找到内心的平静与力量。

2. 敏感的新内涵

我似乎天生就具备一种敏锐的特质，如果让我重新选择职业，我相信只有侦探能发挥我这一特点：一旦让我发现任何细微的线索，我就会顺藤摸瓜，一路深入追查，直到揭示出事情的全部真相。

我的敏感并不仅仅局限于解决问题上，它更像是一种全方位的感知。我常常对生活中的各种事情有强烈的预感，这些预感往往会按照我想象的那样，以惊人的准确性发生。

但同时，这种敏感性也给我带来了一些困扰。在经历困难和挑战时，它让我更加深刻地感受到痛苦和失落。还会让我过于关注他人的反应，过于拘泥于自己的言行是否得体。这种过度的在意，有时会使我在人际交往中显得紧张而小心翼翼，甚至影响到我的自信与表达。而且，当我的身体出现哪怕一丁点微小的不适时，我都能够立刻察觉到，并且会不自觉地开始过度解读这些信号。继而陷入一种自我猜测的循环里，不断地在网上搜索与这些症状可能相关的疾病。我每天在不同的症状之间来回跳转，试图自己诊断自己，结果往往都是把自己吓得半死，还没有看过医生就已经因为自己的想象而身心俱疲。

我深知这种内耗对自己的病情并无益处，但与生俱来的敏感多疑又难以摆脱，很长一段时间我都对自己的"敏感体质"深恶痛绝。但实际上，敏感像是一扇敞开的窗户，把痛苦和困扰透过来的同时，也让我更加清晰地捕捉到生活中的细微幸福。

比如，我时常在和孩子们相处时因为一些小细节而感动。我跑步时，女儿骑着滑板车在后面追我，一回头就能看到她红扑扑的小脸。我笑着大喊：

"宝贝，追我呀，小短腿！"这种与孩子间简单纯粹的互动，让我觉得生活中满是幸福。

敏感也让我能够更加敏锐地感知到孩子们的需求和情感变化。之前，俩孩子都是自己睡自己的床，但前段时间他们生病了，就都跑到我房间来了。我儿子尤其黏我，晚上睡着了也得摸摸我在不在身边。要是摸不到，他立刻就醒，翻身就往外跑，边跑边喊"妈妈"。有一次，他感冒打呼声音实在太大，我根本睡不着。等他和姐姐都睡沉了，我就跑到他房间去睡。可没想到，半夜我就听见他小脚丫噔噔噔地跑过走廊，嘴里还嗒嗒地喊着"妈咪妈咪"。我赶紧打开房门叫他，他一进房门就栽倒在床上睡得呼呼的，看那样子已经困得不行了。没过一会，他大概睡得不安稳，开始乱动。我轻拍着他说："妈妈在这里呢，别怕，别怕……"他听了立马安静下来，又呼呼睡了。

只要我说："妈妈起床了，你再睡会儿吧。"他立刻就会迷迷糊糊地坐起来，半睁着眼睛看着我说："不睡了，我也起床。"我问他："那妈妈陪你再睡会儿，还是起床？"他抱着我的脖子，撒娇地说："再睡一会儿吧。"儿子的纯真和爱意，像火焰般点燃了我内心的温暖。明明前一天晚上我还因为他调皮训了他。

这种高度敏感的特性，还数次在危急关头挽救了我的生命。

一次发生在我刚到美国不久，我差点因为自己的无知和粗心大意没能从死神那挣脱。那时，我在工作中需要使用一种杀虫剂。这种杀虫剂的使用方法是封闭门窗后打开罐子，让烟雾弥漫整个屋子以起到杀虫效果。在这之前，我从来没接触过这个产品，再加上不认识英文，我无法看懂说明书，只是简单地听别人描述了使用方法。但重要的是，没有人告诉我在使用过程中人不能留在室内，没人说自己也没往这个方面想更没有这些常识。

按照指示操作之后，没多久我就感觉头晕目眩，呼吸困难。我意识到情况不妙，挣扎着向门口移动，想尽快逃离这个空间。当时我心里只有一个念头：我不能就这样死了，没有人知道我在这里，我必须靠自己的力量逃出去。但还没走几步，我就已经无法控制自己身体，栽倒在地，失去了意识。

当再次醒过来时，我发现自己躺在外的草地上，房门敞开着，大半个身体已经爬到了外面。我竟然在失去意识之前,凭借求生的本能爬到了室外。尽管没办法回忆起具体的逃生过程,但可以确定的是,是强烈的求生欲望驱使我逃出了生天。

我慢慢爬到更远的草地上休息,意识完全清醒之后。拖着并未完全恢复的身体,起身继续工作,完毕。去工具店购买所需的工具。店主注意到我的异常,惊讶地问我为什么脸和脖子都通红。我当时只是微微一笑,没有多说什么。因为那种惊心动魄的经历所带来的深刻感受,是我时至今日也无法用言语来形容的。

大概是劫后余生的庆幸吧。在封闭的屋子里,被有毒的烟雾包围,呼吸困难,意识模糊,那种无助和恐惧至今仍历历在目。而当我恢复意识时,却惊喜地发现自己竟然逃出了生天。生命是如此的脆弱,在一瞬间可能就会失去;但同时,生命又是如此的顽强和坚韧,即使在绝境中,也能爆发出求生的本能。

我的生命,就像被重新点燃的蜡烛,虽然微弱,但是顽强。那是我又一次见证生命的韧性,我没有理由随意浪费。

还有一次也是发生在很多年前。当时我在重庆下飞机后需要转车回老家,但是因为临近年关,时间又很晚了,已经没有其他交通工具可选,只有黑市汽车了。无奈之下我只能上了一辆11座的车,选了驾驶室后面第二排的单人座位坐下。没过多久一个女孩也上了车,坐在我前面。聊天中我们得知,她跟我乘坐的是同一班飞机,更巧的是,我们的老家竟然在同一个地方,她在离市区很近的一个小县城。我们俩都觉得很有缘分,就互相加了微信。在众人陆续上车的过程里,有一个人引起了我的注意。他带了一个钓鱼包,上车后动作非常熟练地把包塞进了车门正对的两排联排座位的下方。跟着他的动作我发现那里还放着一根空心铁棍。然后他走到车厢最后,选择了一个单排座位坐下。坐下后,他的眼神在车内四处游移,从头到尾地扫视车上的每一个人。那眼神仿佛一台扫描仪,能识别出每个人衣着打扮价值几何。

没过多久,又上来了一个男孩。这个男孩一上车就显得嬉皮笑脸,一直在那边笑,笑得人不寒而栗。他还特意看了一眼放着钓鱼包的座位下面,就这一看让我警惕。而且我注意到，他看向之前那个放东西在座位下的男子的眼神非常奇怪。更让我感到不寻常的是，尽管车内并不算很吵，大家都在有一句没一句地闲聊，但每当那个嬉皮笑脸的男孩发一条信息，拿着钓鱼包的那个男子的手机就会"叮咚"响一声。而每当拿着钓鱼包的男子回复信息，嬉皮笑脸的男孩的手机也会随之"叮咚"作响。这个微小的细节被我捕捉到了，我察觉到情况有些不对劲，立刻警觉起来，发信息给坐在我前排的女孩。

那个女孩子看了我的信息后，也开始仔细观察确认情况。过了十几分钟，她回复我说："的确，事情看起来确实有些不对劲。"女孩决定试探一下那个嬉皮笑脸的男孩。她故意问了他一些问题，比如住在哪里、要去哪里、老家是哪里等等。男孩的回答虽然看起来镇定自若，但是女孩就是他所回答那个地方的本地人，知道他说的明显有出入，发消息告诉我嬉笑男的确有问题。还好，车上的大家都在聊天，男孩完全没有察觉到女孩的试探。

很快，我们的车到了加油站。趁着加油的时候，大家都去上厕所或下车透气了。我和女孩也从加油站的工作人员那里得知这一带经常发生麻抢事件，就是把一整车的人都麻醉了，然后再抢劫他们。听到这些，我们俩决定不再上车，女孩立刻打电话给他爸爸，让他开车来接我们。大概40分钟之后，司机在一个很安静的环境下打电话给我，问我们出发了没有，说他们已经到目的地了。按照时间计算，他们至少需要两个半小时，根本不可能现在就到。再加上他那边的环境异常安静，安静得诡异。这时，我们几乎可以肯定他们是一伙的。

回想起这次经历，我深感自己的敏锐和果断行动是多么重要。这大概就是"硬币有两面"吧，敏感赋予我更深刻地感知世界的能力，也让我更容易受到伤害，更容易被外界所影响。真希望拥有一个掌控敏感的开关，既能细腻温柔地享受生活，又能在面对伤害和不快时一笑而过。想要和"敏感"友好相处，我还有很长的路要走，希望我们都能在敏感和顿感之间从容切换。

3. 破旧立新，解放思维

送女儿去游泳队的时候，我们的车总会停在一个固定的位置上，然后绕一大圈从前门进去。到现在为止，她在那个游泳池两三年了，将近三年的时间我们都是走前门。直到前几天我忽然得知我们停车的位置就是侧门，只需要一推开门，我们就可以直接到达车旁。我非常诧异地问女儿："宝宝，你知道从这门也可以进去吗？"她说："知道呀！""那为什么我们还要每次绕那么远？走侧门这里更方便呀！""我知道这里可以出来，但是我们已经习惯走前门了不是吗？"

这件简单的事情让我开始重新审视"习惯"这件事。"习惯"很多时候会让我感觉到舒适和自在，积极的习惯还可以帮助我们保持稳定和连续性，成为我们前进的动力。然而，一旦某种习惯根深蒂固，就有可能阻碍我们有更好的选择。

提及惯性思维，我不由得想到女儿同个画室同学的妈妈 Jenny。她在面对问题、解决问题时总是保持开放的态度。哪怕她老公是一名西医的 ICU 重症监护医生，在她头痛时我建议她去看中医，看马医生，她也欣然接受并且积极尝试。她对新事物总是充满好奇，我们俩在同一个拳馆打拳，我跟她讲有另外一家拳馆氛围更好，她很快就去体验，不会固执己见。看到她如此乐于接受新鲜事物，我也深受启发，觉得自己也应该去勇敢尝试一下新的事物，否则很可能会错过许多美好的东西。

惯性思维是我们生活中的常见现象，它像是一种思维定式，让我们在面对新问题时，总是倾向于用过去的经验和知识来解决。陷入惯性思维后，我们会不愿意去尝试新的方法和思路。比如在短视频平台，有些人穿着白大褂、拿着保温杯泡枸杞水，我们总会习惯性认为他们是医生，对他们的言论和产品深信不疑，这就是惯性思维和刻板印象在作祟。

在抑郁症患者中，消极的惯性思维更是常见。它就像一个不断循环播放的负面磁带，反复强调患者的无能、无价值感和失败。它不断地侵蚀着患者的自我认知，使我们难以看到自己的优点和成就，甚至对自己的存在意义产生怀疑。在这种思维的影响下，患者可能会对自己所做的一切事情都持有否定态度，无论这些事情是否真正值得肯定。

惯性思维在抑郁症患者寻求和接受新的治疗方法时，也可能成为一道难以逾越的障碍。抑郁症患者可能曾经尝试过某种治疗方法但效果并不明显，于是便对这种方法及其相关的一切产生先入为主的成见。这种偏见会让我们忽略其他可能更有效的治疗方法，从而限制了康复选择。比如我曾经因为药物的副作用格外痛苦，以至于在后续治疗中都尽可能避免使用药物。

那我们该怎么避免惯性思维呢？首先，保持开放的心态是关键。在遇到新的观点和建议时，不要急于否定。回想女儿在游泳队训练的两三年里，她也许曾经试图跟我分享侧门的捷径，但都被我的"急性子"打断了也说不定。其次，我们要尝试从不同的角度和立场去思考。就像站在场馆设计师的立场，我们会明白，偌大的一个游泳场馆，怎么能只设置一个出入口呢？最后，持续学习和成长才是避免惯性思维的重点。通过不断的学习和积累经验，拓宽自己的视野和认知，增强自己的思维灵活性，积极适应变化的环境和挑战。

惯性思维或许是我们大脑的一种自然倾向，但并不意味着我们无法克服它。希望我们都能保持一颗好奇的心，持续探索和学习，成为更好的自己。

4. 巧克力启示：珍惜当下

朋友从迪拜带回来一盒巧克力送给我女儿。每一块小巧克力都是独立包装的，有紫色和银色两种。银色巧克力的口感略微苦涩，紫色的会更甜润一点。

我女儿和儿子在尝过之后都很喜欢，尤其对甜甜的紫色情有独钟。于是，我决定允许他们每人每天可以吃一块。吃到最后的时候，盒子里只剩两块银色的巧克力了。拿给我儿子的时候，他很不开心："为什么是讨厌的银色啊？

我再也不要吃银色了。我要吃紫色，紫色的好甜。我现在很不开心。"

看着他紧锁的眉头和噘上天的小嘴，我试着引导他换一种思路。我轻声问："宝宝，你觉得现在还有两块银色巧克力可以吃，是不是也挺开心的？如果连这两块银色巧克力都没有了，你会更不开心吧？"他想了想，点点头说："嗯，是的，还有两块银色巧克力可以吃。"

看着儿子满足地吃着那块银色巧克力，我不禁佩服自己的智慧，短短两句话就避免了一场"纷争"。庆幸的同时，我惊讶于自己心态的转变。如果在以前，在这样的情况下我会和儿子有一样的反应。因为我们常常会被追求美好和避免痛苦的本能驱使，容易忽视和抱怨那些不符合我们预期的事物。对银色巧克力的不满也不过是人们在面对生活中的不完美时的自然反应。但经过生活历练后的我逐渐意识到，美好并非只存在于我们深爱的紫色巧克力中，那些不那么引人注目的银色巧克力，同样值得我们去品味和珍惜。

这场关于巧克力的小小对话，引出了一场关于"活在当下，珍惜眼前"的思考。

活在当下，珍惜眼前是一种生活智慧，它要求我们把注意力集中在当前的生活上，不被过去的遗憾或者对未来的过度担忧所困扰，享受现在的美好。来世不可待，往事不可追，我们所能真正掌握的，唯有此刻。人生其实无所谓幸运和不幸，这只不过是两种不同境遇的比较罢了。人生最悲哀的事情，莫过于在比较中错过幸福，在犹豫中错过了最好的时光。一定会有"更好的"，但"最好的"一定是我们触手可及的当下。

活在当下，珍惜眼前还需要我们保持一种开放和乐观的心态。悲观者眼中的世界总是少了些许色彩，多了几分沉重，容易因为小小的不如意而感到沮丧，对未来缺乏信心和期待，就像曾经的我。而乐观的人却能从同样的情境中汲取到不同的力量，看到生活中的积极面。看到剩下的银色巧克力时，他们心中涌起的会是感激和庆幸，会觉得还有两块巧克力可以吃这本身就是一种幸福。他们懂得欣赏生活中的美好，也能够在面对困难时保持坚韧和乐观，比如现在的我。

不由得想起《阿甘正传》中那句关于巧克力的著名台词："Life was like a

box of chocolates, you never know what you're gonna get.(生活就像一盒巧克力，你永远不知道下一块是什么味道。)"生活充满未知和变数，我们没办法控制每一块巧克力的颜色，但我们可以选择以何种心态去品尝它。

5. 相信世界的善意

昨天，我去买东西遇到一点小麻烦。自助付款结账的时候，我不小心提前把卡拔出来了，没能付款成功。系统提示我需要重新操作。但对我来说，这个过程有些过于复杂了。我在自助结账机前折腾了好一会儿，那会估计真是忙的时候，没有工作人员立即过来帮我。这时有一个已经下班的员工路过，注意到了我的窘境。他主动停下来询问我是否需要帮助。我向他解释情况后，他耐心地指导我重新输入信息，并尝试再次付款。而且，他第一次也没成功，他立刻又帮我进行第二次尝试，直到最终付款成功。

我最近遇到了不少事情，情绪有些低落。但在那一刻，看到一个陌生人，即使已经下班，仍然愿意花时间帮助我，这份善意让我感到非常温暖和感动。毕竟在美国的文化中，下班就是下班，不会再理会你任何事情，大多数人都是如此。他愿意对我伸以援手不是因为工作要求，也不是出于对我的特别关注，而是因为他是一个好人，一个乐于助人的好人。

就在这天早上，因为搬家去办理 Wi-Fi 业务时，我遇到了一位非常负责任的女士。按照这边的办事流程，顾客需要在工作人员旁边等待，哪怕这个过程可能要耗费数个小时，不然人家不会帮你办理。我已经在这位女士的协助下办理了一个多小时了，还需要联系另一家公司来协助完成一些手续，比如转线。整个过程异常烦琐，对方公司的效率还很慢，不断地让我们等待。幸好，整个过程中，这位工作人员一直耐心且尽职尽责地帮我弄。然而，我的闹钟很快就响了，提醒我女儿放学了。我只能向这位女士说明情况，说我必须去接我女儿了。她立刻表示理解，说她也是一个母亲，能够理解我的处境。我说，能不能和她进行三方通话，以便我不在场的情况下她也能继续帮我办理业务，她很爽快地就答应了。最终，业务办好了，也没有耽误我接女儿放学。

这些小小的善意，不仅解决了我眼前的问题，更让我的内心得到温暖。它们提醒着我，无论我们来自何种背景，善意和乐于助人的心总是能够跨越障碍，温暖他人。只要我们用心去发现和感受身边的美好，就会发现生活中处处都有令人感动和惊喜的瞬间。这些美好的人和事会让我们更加热爱生活，也会让我们更加坚定地走向未来。

6. 允许自己轻松

前几天，我不小心扭伤了腰。那天正好是一周一次上门按摩的日子，当晚经过大姐的按摩治疗，我的疼痛稍微得到了缓解。但到了第二天，我仍然很担心，唯恐自己伤到了骨头，于是我又去做了按摩治疗。这次是个男按摩师，他的力气很大。虽然当时感觉很舒服，但第二天疼痛却变本加厉，让我痛不欲生。我赶紧去拍了 X 光片，医生诊断后告诉我只是肌肉拉伤，并没有伤及骨头。最后我还是去找了马医生，解决了腰的问题。

没过几天，我又因为脚痛险些拨打 911。那段时间我的脚可能是变大了一些，送孩子去上钢琴课的时候，我偏偏穿了一双稍微紧些的鞋子，穿了大约三个小时。在开车回家的路上，左脚脚背特别痛。我想着还有半个小时就到家了，再坚持一下吧。结果回到家之后脚背越来越痛，越来越严重。我有些懊恼，责怪自己为什么不穿一双合脚的鞋呢，明明知道脚变大了还硬要挤进小鞋里。疼痛难忍的时候，我突然出现了焦虑的症状，开始发冷、发抖、冒冷汗、心慌、想吐、口渴、想去厕所，甚至胸口变得通红一片。我的第一反应就是拨打急救电话 911，担心自己可能需要紧急送医。同时又担心如果自己去了医院，家里的两个孩子该怎么办？我无法预测医生何时会让我回家。

在无奈和慌乱之中，我尝试上网搜索了止痛方法和应急处理措施，又联系了之前在美国看过的跌打医生。他告诉了我如何进行应急处理，并为我预约了第二天早上的诊所时间。我慢慢冷静下来，意识到这可能仅仅是一次普通的扭伤，或者是因为鞋子过小导致的挤压肿痛。想到这里，焦虑的症状也随之消散。

我深知自己在生活中一直过度紧绷。每次遇到突发事件，我总是过于紧张，甚至在一些小事情上也难以放松。就像刚刚，脚的肿痛竟让我一度联想到了死亡。这很大程度上源于对未知的恐惧，我时常感觉自己在生活常识方面就像一个白痴。除此之外，还与对结果的过度期望有关。我总是担心事情会出错，或者结果不如预期，这种担忧让我无法放松。这种紧张状态不仅影响了我的心理健康，也给身体带来了不必要的压力。

我很需要"放轻松"。放松能够显著降低身体的应激反应，有助于减缓心率、降低血压、减少肌肉紧张。我发现，深呼吸、冥想和瑜伽是最有效的"放轻松手段"。我能明显感受到身体的紧张和疲惫被逐渐释放，睡眠质量也得到改善。放松不仅缓解了身体的紧张，还在心理上带给我巨大的益处。在放松的时刻，我能够暂时抛开日常的烦恼和压力，让自己的思绪得到真正的解放。

一个习惯了紧绷状态的人不会在一夜之间就能完全放松下来。这需要时间，需要耐心，更需要自我觉察和调整。希望我能够逐步让自己变得更加从容、自在。

7. 欲望：追求和满足的平衡

在人类的心灵世界里，欲望扮演着一个复杂而又充满力量的角色。它是推动我们前进的引擎，也是我们内心诸多挣扎的源泉。这个简单的词汇，承载着对知识的追求、对成就的渴望，以及对亲情、友情和爱情的向往。它既能激发我不断超越自我的潜能，也在不经意间成为我的枷锁，将我困在无尽的追求和比较之中。

比如，我已经学习了三四个月的 ESL 课程，曾经有人跟我说，只需要三个月的时间，我就掌握英语并自由地与人沟通。但是，现实远比预期中的简单承诺要复杂得多。我目前的听力水平按照标准化考试的等级来衡量大约只有四级。面对真实的沟通场景时，我感到力不从心，没办法流畅地和人交流，更多时候我需要依赖翻译器，而翻译器往往无法完全且贴切地传达我的意图。这种挫败感让我时常质疑自己，犹豫还要不要继续 ESL 的课程。

就在前两天，我因为搬家需要处理一系列电力、水费、垃圾费等的转移手续，我惊喜地发现，完全理解办理页面上的内容对我来说有些难度，但是我已经能够看懂其中的一部分短句了。我忽然意识到自己并非毫无收获。当初报名 ESL 课程，我就是秉持着一个不断进步的态度，希望自己有勇气克服对语言的恐惧。但随着时间的推移，当学习状态没有达到预期的效果时，我发现自己失去了平常心。

类似的情况还有很多，我往往会质疑自己的能力，甚至产生一些不切实际的幻想，希望自己能够拥有超能力，比如成为吸血鬼那样能力出众的种群，拥有强大的学习能力、身体素质和永驻的青春；又或者在大脑里植入芯片，一夜之间就能拥有流利的英语口语。但现实是，我们都不是超人，这些想法不过是逃避现实的借口。学习本就是一个漫长而艰难的过程，它需要我们付出时间和精力才能看到结果。想明白这一点后，我选择继续 ESL 的学习之旅。虽然我真的很忙，我的一天里只有早上的时间是可以自由支配的，下午的时间几乎都被孩子们的活动所占据。但是我仍然坚持利用宝贵的早上时间学习英语。我告诉自己，即使每天只学习一个单词、一个句型，或者练习一种表达方式，都是在加深我的记忆和理解。当然，这样的坚持不仅仅是为了提高语言能力，更是为了享受学习和成长的过程。欣赏自己的每一次勇敢尝试，不论成功与否，不要让欲望和功利心冲昏了头脑。

在追求自我提升的路上，我经常给自己设定极高的标准和期望。这种内在的驱动力有时也不可避免地投射到孩子们的身上。作为一个母亲，我衷心地希望孩子们能够健康、快乐，但是随着他们长大，逐渐展现出自己的才华和潜力时，我心里又不由得出现一股特别的期待。

记录此时，我的儿子虽然才4岁，但是接触过的每个老师都会夸他，说他很聪明，尤其是专注力很出色，三岁就能稳稳当当地坐在那，认认真真地上完一个小时的课。无论老师提出什么样的问题，他都能从容地回答。这不禁让我对他的期待越来越高。甚至于一加一等于二，他如果不知道的话，我都会觉得很吃惊，因为在我心里，他早就应该已经掌握了。我耐心地教他用手指理解十以内的加减法，慢慢地他学会了个位数的加减法可以掰着手指得出正确答案。开心之余，我想象，或许明天他就能学会更复杂的两位数加减法。不经意间，我开始用自己的预期来约束、要求他的成长速度。

又比如前两年，女儿的游泳老师建议她加入游泳队。但是训练时间太晚，考虑到她需要充足的睡眠，我就没有同意。结果，女儿一直坚持，表示自己真的很喜欢游泳，最终我决定支持她的兴趣，让她加入了游泳队。她游泳速度越来越快，身体也变得更加健康，这些都是意外之喜。教练还经常夸赞她有游泳方面的天赋，让我最开始单纯地希望她开心地游泳的心泛起了一些波澜。再比如女儿一直在坚持学习绘画，也参加了一些相关的比赛。最近，我收到了来自比赛机构的邮件，通知我女儿的作品经过严格筛选，成功入选了全美儿童作品选集。邮件里还特意说明，这本选集将展示来自全美国各地孩子们的优秀作品，并不是每个孩子的作品都会入选，问我同不同意他们使用。虽然我原本就希望她能在比赛中脱颖而出，我也对她有信心，但是得知她的作品能够收入这样一个有声望的作品集时，我还是感到非常意外和惊喜，仿佛所有的努力和期待都在这一刻得到了回应。这份荣誉不仅仅是对我女儿艺术才能的肯定，也为她的未来描绘出更加光明的前景。她对数学的那份热爱也让我不由得产生了一些高期待，希望她以后能在学术上有所成就。

女儿在一所私立学校就读，这所学校以学术成绩优异著称。比如，如果孩子是一年级的学生，学校会采用二年级的教材，这样的安排让学校的教育水平和普通学校拉开了差距。我女儿现在是二年级，她的班主任在期中考试后告诉我，她的英语水平仅相当于学前班。这个消息让我不能接受。我女儿的学前班阶段就是在这所学校，她已经在这里连续读了三年——包括学前班、一年级和二年级，现在跟我说她的英语能力只有学前班，学校还声称他们最重视学术。

这个消息给我的冲击是巨大的，我感到了前所未有的压力和焦虑，毕竟在英语环境中，如果英文水平跟不上，我担心会影响到她其他学科的学习，甚至影响她的人际交往。为了帮女儿提高英语水平，我开始给她找私教进行课外辅导。经过大约半年的密集补习，最近的一次考试里，女儿的英语水平终于达到了与她年级相符的程度。

在女儿补习的这半年时间里，我心里充满了焦虑，常常在想：为什么她的成绩还没有明显的提升？什么时候才能达到我期望的水平？我过于急切地想要看到补习的成效，仿佛期望她能在一夜之间突飞猛进。我忽略了学习是一个循序渐进、点滴积累的过程。就如同我学习英文时那样，心里着急，总觉得进步缓慢。但实际上，不管是我还是我女儿我们都在一点一滴地进步。而且，相比之下，我女儿的学习速度其实比我快太多了。

也是因为这件事，我有了让女儿转学的念头。千挑万选之后，选定了一个所有人挤破脑袋都想去的公立学校。这也意味着，如果想申请就读那所公校，我们就必须搬到公校所在的那个区。说实话，以前我从未考虑过公立学校，因为大家都说私立学校如何如何好。而且师生比例公校少一半，老师能有更多精力去关注到每一个学生，所以在老师告诉我她就读二年级却只有兴趣班的英文水平之前，我从未认真研究过哪个学校最好、最适合她。而这所公校会为她提供一个更好的学习环境，让她在各方面都能得到更好的发展，而且马上弟弟也要上学了，这是一个对他们两个人的未来都有益的重要选择。

搬到新社区之后，我像以前一样外出跑步。虽然同在一个社区，但是这里的房子按照位置和品质有着明显的等级划分。跑着跑着，我就到了最豪华的那个区。我能感觉到，一股强烈的欲望在我心中瞬间燃起。那里的房子宽敞到连院子都比我现在住的整个房子的占地面积还要大得多，光是大门看上去都不一般。我一边跑步，一边忍不住想象，我要努力在这里买块地，盖更大的房子，里面有网球场、壁球室、一个给我女儿游泳的恒温游泳池、一个超大的健身房……但是转念又想，即便住到这样的豪宅里，也还有人有更好的房子。如果一味地继续追求更高的物质生活，那我的心将永远处于不满足的状态，永远在追逐欲望的漩涡里挣扎。

我突然觉得，我应该静一静，反思一下自己的欲望，无论是对自己的，还是对孩子们的。我要学会控制它们。

我对孩子们这种期望的传递可能并不是总出于最建设性的动机。它可能源自我对他们未来的深切关怀，以及希望他们能够拥有成功和幸福人生的渴望，这是天下所有父母最常见不过的现象。但是这些期望不应该成为孩子们成长道路上的负担。我不希望我的欲望影响到孩子，让他们觉得充满压力或不安。每个孩子都是独一无二的个体，他们有着自己的兴趣、天赋和成长速度。我只能努力调整自己的心态，尝试从一个更加平和和理性的角度来看待孩子的成长。不再单纯追求他们快速掌握技能或知识，而是更多地关注他们是否在学习过程中感到快乐和满足。鼓励他们去探索自己感兴趣的领域，即使可能不会收获名利和成就。

爱和理解或许比任何期望都更加重要。我只能尽力为孩子们提供一个充满爱和支持的环境，让他们能够自由地成长，成为他们自己想成为的人，选择自己想要的生活。

欲望是推动我们前进的动力，但过度的欲望只会让我们迷失方向，忘记真正的目标和价值。所以，我们需要走走停停，在前进的道路上不断审视自己的内心，能够更加理性和平和地看待生活，确保自己的欲望在可控的范围内。如果过分地超越自己的极限 那么等待自己的只能是毁灭了。

这场"自我革命"不仅仅是对内心世界的一次洗牌，更是在抑郁的挑战中寻找到的一股不屈不挠的力量。我学会了如何面对内心的恐惧，学会了如何打破心灵的枷锁，学会了如何在逆境中培养出更加坚韧积极的自我。每一次自我革命的成功都让我站在成长旅途的一个新的起点。

记住，无论外界如何变迁，我们都有能力引领自己的"自我革命"，成为自己命运的主宰。

第八章　随笔杂感

在人类历史的长河中，抑郁症作为一种深刻的心灵体验，激发了无数艺术家和作家的创作灵感。从古典文学到现代电影，从绘画到音乐，抑郁症的主题贯穿于各种艺术形式，成为探讨人性、情感和社会现实的一个窗口。每一部作品都是一个独特的宇宙，它们以不同的方式讲述着人类的故事，反映着生活的多样性。

在这个章节，我将记录下这些作品在我心中的回响，无论是深刻的思考，还是简单的感动，都是我与这些作品之间真实的对话。这里，没有严格的理论框架，也没有固定的分析模式，只有真挚的情感和随性的笔触。我们将一起探索那些触动心灵的电影和书籍，分享它们给我带来的启示和感悟。

《被讨厌的勇气》读后感

《被讨厌的勇气》是一本由岸见一郎和古贺史健合著的书，它介绍了奥地利心理学家阿德勒的心理学理论。这本书采用对话的形式，讲述了一位青年和一位哲学家之间的五天对话内容。以简洁而深入的方式，呈现了阿德勒心理学的核心思想。它鼓励我们把握自己的命运，勇敢追求自我实现和完善。

被讨厌的勇气，顾名思义，就是可以接受自己被他人厌恶。想要拥有被讨厌的勇气，是因为我们想做一个自由的人，而这里的自由不是指从家庭、群体、社会中跳脱出来，而是指可以毫不在意别人的评价、不害怕被别人讨厌、不追求被他人认可，我们都期待有这样自由的生活方式。

书中的"哲人"与"青年"的对话，仿佛就是我与自己内心的对话。阿德勒的心理学理念，让我重新审视了自己的人生和抑郁症。阿德勒告诉我，抑郁症并不是因为过去的经历所致，而是因为我们不愿意从过去走出来，我们一直在寻找不让自己前进的理由，试图在过往的经历中找到安慰。

心理创伤，我曾经深深地受其困扰。我总是在回忆过去，试图找出那个让我陷入抑郁的根源。但是，阿德勒告诉我："无论之前的人生发生过什么，都对今后的人生如何度过没有影响。"决定自己人生的是活在"此时此刻"的自己。

接纳自我，这是一个我从未尝试过的概念。我一直试图逃避自己，逃避那个不完美的我。我从来不会一个人去洗车，因为我开不上洗车店的轨道，后面的人会不停地按喇叭，而且我完全不会英文，所以也看不懂支付方式。另外，作为深度咖啡爱好者的我因为语言障碍也不敢去店里买咖啡，只好买了咖啡机自己在家做很难喝的咖啡。

但是，阿德勒告诉我，改变的第一步，就是接受自己，拥有坚定的自我认同感和价值观。不管现实如何不尽如人意，我都要告诉自己，我允许自己这样。因为只有真正接受了自己，我才能找到改变的动力和勇气。接纳自我的第一步，坦然接受了自己不会英文这件事，承认自己对于语言学习的抗拒。因为害怕在学习过程中出错，害怕被人投以异样的目光，所以我提前否定自己，拒绝学习英语，杜绝这样的情况发生。

认清这一点之后，我试着将注意力集中在自己能够掌控的事物上，而不再过分关注外部环境和其他人的评价。我开始尝试自己去洗车，哪怕后面的车因为我付款耗时太久而按喇叭示意不满。随着去的次数增多，我对整个流程的操作更加熟练。而且我发现，有很多本土的讲英文的人有时候搞半天也弄不好，需要叫工作人员来帮助完成。

我鼓起勇气报名了 ESL 的网络课程。ESL 就是 English as a Second Language，是美国、加拿大等英语系国家针对母语不是英语的人士开设的专业英语语言课程。每节课两个小时，有时候两个半小时，前一个小时老师通常是在读一段英文，我总是听得很糊涂。这种"不受掌控"的感觉再次勾起我的抗拒，很多次都想要放弃。后一个小时，老师把这些内容讲解得清清楚楚，我理解吸收之后，那种压迫感、那种喘不过气的感觉才得到缓解。庆幸自己刚刚没有放弃，今天又学到了新的东西，要不然我自己的成长就被我自己耽误了。

我还记得有一节课讲了一个语法，我一直不能理解。课后的家庭作业，我交了白卷。随后，老师在评语里留下了正确答案，我照着答案填写以后又重新提交了。第二天看着老师回馈的"100分"，我完全不记得昨天写了什么东西，对那个语法更是一点印象都没有。

在和普拉提翻译复习考试内容的时候，我拿出这道题，请她帮我讲解。翻译先给我讲解了两个例题，然后问我这道题应该填什么。我说不知道。"不，你知道的！"她语气有些坚定。"我真的不知道。""不，你知道！"她过于肯定的语气让我有点委屈，我真的觉得自己不懂。我强迫自己再一次认真地看那道题，告诉她答案。"对！你是不是能做到？！"那一瞬间我真的想哭，有些自责，觉得自己对学英语这件事没有用过心才觉得自己做不到，没有付出全部的努力。

这件事也恰恰印证了书中提到的"责任担当"，我们应该对自己的言行负责，承认自己在生活中的选择和决定对自己的影响，并愿意为这些影响负责。我选择了一个"名不副实"的100分和轻松的学习过程，就要承担无法学会这个语法的结果。学习本就是一个需要耐心和毅力的过程，没有任何一种方法能够让我们一蹴而就。即使我们学会了某个知识点，也需要通过不断的沟通和练习才能真正熟练掌握。否则，我们很容易陷入一种"学了就忘、忘了再学"的恶性循环中。

在我年轻的时候，我总觉得自己年纪还小，身体很好，过于放纵自己，没有好好爱惜自己的身体，导致现在时常感觉到一些疼痛。我猜测这些疼痛可能和当年的一些行为有关系。比如，当初我在手臂上割过很多条伤口，甚至割断了里面的筋。现在我总会觉得左手的经络特别的疼，有时候感觉像是没有得到充分的拉伸，有时甚至感觉整个经络像是断掉了一样。

现在回想真有后悔的事，那就是年轻时做事太过冲动，盲目地追求短暂的快乐与满足，不爱惜自己的身体，伤害自己身体。如今，身体的疼痛成为我年轻时期冲动行为的直接后果，让我深刻体验到了不负责任的代价。真正的成熟，不仅仅是做出选择，更是要为这些选择负责。这就意味着，在做出任何决定之前，我们应该深思熟虑，预见可能的后果，并准备好承担这些后果。现在，我更加珍惜自己的身体，积极地通过锻炼来弥补年轻时的冲动。

书中关于人际关系的探讨也让我深受启发。"人际关系，是一切烦恼和不良情绪的源头。"面对人际关系的复杂性时，我们发现自己常常会陷入由他人期望和自身需求之间的矛盾所带来的烦恼和焦虑之中。

书中提到的"课题分离"概念，为我们更好地处理人际关系提供了清晰的思路。课题分离就是指区分什么是你的课题，什么是他人的课题。简单说就是，每个人都有自己的问题和挑战需要面对，而不必过度介入他人的问题，也不必让他人过度介入我们的问题，大家专注自身就好。

当然，尽管我理解并认同"课题分离"的重要性，但在实际生活中，特别是在对待孩子们的问题上，我往往会忘记这个原则，过度地约束他们。或许是因为作为父母，我们天然地希望保护和教育孩子，希望他们避开危险，少走弯路。然而，这种过度的保护可能会成为他们成长的绊脚石，阻止他们独立思考，独立解决问题，体验失败和成功。他们需要我们的指导和保护，但同样需要自由和空间去探索这个世界，去锻炼自己的独立能力。

有一件事我印象很深刻，我的身体因为幽门螺杆菌不舒服，甚至严重到吐血，家中叫来了两辆救护车。在这紧张的时刻，我女儿却像是在看一场精彩的表演，兴奋地趴在窗户边喊着："哇，来了两辆救护车耶！"真是哭笑不得。反倒是年纪更小一点的儿子，会疑惑地问妈妈发生了什么，为什么妈妈会躺在救护车上。我女儿总是那么活泼好动，甚至在这种关头也毫无顾忌地玩耍打闹，这让我深感焦虑。如果她一直这样天真烂漫，不知人间疾苦，如果我怕现在突然离世了，她是否能够独立应对生活中的困难呢？她是那样善良的一个孩子，很容易就原谅伤害她的人，总是轻信所有人的话语。如果我不在了，她是否能够处理那些复杂的人际关系，解决那些棘手的问题呢？现在，我完全理解当初祖祖对我说的那句话了："以后祖祖不在你身边你该怎么办呀？"我深深地体会了祖祖的焦虑。

这些担忧让我更加明白，我需要教会孩子们独立，教会他们如何面对生活的困难和挑战。当发现自己在过度约束孩子们时，要立刻停下来，反思我们的行为。我们需要问自己，我们的行为是出于对他们的保护，还是出于自己的焦虑和恐惧？更或者是想要孩子们成为你心中理想的样子呢？只有真正认清自己的动机时，我们才能做出改变。"课题分离"的实践很艰难但也很重要，希望我能够坚持下去，不管是为了孩子还是为了自己。

总之，全书都在传递一个观点，就是鼓励我们做自己！在抑郁症的治疗过程中，这种"做自己"的思维方式尤为重要，对于抑郁症患者来说是一种解放。抑郁症患者常常陷入自我否定和焦虑的漩涡，他们过于在意他人的看法和评价，以至于忽视了自己的内心需求和情感。而"做自己"的理念，鼓励患者接受自己的真实状态，关注自己的内心世界，不必刻意去迎合他人的期望，不必为了取悦他人而扭曲自己的真实感受，要求他们重新找回自我，勇敢地展现真实的自己。

在这个过程中，我们会逐渐发现，真实的自己并非别人所期望的那样完美无缺，但它却是最真实、最自然、最有力量的，才是值得被爱和尊重的。当我们开始接受并珍惜自己的真实状态时，内心的负担和焦虑也会逐渐减轻。在追求真实的自我中，找到治愈抑郁症的希望和勇气。

《情归新泽西》观后感

《情归新泽西》是扎克布拉夫自编自导自演的小成本独立电影，让他本人在当年的美国影评界颇受好评。浪潮般的好评让我这个不怎么关注电影的人也产生了好奇，而且听说是部轻松的爱情喜剧电影，内容离奇搞笑，于是我在孩子们都入睡后打开了这部影片。没想到，收获了一个温暖的夜晚。

故事围绕男主人公回家参加母亲的葬礼展开。26岁的青年安德鲁心中有个演员梦，独自在洛杉矶打拼多年也不过跑了一些龙套，始终与灯红酒绿的洛杉矶格格不入，在餐厅打工时还要被客人讥笑嘲讽。正当安德鲁为自己的前途感到迷茫时，他的"心理医生"父亲打来了电话，瘫痪多年的母亲去世了。这对安德鲁无疑是一个沉重的打击，但是如他自己所说，他没有流泪。无论如何他也哭不出来。

安德鲁的童年并不幸福，那是一个灰暗且充满病态的时期。因为他小时候过于调皮，父母对他非常严厉，甚至认为他有问题。为了约束他，控制他的情绪，父亲让他长期服用药物，直至今日。这些药物已经对他的生理造成了不良影响。由于无法忍受父母的过度干涉，安德鲁心中甚至产生了让母亲离世的念头，并在一次偶然中，导致了母亲终身与轮椅为伴的悲剧。也因此父亲将安德鲁送到了寄宿学校。在那里，同学们将他视为异类，他自己也深感如此。高中毕业后，他毅然决然地离开了家，告别了朋友，独自前往洛杉矶追寻演员梦。在这段时间里，他从未回过家，与父亲的关系也愈发紧张。"父亲"这个本应该充满温暖的词语，对于安德鲁来说，却意味着冷漠。

在母亲的葬礼上，安德鲁遇到了儿时的朋友。这些朋友带着他参与各种热闹的派对，结识了形形色色的人物。然而，童年的阴影似乎仍在他心中徘徊，他始终觉得自己被一种无形的力量束缚。这时候，女主角萨曼莎走进了安德鲁的生活。这个女孩有些神经质，甚至可以说是多动症，但这并不影响她散发魅力。她善良、充满爱心，收养了许多小动物。而且，她身怀绝技，有成为奥运冠军的潜力，却从不张扬。

安德鲁的内心世界充满了对自我价值的怀疑和对亲情的冲突。他的童年经历让他对父母产生了强烈的抵触，间接导致了母亲的悲剧性事故。这样的心理创伤成了他无法逃避的阴影，迫使他不断寻求解脱。他对药物的依赖，正是他试图逃避现实、自我疗伤的一种不理性的手段。这不仅是对抑郁症患者的真实写照，更是对每个在现代社会中感到迷茫的人的深刻反映。

在这短短几天时间里，朋友们为安德鲁创造了一个可以袒露心声的环境，让他能够摆脱药物，真正面对自己的内心。安德鲁也逐渐学会了释放自己内心的束缚，原谅了父亲过去的严厉和误解。他走出了生命的怪圈，开始以全新的眼光看待自己和周围的世界。这段经历不仅让他找到了真爱，也让他重新找回了生活的意义和价值。

随着电影落幕,我也开始反思自己的生活和内心。在安德鲁的故事中,我得以窥见一个被过往阴影笼罩,却又最终挣脱束缚、找回生活真谛的历程,这和我自己何其相似,主人公经历的种种抑郁症状我也曾经历过:长期的失眠,夜晚辗转反侧,眼睛盯着天花板直到天亮。焦虑如同影子般不离不弃,伴随着心跳加速、呼吸急促,在平凡的日常中也感到窒息,甚至出现恐慌发作。头痛、胃痛、肌肉疼,没有任何生理原因地就找上门来。情绪低落更是常客,悄无声息地夺走一切快乐和激情。而最让人疲惫的莫过于对生活失去兴趣和动力,曾经的爱好和追求变得索然无味,甚至简单的日常任务也变得难以承受,只想逃避一切社交活动。

更不要提,时至今日我仍然没办法像安德鲁一样与生父和解。

安德鲁的故事给了我信心和勇气,我决定用自己的方式和过去告别。我不再纠结于他们的过错,也不再期待他们会有所改变,我选择放下这些包袱。生活是用来成长的用来珍惜和成长的,而不是用来怨恨和纠结的。人不能永远停留在过去的阴影中,继续纠结于他们的所作所为,只会让自己活在怨恨之中,无法前行。保持一定的距离,避免过多的交集,专注于自己的生活就好。

萨曼莎和朋友们对安德鲁来说无疑是生活中的救赎,他们为安德鲁带来久违的温暖和关心。在这个喧嚣的世界里,我们或许都会感到迷茫和孤独。但只要我们愿意打开心扉,去接纳那些愿意走进我们生活的人,去理解和包容那些不同的声音和观点,我们终归能找到属于自己的温暖和力量。生活都是孤独冰冷的,倘若有人能给你带来一点推翻过去的力量,让你觉得生活和情感变得具体可感,这必定是世间最动人的感情降临的一刻。

这部电影不是简单的爱情喜剧,也不仅仅是对抑郁症的描述,更是一部关于人性、爱与救赎的赞歌。无论现在的你在何种心境下都值得一看。

《运动改造大脑》读后感

在忙碌的生活中，我们常常因为种种原因而忽视了运动的重要性。当压力、焦虑、抑郁等负面情绪袭来，我们往往寻找药物或其他外在的解决方案，而忽略了一个简单却极为有效的途径——运动。

在《运动改造大脑》这本书中，作者以生动的笔触、严谨翔实的科学研究和丰富的现实案例，向我们展示了运动如何重塑大脑，如何帮助我们更好地面对生活中的种种挑战。关于有氧运动，书中详细阐述了其对提高认知功能的作用。如慢跑、游泳和骑自行车等，能够促进身体内的血液循环，增加心肺功能，帮助大脑获取更多的氧气和营养，提高大脑的工作效率。此外，有氧运动还能够刺激大脑神经元的生长和连接，增强大脑的认知储备，有助于延缓认知衰退和提高记忆力。关于力量训练，不仅能够提高肌肉质量，提高身体的力量和耐力，还能够通过促进血液流动和释放大脑激素来改善情绪状态，减轻焦虑和抑郁症状。力量训练还能够增强大脑神经元的连接，提高大脑对信息的处理能力，有助于改善认知功能。还有平衡训练，如瑜伽、太极和舞蹈等，可以提高身体的稳定性和协调性，降低摔倒的风险，进而保护大脑免受损伤。书中还提及了我一直在学习的普拉提运动，比如普拉提的弯曲动作在提高身体协调性的同时，也促进了大脑神经元的连接和交流，有助于提高认知能力、反应速度和注意力。

在预防和治疗一些心理疾病方面，运动也发挥着积极的作用。例如，运动可以相当于一定剂量的精神药物，有助于治疗焦虑症和抑郁症等心理疾病。对于那些正在戒烟、戒毒或戒瘾的人来说，运动也能提供有效的帮助。例如，身为职场人士的约翰，经常感到压力巨大，情绪波动严重。通过坚持每天晨跑，焦虑和压力都有所减轻。这对很多职场人士都很适用，简单高效地缓解工作压力和焦虑。还有年轻人艾米，她在学业上遇到了挑战，感到自己的学习能力下降。通过增加体育活动，特别是有氧运动，艾米发现自己的注意力和记忆力有所改善。这个案例告诉我们，运动不仅对身体健康有益，对于学习和认知功能的提升也是至关重要的。至于中年人大卫，因为工作原因，长时间坐在办公桌前，导致的体重增加、心情低落也因为规律的锻炼得到缓解。而年长的莉莉女士通过参加社区的运动团体，结识了很多新朋友，整个人都更加开朗乐观。

每个主人公案例都展示了运动对于大脑健康的积极影响。除此之外，还有一个主人公的经历让我印象最为深刻。他因为婚外情与妻子分居，工作上也不顺利，生活节奏全部被打乱，陷入抑郁状态，本身他就有多动、注意力不集中的问题。医生为此给他开了药，但药物带来的副作用让他感到非常不舒服，出现了全身肌肉疼痛、头疼、胃疼等多种不适症状。医生后续又针对他的情况提出更换新的药物。在聊到新药的作用时，他开始不停地呕吐。他非常不喜欢药物进入身体后带来的种种不适，打算停止服用导致呕吐的药，决定通过运动来调整身体状态。再次复诊是两周后，期间他坚持每天长跑，医生看到了他的身体和情绪已经有所变化。紧接着又过了一个月，他的状态几乎完全恢复，新的工作和生活也变得更加有序。

他对药物带来的副作用深恶痛绝，这和我当时的感受如出一辙。2021年刚入秋的时候，我的家庭医生建议我不要停西药，她认为西雅图接下来连绵不断的雨季和冬天会让我更加抑郁。我当时非常肯定地和家庭医生说："不，我不能再依靠药物维持情绪了。我要逐步停止药物了，我深信运动可以帮助我改变这种状况。"所以，我深知抑郁症患者对药物的依赖性，所以当他决定不再依赖药物，完全依靠运动来改善身心状态时，我真心佩服他的决心和毅力。

在看这本书前不久，我刚刚停止了最后三十分之一的药物，到此为止我彻底走出了依靠西药维持情绪的处境。现在，我已经养成了定期运动的习惯。每当有空闲时间，我都会去跑步或打壁球。孩子们去上兴趣班的时间也被我利用起来，哪怕在路边跑上二十分钟就要接孩子，我也心满意足地享受着运动带来的快感和自由。通过运动，我感受到了身心的和谐与平衡。我不再一味地依赖药物，一旦失去药物就紧张焦躁，反而学会通过运动来释放负面情绪。运动让我变得更加自信、乐观和坚强，也让我更加珍惜和享受生活的每一个瞬间。当然不排除我之所以要切分那么细小的来停药和我的敏感有极大关系。

书中主人公有着与我相似的病症和康复经历，甚至他的遭遇比我更加坎坷，这让我意识到世界上还有无数饱受抑郁症或其他疾病折磨的患者，他们的经历或许比我们更为不幸。希望我记录下这段故事和感悟可以让更多的人看到，看到《运动改造大脑》这本书，了解到运动对身心健康的重要性。也许是他的好友，也许是他的亲戚，受到触动，去鼓励并劝说他开始运动，帮助他有机会摆脱那些痛苦。

客观来说，书中也存在一些我无法理解之处。比如，部分理论知识较为深奥，大量的医学专业术语对于非专业读者来说可能存在一定的阅读难度。此外，虽然书中列举了大量的实验与案例，但个别案例的描述可能不够详细，难以让读者完全理解其背后的科学原理。但这并不妨碍它是一本值得一读的好书。

当然，我并不主张正在服药的患者擅自停药，盲目进行运动健身。一切康复过程都应该在医生的专业指导下进行。

在这些随笔中，我分享了自己的感受和思考，它们或许并不完美，但却是真实而深刻的。我希望这些文字能够激发读者的共鸣，也许在某个不经意的瞬间，你会发现自己的影子，感受到心灵的触动。

生活本身就是一部丰富多彩的作品，我们每个人都是其中的作者和读者。希望在未来的日子里，无论你遇到什么样的故事，都带着一颗开放的心去体验，去感悟，在生活的大书中，书写属于自己的篇章。

后记

当我为这本书画上最后一个句号时,心中涌起的情感难以言表。这不仅仅是一本书的结束,更是我个人旅程的一个里程碑。回望过去,那些和抑郁症对抗的日子仿佛就在昨天,但此刻的我已经站在了一个全新的起点。未来也许有更多挫折要经历,但我坚信自己不会被任何消极情绪所打败。

回首过去,抑郁症曾是我生活中的一道深深的伤痕。它让我痛苦、迷茫,甚至失去了对生活的热爱。然而,正是这段经历,让我更加深刻地理解了人性的脆弱与坚强。我学会了在困境中寻找力量,在黑暗中寻找光明。

当我迈出步伐,不再把自己困在自己的房子的时候,感觉这个世界太美好了,新鲜出炉的披萨滋味无与伦比,餐馆里现场烹饪的意面,其风味远胜于打包带回家的那份。随着出门的次数增多,心中的焦虑渐渐消散,变得愈发微弱。这份日益减轻的焦虑感,让我仿佛预见到自己即将与世界和谐相融。即便我不会英文,我也能做到很多东西,我也能开心快乐的生活,也能吃到美味。

在撰写这本书的过程里,我经历了无数次的自我剖析和反思。每一个章节、每一段文字都凝聚着我对那段经历的思考和感悟。我希望通过我的故事,能够唤起更多人对心理健康的关注和重视,为那些正在经历困境的人们带去一丝慰藉和勇气。

我要感谢我的家人和朋友,是你们的爱与陪伴让我有勇气面对自己的过去,有力量走出那段黑暗的日子。你们的理解和支持,是我走过这段旅程的最大动力。同时,我也要衷心感谢那些帮助过我的医生们,是你们的专业知识、无私奉献和耐心倾听,让我逐渐找回了自己。感谢每周都通过电话疗愈我心灵的心理辅导师,即使是在晚上 9 点后——她的非工作时间——每当我情绪很不好的时候，她也会安抚我的情绪。还要特别感谢马医生，他不仅是我身体的疗愈者，更是我心灵的引路人。感谢每一位在我康复旅程中给予我支持和帮助的人。是你们让我相信，无论生活多么艰难，总有希望和光明在前方等待着我们。

最后还要感谢所有正在阅读这本书的人。你们愿意花时间了解我的故事，这本身就是一种珍贵的连接。

"人生海海，山山而川，不过尔尔。"生活或许充满了曲折与荆棘，但请相信，每一次的跌倒都是成长的契机，每一次的黑暗都是黎明前的预兆。就如同抑郁症的阴霾之后，是那重新拥抱快乐与希望的曙光。愿我们都能勇敢地面对内心的挑战，学会在逆境中寻找力量。

记住，无论前方的道路多么崎岖，总有一束光在等待着我们去追寻。

Notes on Depression
Self-help

Chapter 1 Echoes of the past

The past years beat gently on the door of memory, like echoes in a distant valley, now faint, now clear, but never haunting. These echoes are who I am, an individual shaped by my experiences. They are the starting point of my story and the key to understanding who I am today. Through the tunnel of time, back to the moments that defined me, challenged me and ultimately shaped me.

I was told that I had been abandoned by my biological father because of my gender, and that my biological mother had no interest in taking care of me, so she paid for living expenses and entrusted someone else to take care of me. Fortunately, some people are willing to take care of me, but I was just born like a thin monkey, arms only adults thumb thick, also do not eat, everyone is afraid to keep alive. So, I was passed around foster care, this family for five days, that family to see a week.

Pushing and pushing, just when I had no place to live, I was glad that my Zuzu -- my biological father's grandmother, took me in. I finally had a stable "place to settle", and finally did not have to be kicked around by those foster families like a ball. There were already seven people in my family, including Zuzu, Yao grandpa, Yao grandma, their three daughters and a son -- big dad, second dad, third dad and Yao dad (in my hometown, "dad" is also used to refer to a woman), and now there was me. As the elder male in the family, the kindly grandpa Yao does not meddle much in the family trifles. And I, a baby who can only cry and need to be taken care of, undoubtedly added a lot of burden to

Chapter 1 Echoes of the past

Grandma Yao. Grandma Yao is always very fierce, no smile, speak loudly, but also like to swear, the house reverberated with her voice can not be quiet.

I didn't know what kind of feelings it was, maybe I was sensitive when I was young, sometimes I felt bullied, sometimes I felt loved by my relatives such as treasure, sometimes I felt like they were used as toys to amuse myself. They loved me but maybe they hated me a little bit, thought I was a burden, or a doll to be manipulated at will... Too complicated emotions. I want to thank them, of course, for helping Zuzu pull me up when no one else would adopt me.

I don't know how Zuzu pulled me up, she is very old, very thin, the skin of the whole body are wrinkled, the skin of the chin and neck has been loose to completely hang down, I often like to touch the skin of her chin hang down, soft and smooth is very comfortable, good fun. Zuzu's feet are very small, very small, she has been wrapped in small feet since childhood, with a wrapping cloth to wrap the feet tightly. The little toe was bent, like a hunched person, and pressed tightly against the fourth toe. And the fourth toe is tilted and firmly against the third toe. The five toes are close together to form an uneven triangle. Zuzu and I sleep, and I sleep at the other end, opposite Zuzu's feet, which are the size of a five - or six-year-old child. Ha, ha, what small feet.

Zuzu often said to me: "Don't blame your mother, it's your father's fault, don't hate your mother..." In fact, there is no point in talking to me about this, I don't know what is mother, what is father, it is just a vague pronoun for me. For example, mother is the person who occasionally comes to see me, grandma represents very fierce, three father represents smiling happily, for other family members I am more vague, especially dad, what is that? Only Zuzu, kind, beautiful, even if her wrinkled skin is also beautiful. She has no temper towards me, only patience and kind smile.

Later I grew up and went to school. Once when Zuzu gave me breakfast money, she took out a handkerchief wrapped in layers. After she opened it, the innermost wrapped was money, and she gave me a ten-piece piece as two pieces. I calmly took the money and went to school. But I did not intend to tell Zuzu. On the contrary, I wonder if Zuzu will give me the wrong money for breakfast next time. What should I buy next time? I'm looking forward to my next ten bucks.

I remember one time my big dad scolded me because she caught me and lit a chopstick to smoke, and then went to a dark place to light the chopstick as a sacrifice to a ghost. Yes, I believe in ghosts rather than Buddhas, because I think the world is ugly and nothing is beautiful. It is false to say that God can help you. What really exists is ghosts, ghosts in the dark. At that time, Big Dad was really angry. He kept scolding me and beating me. Zuzu could not see past it, so he found a bamboo pole, which was very large and long, with one end cut into a strip, and was called a broken pole. I do not know exactly what it was used for. I only know that Zuzu hit me with the broken pole, as if it hit me and as if it did not hit me, because I forgot whether it hurt at that time, and the broken pole sounded very loud and overmighty. I looked at Zuzu angry look very surprised, why so loving Zuzu will hit me? She hit me twice and then burst into tears. She didn't cry, but the tears ran down her wrinkled cheeks. When I went to sleep at night, she hugged me and said, "You know, I'm not really going to hit you, I'm cheering, I'm so angry, I'm too old to protect you, you have to grow up and protect yourself. They bully you, don't like you, Zuzu gas, Zuzu is not around you later what should you do?" At this moment, I can not hear Zuzu's anxiety about my growth path.

One day, I saw Zuzu struggling to get up from the ground and sit on her cane chair. I asked her what was wrong and why she had fallen. Zuzu was reluctant to speak at first, hesitating. I kept asking, "You can't fall down on your own, can you?" Zuzu finally revealed that it was the big father who pushed Zuzu to the ground after arguing with her and walked away regardless of his head. Instantly exploded my small universe, I was angry, immediately turned and rushed out of the house, lunged along the road to catch up with the big father and wife who were ready to go home after dinner. After about 1 kilometer, I saw the back of them. Impatiently, they sped up and flew forward with a kick, kicking at my big dad. At that time, my eldest father was pregnant, and her husband hastened to stop me, but my anger could not be calmed, and I still jumped up and kicked over. All my anger was directed at the leg I had kicked. I hate her. My great-great-uncle is old and his body is no longer flexible. She can only rely on the cane chair to move slowly. Each time, she had to push the chair with difficulty, and then put forward her trembling feet and moved forward little by little, with each step requiring some effort. Big dad was so cruel that he pushed Zuzu to the ground and did not help him up. When I was young, I had already begun to fight violence with violence, to fight tooth for tooth. Later, my father gave birth to a child with a slight cross eyes. Every time I saw him, I always thought, was it my flying kick that broke him? I always hid a little guilty feeling in my heart.

Now think about my childhood probably really naughty, always like to wander outside, like a boy on the tree to dig a bird's nest, down the river to touch crabs, drilling black holes, after all, just came to this world soon, many have not seen, full of curiosity about life. However, whenever I immersed in these adventures, there was always a severe reprimand and punishment from my grandmother. Once, I went to watch others kill eels because of curiosity to see that it was nearly dark after dinner, or grandma Yao to the market to find me to go home, after going home was punished to kneel on the roof. Now, I have become a mother myself, only to finally understand why grandma Yao kneel me.

Zuzu at that time, all meals were cooked with cabbage. There was no meat, the rice was cooked very badly, and the dishes were also cooked rotten. I think the rice was very delicious. I was not in good health, very thin and did not like to eat, so Zuzu steamed soup with mirror grass, chicken fungus and rhizome. It was the best soup I had ever tasted. She said it nourished my spleen and stomach. I still remember that we lived in a bungalow at that time. The house was built a little strange, because the house was concave, as if it had sunk. Now I can still think of Zu Zu holding a steaming soup of mirror grass, broken ear root and chicken fungus, standing at the door and calling me to drink soup: the sunken door made her look shorter, she carefully carried the soup: "Come here, drink the soup while it is hot, warm just right, this is nourishing the stomach." Small steps to move the ground while walking called me, for fear of soup spilt.

Remember that once the heavy rain for a long time, we live in the sunken house filled with water, my grandparents live next to a step away from the red brick four-story building on the second floor, that is, my grandfather's brother, someone came to pick us up. Only to hear Zuzu tried his best to shout loudly: "You first hold her up, quickly give her a change of clothes, wrapped in the quilt, wrapped tightly ha!" Don't catch cold!" Heard her use her strength to shout, my heart is warm, every word is filled with Zuzu's love for me, I am Zuzu's heart meat, she does not allow me to have any damage.

Zuzu, I love you, love very much, but when I was young, I did not understand life and death, for this deep love, but unknown in a few years will never see my beloved Zuzu.

Later do not know when we moved, Yao grandpa built a two-story building, the second floor is their family plus I live place, the first floor is separated into several small rooms, for rent. It was a little dramatic, abandoning my biological father and renting it separately with my mother, who was responsible for my living expenses every month. They lived just below me, but they did not ask or care about me. It is not too much to use the analogy of being strangers, and they did not understand why they would appear here together when they each had their own homes. They live their own lives downstairs, their mother is single, and their father takes his friends with him. I once heard my mother mention my father when chatting with my third father: "He always finds various excuses to come to my room, either to borrow water or to borrow paper..."

Just as I was about to accept the fact that we were strangers, my biological father suddenly broke the surface of calm. That day, as usual, I came down from the upstairs to play with some children nearby. When I passed the long corridor on the first floor, my biological father suddenly came out of his room, pulled me by his hand, and went to his room with a bright smile.

Probably the first time I saw my biological father smile at me, now I think of that smile is really obscene and ferocious, disgusting, and it is also this smile that makes me feel sick and disgusted when I see people who look similar to him. At that time, I was really stupid and obediently stood there like the two idiots. His room was not spacious, and it was a little messy. As I stood in the open door, a dull air filled the room. I stood stiffly in the doorway, afraid that any action would disturb the intimacy of the scene. He loosened his grip on me and walked to the head of the bed, where I noticed another woman under the covers. He sat down, then smiled and waved to me. "Come on, why are you standing so far away?" I shuffled along, eliciting an impatient "tut, come here" from him. I still had no intention of speeding up my pace, taking small steps and watching from the far end of the bed.

"Look at your little mother's boobs, white or not, big or not?" With these words, he suddenly lifted the quilt on the woman's body. The naked woman lay on her side, propping her head on her arms, smiling and shaking her flowers. The man's laugh mingled with the woman's, and chased me out of the darkened room like a viper. I was about five years old.

After that, every time I passed the door of that room, I ran, afraid that a hand, black, hairy, with sharp claws, would pull me in. In the years that followed, that darkened room seemed like a dark abyss, trying to swallow me up. As I grew older, I often wondered if all the men in the world were just like my biological father... Are they terrible?

It was then, too, after eleven o 'clock at night, yes, after eleven o 'clock at night! He asked me to go to the train station to buy melon seeds for her big boobs. His birth mother, who lived next door to him, heard me. Luckily, she thought I was too young to go and stopped me.

My mother is a very negative person, she doesn't like to communicate, whenever I talk she will tell me to shut up and leave her alone. This attitude started when I was a child and has continued to this day. Perhaps because of this, I also developed the habit of not liking too much gossip and not being good at proactive communication. No matter what she encountered, she would always speculate and interpret it from a negative perspective.

My mother didn't know when she was getting remarried. When I was seven years old, my mother took me away from my youngest grandfather's family for some unknown reason and took me to my grandfather's family to live with my aunt's family. Also from this year, I almost every day by varying degrees of beating and scolding, better just one or two slap in the face, if they do something wrong or meet them in a bad mood will be covered with bruises or purple bruises, normal like beaten than rice point is also on time. A very strange phenomenon is that my aunt will suddenly smile and give me a slap when she is talking happily... Notice that this slap was so hard that my head was turned to the end of the other direction. If I could turn it, I would have to turn it five or six times. The marks on my face were clearly visible. This sudden slap was, love?

I still remember the first day to my grandfather's family I actually insomnia, a seven-year-old child insomnia. I picked up a small rectangular four-legged low wooden stool to the door of the backyard room, more than one meter away from the vine rack, there are a lot of flowers in the yard, there are four seasons begonia, rose, gardenia, etc., fragrance. But at this time young I did not want to

Chapter 1 Echoes of the past

enjoy the flowers, one hand across the knee, one hand holding up the chin looked up at the high moon, until now I still remember the moon that night special round special bright. The side of the hand holding the face felt wet, um, I cried. The tears ran uncontrollably down my chin and down my neck in a single, unbroken line, ticking over my other hand and leg, which lay across my knee. But no sound came from me, as when Zuzu hit me with the broken penny, and the silent tears poured down like rain. I felt a dull pain in my chest, and the pain dragged and grew more and more painful. Looking at the night of the moon as if to see Zuzu smiling face, wrinkled smiling face, want to touch her chin wrinkled down the skin ah, and those child-like feet, Zuzu I miss you. My Zuzu must also miss me very much.

For the next period of time, my chest has been very painful, I feel unable to lift breath, chest shortness of breath. After telling the adults, my grandfather decided to give me a kind of syrup to drink. After drinking it for about two months, it no longer hurt. Recalling the time when I was by Zuzu's side before, I was just in bad health, and there was no pain or I could not remember.

My grandfather has trouble with his legs and feet. It is said that he was injured when he was young. In my childhood memory, he is a relative who does not have much affection for me. Because when he died, I didn't feel the pain of loss. My aunt's family had two sons, my mother remarried and had another son, and my uncle's family had another son. As the only girl in the family, I was, of course, a thorn in my grandfather's side. My grandfather's eyes, always like the winter wind, sharp and cold. Although I was still young at that time, I understood that my grandfather's eyes were helpless and dissatisfied with my gender. I did not feel the kindness that a grandfather should have in his abuse of my gender. My grandfather would often give his cousin and my half-brother vitamin C tablets and then laugh as he watched their faces twist with acid. My grandfather's favorite is my eldest cousin, who is my uncle's son. Because they share the same surname, they are called Neisun. The three Cousins often play on my grandfather's bed, and my grandson recklessly takes the money in the envelope next to my grandfather's pillow and the peach cakes and snacks near the wall beside his bed. I wondered if that bed was more fun than any other place. They were so happy. Although my grandfather's legs and feet are not easy, it does not prevent him from beating me. He called me to lie on the corner of his bed. His second daughter pressed hard on my body to keep me balanced and easy for her father to operate, and lifted me high and fell heavily with his brown dragon crutches that were more than one meter long and hard. Every time I lift, I can see the large bruises left by the previous fall, and I will give up until the whole buttock is bruised. He always said: "Daughter is a loss of money, married daughter is poured out of the water, sooner or later is someone else's people..."

My grandfather is from the north. He does not eat southern food. He only loves pasta. He always gave the leftover dumplings and pimple soup to his Cousins, and occasionally I could have a bite or two if they didn't eat them. Growing up, I hated dumplings and pimple soup, and I didn't eat peach cake. When I was a child, snacks or fruits were divided by my grandfather, divided into portions, and then my Cousins chose the first one, and the rest was mine. Each of them has three hands. While taking away their share, each of them will take my share away a little, and finally the rest will give me no need to elaborate. The grown-ups smiled at each other with no intention of saying anything, just crossed their legs, eating sunflower seeds and watching the fun.

His eldest daughter, my mother, was just as good as him. She told me to roll up my pants and kneel on the ground. She lashed me in the shins with a cane. The bruise on my buttocks had not healed, but both my legs had turned purple again. Seems this family has a passion for purple? I don't know if my dark skin is due to frequent beatings as a child, and every inch of my skin is too purple, so-called pigmentation? She did not want to stop the meaning, the more hit the top, the more hit the more hard, is probably to find the pleasure of venting, and I have cried. There is no need to describe how I walked for the next few days to recover. That's why I hated purple when I grew up.

Once, when I was seven years old, my aunt let me and my older cousin, who was eight, cook together. In those days, there were no things like rice cookers, they were all cooked on a stove, but how could we control the stove when we were young? No experience at all, not surprisingly, the rice burned. When my aunt saw the charred rice at the bottom of the pot, she was immediately furious. She actually picked up the kitchen knife on the chopping board and cut down on me and my big cousin: "Two black sheep, do not do a meal well, what use are you? I cut you both to death......" Cousin and I didn't even get a chance to react. What did we do to deserve to be killed? We were scared and running. We ran next door to my uncle's house and hid. My uncle's wife was at home. She stopped my aunt at the door and kept telling her that they were too young after all. At that time, hiding in the room shivering, I was glad that my aunt was not only targeting me.

From that time, I planted the seeds of "doing housework badly is to be cut by a knife", and after sprouting, I decided that "there is no problem that can not be solved by force", as long as you are fierce enough, you can conquer all. So when I was at school, I liked to play with violent boys, and a fight could break out at any time, so as to show their skills and mercilessness that they taught me by example. This led to me being asked to be a parent from time to time.

Like Grandma Yao, my aunt was very loud and liked to make me kneel. But I prefer to grandma Yao, because she just scold me and punishment kneel, and aunt scold me after I began to keep slapping, sometimes came is a few slaps, what will not say to you, too happy is also hard a slap to reward you. This also led to the formation of me now can do absolutely not move the character. You know, I have a cousin who's about my age, just a few months older than me. Her parents abandoned her, is our real father adopted her, in my opinion, the big father family is relatively gentle, maybe when things are reasonable will not start, cousin now personality is quite gentle, everything is softly spoken patiently reasonable. Once, I knelt for a long time next to the four-sided Beijing iron stove burning coal. I felt the rush of convenience getting stronger and stronger. I could not help but beg for mercy many times: "Let me go to the toilet, my stomach hurts so much that I can't hold it anymore. However, my aunt, who was knitting a sweater, screamed at me, "Don't think I don't know what the hell you're thinking! Just kneel down!" The increasing discomfort made me feel that my chest was short of breath, and my aunts just ignored me. In the end, the long kneel ended when I was forced to pass out.

In fact, my aunt had feelings for me. Although she beat me and scolded me, she often cried for me at night and pitied me. But that was when I was an adult. She pitied me for being alone, worried about my future, and pitied me for not being cared for.

As I grew older, I often wondered if my grandfather would have changed his mind about me if I had been a boy. Would I have been loved and approved by him like my brothers and brothers? But that is a question that can never be answered. Of course, when I grow up, my grandfather and aunt's attitude to me has changed a little, not every day to beat and scold, I also occasionally reflect, maybe the punishment of grandma and aunt kneeling, scolding because I was too naughty in childhood, maybe big dad they are really love me, but not careful and patient enough... Yao grandma is old, she has changed, she is kind, smiling all day, speaking volume is still very high but the tone has been softened a lot, probably no longer have the ear of children chirp and keep making mistakes to annoy her, so she became calm, the two pear vortex mouth is very good-looking. My aunt also has two pear vortices in her mouth, but she is still so angry and cranky. They were both fat and tall and fierce. Now that I have children, I can understand why

Chapter 1 Echoes of the past

the house is always filled with the cries of old mothers.

When my mother took me to my grandfather's house, she arranged for me to study in a nearby primary school, about three kilometers away from Zuzu's house. Every day I go to grandma's home after school, grandma sent me back at night, I gave my grandma said I don't want to go to grandpa's house, pointing to the pole said grandma you see I wrote down grandpa. At that time, I think that the people who blocked my return to Zuzu side is my grandfather, stupid thought that writing a few words can go back to the past, of course, living in my grandfather's home during that time also have a lot of happiness, the children in the yard is particularly many, we play together to drill a black hole, climb trees, run switches, write Wang words and so on. Of course, this series of play down the butt of course also can not miss the cane beating and a variety of corporal punishment, I often miss Zuzu and can not sleep, sitting in the yard to see the moon. The moon is so round, so bright, as if it can illuminate the darkness in my heart. Is Zuzu thinking of me, too?

When I recall my childhood, my favorite and happiest things are the time I lived with Zuzu. Follow Zuzu, do not have to do any housework, even the very fierce MAO grandma did not shout to me to do housework, did not beat me because of anything, more will not cut me, mistakes are only punished to kneel. At this time is missing Zuzu. Why do adults move me around without asking me how I feel? During a recent argument with my mother, I mentioned, "Why did you send me to my aunt's house instead of being with Zuzu?" She said that she had asked me and that I had asked to go. She really came with her mouth open and was always full of words. She talked to my friend and said, "I hope she can take care of her brother for the rest of his life after I die…"

Indeed, I never refused their endless demands, and it was because of this that my mother thought I should give her all I had. During the epidemic, a friend called and said that life insurance was very good, so I casually said to my mother,

抑郁自救笔记
Notes on Depression Self-help

"I'll buy an insurance policy, and if I die, you will get one million dollars, OK?" Mother said excitedly: "Great, thank you, sincerely thank you!" That smile is really more brilliant than flowers, my own mother is thanking me...... She probably wished I'd die as soon as she bought it. This reminds me of many years ago, because my work requires me to fly often, once she saw that the ticket did not buy accident insurance and scolded me: "How come you have no conscience? You don't buy accident insurance when you fly. The plane is so prone to accidents, and you don't buy accident insurance? Have you ever thought that you bought insurance, if you die can leave money to me, raise you so big at least a little return scatter......" This got me thinking, if you really think that flying is so dangerous, why don't you just persuade me not to take it, instead of asking me to buy accident insurance? In addition, there were too many small things and indifference in her life to me, so once I cut my own wrist after drinking too much, thinking that I should give my life back to them, stop torturing me and using me! But, Zuzu bless me, wish me peace all my life.

Primary school I mathematics is very bad, although now back the multiplication table is not good, at that time was no less by the math teacher ears torn skin of that kind of students, every time when the ears are pulled hard to twist my whole expression is distorted, feel her strength is born again will guarantee that it can be successfully pulled down, very ruthless, not blood she is not willing. My mother bought me a lot of fairy tale books, I like to read story books, and I once dreamed of becoming a writer when I was young. When writing a composition, I often narrate the story inside, and sometimes I was sued by my classmates and my teacher for copying the book if I wrote too carefully. But when I grow up, I don't know when I don't like to read books. I feel dizzy when I see a little more words. But our Chinese teacher still like me, she is our class teacher. To say that she likes me is not so far, she just does not hate me. See I am tall in the class to choose me to run 1500 meters, usually did not let me go to the special practice let me run, the result of four hundred meters when I was already tired to go, and finally took the first place, but is the countdown, haha, can walk is also powerful. However, after the end of the game was the head teacher in charge of a scolding, from then on I hate sports, can lie down absolutely will not sit.

Later, I went to Guiyang Art School with my friends and saw that the girls of the art school were able to sing and dance and perform, and planted a dream of an actor in my heart. Their dancing is as clever as the spirit, the singing is as melodious as the sound of nature, every word is floating into my heart, knocking the dream. In other words, I have learned dance with dance skills, primary school mother once let me learn two days of dance, yes, a total of two days of time. Unfortunately, in this precious two days, my mother saw that I had no progress, determined that I was not dancing material, shaking her head and saying: "TSK TSK, ah... No talent." So there was no further reading on the matter.

At the age of 14, I had dropped out of school and was sent to my dad's garage by my mother, who somehow inspired her to think that I would be a great mechanic, or that I had accidentally shown a talent for fixing cars at some point. Hanging out with a bunch of mechanics for a long time, drinking and smoking, and being even less interested in studying, it was at this time that I started my smoking history, and my personality became more and more "masculine". Coupled with my calm and natural eyes looking out into the distance, my smoking posture became more and more handsome.

At that time, the biological father conditions are very good, the small life is very leisurely, he suddenly thought of me one day, do not blame him for thinking of me, because the garage is his elder sister, he always in and out there to see me, see I wear soil said, want to take me to the provincial capital to play for a few days to buy a few sets of clothes, "lost his face?" I was very reluctant to go, wearing my aunt woven a new green and white checkered sweater, mother bought black and white checkered new shoes to go. Maybe plaid was in fashion that year. His woman took me shopping for clothes and kept asking me if I wanted this or that. Sorry, I'm actually not familiar or even strange with either of you, so I always shake my head. It's hard for anyone to accept the sudden warmth of a stranger. But he hurled insults at me like a mad man: "You are a pus, a straw bag, a bumpkin, I don't know how to dress you. Even if I dress you in a dragon's robe, you don't look like a human being..." In the end, although his woman rolled her eyes or chose a set of denim clothes to me, the clothes were very close, quite a figure, when I returned home, all the people around me praised me for changing a set of clothes after so beautiful, foreign style. This can be said to be a beautiful dress in exchange for dignity, although it is not what I would like to exchange. He said to take me to play for a few days, in fact, he has never accepted me in his heart, and he is still so disgusted and run. Indeed, it is undeniable that the eyes of the provincial capital are not the same, to pick a set of clothes for me to wear very good-looking, no grid, but I think that a set of grid wear more comfortable. I haven't seen him since.

  Flash forward to the days when sports lotteries were all the rage, and he and his second sister were also my youngest fathers. The family had a dinner at the youngest's house. At that time, he said a lot of touching words, how how sorry I am, owe me. Those words like the warm sunshine into my heart let me feel unprecedented love, suddenly found the father's love, I finally have "dad", unexpectedly was sweet words poured into the heart soft, the flowers in the heart seemed to be awakened by this sweet words, all opened up, surrounded the whole atrium. I decided to forgive him, immediately put the previous unhappiness behind me, I called him for the first time "dad". As a result, he suddenly showed the ferocious smile of many years ago and said to me: "I have calculated the probability of winning the sports lottery, you give me 20,000 yuan, I can win." I won five million will share you one million..." I was shocked and angry at the turn of his words and his ridiculous, unrealistic bullshit, and couldn't understand

Chapter 1 Echoes of the past

how he could even make such a request in this situation. I, who always knew how to fight back, angrily smashed the table, tore my throat and shouted out my anger and dissatisfaction with all my strength: "Fuck you, you give me 10,000, I won 5 million to you!" Slamming the door out of my heart roared: "later also do not see this bastard! Bah..." The flowers withered, too.

Once I read a report on a social media platform about the conflict between a girl and her parents. Her parents were very strict with her and only paid attention to her study. She didn't have any time for herself, let alone for entertainment. When it came to choosing a college, the girl chose her favorite university, and her parents modified her plan to choose another school closer to home. Later, the girl urged her parents to let her go abroad, and she portrayed the benefits of going abroad with great passion, which eventually came true.

Of course, the life after going abroad was not as easy as the girl described. She always worked and studied part-time and called her parents for help when she was really in trouble. After the call was answered, the abuse came from the other end, and her parents accused her: "If it wasn't for the money, you wouldn't have called back! ..." Even if they have prepared the money for the girl, they still have to constantly criticize the girl. This made the girl very cold and cut off contact with her family in anger. In the 17 years since she cut off contact with her family, she not only earned a doctorate in Germany through her own efforts, but also started her own family and had children. When her parents reached her through television, she refused to see her family. Even though she knew her parents were dying, she stuck to her decision not to see them on their deathbeds.

One is a life of bondage and demand, the other is a life of indifference and indifference. I admire her courage, she can bravely cut off all cares, brave to live for themselves.

And my cousin, who was attacked by her own father with an axe and left her head bloodied, came home from the emergency room just as she was being patched up when I heard the news.

Despite so much pain and neglect, she has now chosen to forgive. I admire my cousin's courage and tolerance to forgive the pain in life and forgive those who have hurt her.

I have also tried to understand the position of my biological father and mother, maybe they have their own reasons, maybe they just don't know how to express emotions... I have tried many times to open my heart and let go of those grudges. But every so often, I think of their past indifference and neglect, of their endless demands on me. They see that I am doing well now, and I am sure that there is a series of things waiting for me to deal with, so it is better not to make trouble for themselves.

I can only reconcile in my own way, stop dwelling on what they did and stop living in resentment. But I don't have much to do with them either. This decision may be self-defeating, it may not be perfect, but it is the best choice I can make at this stage. I will continue to strive to live my life and find true happiness and fulfillment in my own way. Now that I am busy with my work and the physical and mental growth of my two children, I don't want any more negative things to disturb my peaceful and happy life.

Chapter 2 Trapped in a Cage

Depression came quietly, like a shadow in the night, slowly enveloping my otherwise quiet life. It not only ate away at my body, but also ate away at my mind and imprisoned me in a pit of despair. I was a trapped beast, bound by invisible chains, surrounded by cold iron bars, and overhead was the heavy sky. I struggled, I roared, but I could not seem to find my way out, and each struggle only made me more tired.

But even in the darkest moments, there was always a spark of intransigence and defiance flickering deep inside me. I wasn't willing to just give in to fate and let my illness define my life. So I began my battle with the disease and embarked on the long and arduous road of treatment.

1. Being seriously ill

I was probably in my late 20s when I started to realize that something was wrong with my body.

At first, I just felt a little unhappy and down, but I didn't pay much attention to it, thinking it was just a normal mood swing, or maybe a naturally short and impatient temper. But as time went on, this became more and more severe and I began to feel constant sadness, anxiety and nervousness, as well as fear, not being able to control my emotions, gradually losing interest in life and feeling bored and bored with socializing, working and even daily activities. At the same time,

抑郁自救笔记
Notes on Depression Self-help

I also began to experience some physical and mental symptoms. For example, I had trouble sleeping. I always had trouble falling asleep or waking up early. I also feel constantly tired and low energy, even when I get enough sleep, I still feel exhausted because of nightmares and night sweats until I'm soaking wet every night. I even started to have problems with my concentration and memory. I couldn't concentrate on things. I couldn't remember anything. There is also a change in appetite, sometimes you overeat, but no matter how much you eat, you will feel hungry within half an hour, and sometimes you have almost no appetite. And physical pain, excruciating pain. The whole back, especially the upper back and neck, is stiff as stone. I have to get massages to relieve the pain a little bit, and it's usually with blind men because they're so strong. All the people who give me massages say they've never had a shoulder and neck as hard as mine, harder than a muscular man. I now know that it was the tense nerves that caused the tension in the meridians not to be relaxed in time.

There were so many symptoms that I felt like I was in chaos. I could not hear any cold words, and loud sounds made me feel irritable and unable to stay calm. When I see crowded places, I will always tremble involuntarily, will not talk to people, and will lose myself in my nameless sorrow and anxiety. I have also tried to concentrate on one thing, but I have failed every time. No matter how hard I tried, my mind would wander and I couldn't concentrate. This feeling really frustrated me so much that I began to constantly doubt my abilities. Every day, I struggled to find an exit, one that would allow me to escape this pain. But, no matter where I go, I can't find a place of peace. Even in the middle of the night, I could not sleep peacefully, and when I did fall asleep, I was haunted by terrible nightmares. In the bloody dreams, there was always fighting, being killed, or hunting down, and occasionally scary scenes from the movies and evil spirits. Every time at this time, I always wake up from the nightmare, sweating. At this time, I am afraid of horror films, even horror films do not dare to look at the promotional pages, especially sensitive to red, every time I see red feel inexplicable impulse and excitement, more and more do not like red.

In this chaos, I seem to have become a bystander, looking at the world around, but can not integrate, participate in it, feeling like a floating leaf, unable to find a home. The days of such isolation seemed to last forever.

The scariest thing about it was that I felt like I was going crazy at any moment. I can't help but recall a crazy woman I saw in my childhood, running down the street naked, laughing shamelessly. There was nothing in her eyes but pure pleasure, without any other restrictions or limitations. I am afraid that one day I will be like her, after the schizophrenia lost self-control, do some terrible things, such as naked in the street, or hurt the people around and so on. But occasionally I would feel that maybe crazy should be better for me at that time, at least no longer be mental torture, crazy is happy.

In fact, I was not so afraid that I would be schizophrenic. Once, someone told my mother that a psychiatric specialist in the provincial capital was sure to get better, so she took me to the specialist. The specialist said to me: "Your disease is like this, you can only take medicine to control it..." What was more frightening was what she said later: "There is a fine line between depression and schizophrenia. You may become schizophrenic the next second." "The next second..." Keep repeating those three words in your head -- next second! Such an alarmist remark, which I now feel irresponsible, no doubt set up another frying pan to torment my fragile spirit at that time... For a mentally extremely fragile person, this is what a big blow! In an instant, the sky was spinning and I was really going mad! The air was so heavy that I couldn't breathe. Ever since then, the doctor's words have hung over me like a huge shadow, leaving me nowhere to escape, dreading every next second. At that time my mother also listened to the doctor, "That's it", so she paid no attention to my condition.

At that time, my understanding of my illness was really very limited, and

抑郁自救笔记

Notes on Depression Self-help

I thought that treatment was the doctor's business, and even if I understood it, I could only listen to the doctor. The word "self-rescue" never appeared in my mind from beginning to end, and I never faced this problem squarely, never thought about whether I should learn about the illness, pathology and means of rehabilitation, let alone what is introspection. Simply think that what the doctor said is right, blindly listen to all the doctors say, on the way to the doctor changed many hospitals and different departments, hoping to find an effective treatment method. However, each doctor gave me different drugs, which usually had very strong side effects. I vividly remember nausea, vomiting, diarrhea, skin rashes, fainting spells, convulsions, alcoholism and mania, as well as the pain of a stiff neck and tight muscles at my collarbones. At the same time, my mood fluctuated wildly, alternating between euphoria and depression, as if I were on an emotional roller coaster. A lot of people have called me moody.

It's exhausting to be alive! Am I the only one who can do this?

I repeated it countless times, almost every day at the time. I began to worry that I would have no future, not knowing how I would face the world, not knowing if the world had abandoned me, or if I wanted to escape from the world.

So I cut myself off from the outside world, not even my family, and of course they couldn't remember me. I shut myself off from the meds that made me terribly ill but did nothing to help my condition, subsisted on computers and alcohol, and drank an entire bottle of beer (12, 650ml) by dawn. During the day, I only ate a bowl of instant noodles, and sometimes I ate nothing at all. I lived a black and white life. I often did not sleep for two or three days, or slept for three or four hours a day before waking up in nightmares. Day after day, so repeated. There was only a bed, a computer, a kettle and a degenerate me in this one-bedroom, one-bathroom rented house. The room was simple, unfurnished and the walls were still rough, and the rent was only 200 renminbi a month. I still remember when I was playing an online game about The Three Kingdoms.

I spent a lot of money in the game, watching the characters grow and fight. The characters in the game seemed to reflect my heart. I was immersed in the group battle of the game all day long. Every battle would bring me endless satisfaction and pleasure. I seem to have found an outlet for my inner anger, mania and violent tendencies. Immersed in the virtual world, I seemed to forget my emotional pathologies with the help of alcohol and online games.

Speaking of this, I must admit that I am really a very impulsive and violent person. Everyone has fantasies, but my fantasies are often immersed in scenes of blood and violence, full of fighting, brawling and bloodshed. I don't like to communicate with people very much. Once I have a difference of opinion, I will choose silence and refuse to communicate with each other, which is a kind of tempo of incompatibility. And whenever there is a disagreement, I tend to take an extreme way to make a conclusion. I only hope to solve the problem through a one-time conclusion, rather than reach a consensus through rational communication. I even fought with people when I was emotionally upset, so I lost a lot of medical expenses. I was taken to the public Security Bureau by the police many times, which has seriously affected my normal life.

Seeing sharp objects, I would have a strong impulse to stab people with them or run into them myself, and there would be a bloody scene in front of me after bumping into them. When standing on high ground, I even feel the urge to jump. These thoughts often float around in my head and make me feel overwhelmed. To avoid these impulsive behaviors, I would avoid going to any height, not even the second floor. Nor do I touch sharp objects, such as scissors, nails, triangular pieces of wood or even toothpicks.

In addition, I get very upset when other people talk loudly. Even when my loved ones talk too loudly or too much, I can't stand it and want to get angry or violent with them. Sometimes, I even have the urge to smash things and fight, as if this is the only way to release my inner depression and anger. There is always a mass of anger in my chest that has nowhere to vent and is ready to explode at any time, and I can't be happy no matter what. This may have something to do with my childhood experience, when adults always used reprimands and corporal punishment to suppress my disobedience. This experience led me to believe that force can solve all problems, and communication is superfluous, just superfluous.

2. Initial treatment

A friend couldn't bear to see me suffer any more, so he took me to Nanjing Brain Hospital and visited almost every doctor in every department. I was discouraged, but he insisted that there were several expert psychologists, whose numbers were not good to hang up, but they had queued up to buy them online, and they could consult me in a week. At this time, I must have trustworthy people around me, afraid of being alone, afraid of strangers, completely insecure, no matter where I go, I have to pull the coat corner of my friend, afraid that I will be swallowed by everything strange if I get separated from him.

Persuaded by my friend, I went to the doctor's consulting room without any hope. At my first visit, the doctor gently guided me, and I gradually opened up about my experiences over the past few years, including bad habits and being a drug addict, as well as my current physical symptoms and mental pain. However, as the conversation progressed, it seemed that I was not in much pain, but I was in a lot of pain. As we talked, I was irritated by the doctor's tone of voice, which was hostile and sarcastic. I tried to keep my emotions in check, tried to keep my sanity, but eventually I lost control and started banging on the table and yelling. To my surprise, this time there was no conflict like the previous ones. Instead, the doctor gently apologized and explained to me, soothing my emotions: "I meant no harm. I just wanted to see what your tolerance level was." I was shocked to hear this explanation, but also realized that the doctor was helping me face my problems in a special way. At the end of my lengthy consultation, I was diagnosed with bipolar disorder, moderate depression and severe anxiety. I was prescribed four or five medications and asked to check in once a week. The visit was the first long conversation I'd had in my many years of seeking medical help. I asked about every detail of my life. Before, doctors would ask about symptoms for only three to five minutes and then prescribe a bunch of drugs without saying much.

The treatment was very different from my previous experience, although the side effects of the medication I had just taken three days earlier made me very uncomfortable, and it was hard to bear the thought that I would not take the medicine again tomorrow. However, with the progress of the medication and review, the doctor would give me a chicken blood encouragement each time, strengthening my confidence in recovery, and I obviously feel that I am gradually improving. My mood gradually settled. What had been a constant feeling of depression, helplessness and hopelessness began to diminish, replaced by a sense of calm and reassurance. Two months later, I was smiling again and slowly returning to my normal routine. Although I was still nervous and broke out in a cold sweat when I went to crowded places occasionally, my overall condition had improved significantly. My doctor has told me that I can gradually reduce the dosage and type of medication.

I was very anxious when I heard this news. I was afraid that if I left the medication, I would return to the chaos I had felt before. The feeling of pain and helplessness left me terrified. The doctor patiently explained that tapering off the medication was a normal part of the treatment process and that I should be able to get through this phase as long as I continued to actively cooperate with the treatment and pay attention to self-management and adjustment. He encouraged me to believe in myself and the effects of my treatment. I remember him very clearly saying, "You can do this. You're the most different of all my patients, and you're strong." That really inspired me and gave me renewed confidence. So, under the guidance of my doctor, I began to slowly reduce the dosage and type of medication.

The process of stopping the drug was difficult, and the range of side effects of withdrawal, including headaches, palpitations, vomiting, diarrhea, sweating, and shaking, was particularly painful. I didn't know it. The doctor said the drug had meth in it, so I had to stop by my own will. At these moments, I remember what the doctor said, you can do it. You're the most different patient I've ever had. Am I really different? Yes, I am! It must be!

Three months later, I was down to my last medication, the one with the addictive ingredient. I was beginning to worry about losing this vital aid. My doctor advised me to reduce the dosage of this last medicine slowly, advising me to take many doses, gradually decreasing one dose at a time. At this time, it was the beginning of 2014, which coincided with my business trip and required me to go abroad. So I arrived in the United States with only a few medications left and a lot of trepidation. My first effective treatment had come to an end.

3. Recurring phases

Before going abroad, I was worried about whether I would be able to adapt to the new environment and lifestyle. After all, it can be a challenge for anyone to leave the familiar environment and family and friends and come to a strange country with no language. I don't speak English at all, and I never studied this subject seriously when I was in school or, of course, any other subject. On top of that, I struggled with depression and anxiety and was worried that I wouldn't be able to cope with the challenges and pressures of my new environment.

Thankfully, the transition away from the familiar and into a new world stimulates dopamine production and gives me the opportunity to see myself and the world around me in a new light, actively or passively meeting new people, and trying to connect with those around me. They come from different backgrounds and cultures, which allows me to try to understand and be open to different perspectives and values. In addition, limited social activities encourage me to devote more energy to my work. The smooth development of the work made me feel more fulfilled and accomplished than ever before. These changes make me seem to forget the haze of the past, forget the depression and anxiety that used to bother me, and become softer and more confident.

Because of the smooth development of my career and the good control of my illness, I decided to live in the United States for a long time. It was also during this time that I met the father of my children and welcomed our first child, my eldest daughter, in 2015. During this period, I can be described as a family career double harvest, at this time the doctor said I have postpartum depression, but I did not feel where the wrong, so did not put in mind, "spring breeze horseshoe disease", I began to drift, feel that days do not have my big, eyes can not accommodate anyone, a earth less I will not turn the gesture. What followed was that I was narrow-minded and had a strong desire for control in my feelings. I was overly concerned with my partner's every move and tried to ensure my status and security by controlling their actions and decisions. Not only did this state of affairs strain and weigh me down emotionally, it also left me feeling exhausted and empty. Perhaps the disgusting side of my biological father from my childhood has caused me to distrust all men.

After getting my green card, I began to travel frequently between my country and abroad. Life seemed to return to its old habits of indulgence and disorientation. Drinking, having fun, the things that had sunk me, took over my life again. At this stage, my illness suddenly relapsed again, and I became extremely dependent on the father of my children. I followed him almost everywhere and wouldn't even allow him to leave my sight. The slightest sound made me irritable and indifferent to my child. I hired two nannies to play with her, and the slightest sound of brushing my teeth or turning over in bed would send me into a rage and out of control. I think anyone's smile is mocking me, and I get the feeling that "if I'm not happy, no one else can be happy." Violent and manic emotions began to occupy my mind again, and I often wanted to take a knife and destroy the world with it.

At this time, I was like a broken China, the sharp shards cutting myself and stabbing the people around me.

The child's father could not bear to see me continue to suffer, and took me to see a doctor at Seattle Specialist Hospital. When we arrived at the hospital, the staff asked us to fill out a list with several options under each question. After reading the list to fill out, the father's face gradually turned pale and nervous. He took my hand tightly until it hurt and hurriedly led me out of the hall. When I asked him what was wrong, there was an unconcealed quiver in his voice. "If you fulfill any two of the items on that list, you will be placed in mandatory isolation. We can't stay here any longer. I need you, our children need you..." With that, my brain went blank for a moment, gawking at the gun-toting guard in the consulting room, grateful that the father of my child had gotten me out of there. I also wondered why he had taken me away.

After returning home, we found the Nanjing doctor who had cured me before going abroad through various channels and returned to China for treatment. However, the treatment was not satisfactory this time. Because of pregnancy, my physique has undergone a very big change, the previous drugs lost their efficacy, but the side effects are more serious, resulting in my whole person weak, shock, the whole person in a state of semi-paralysis.

Before pregnancy, I never had any allergic reactions. After giving birth, my

Chapter 2 Trapped in a Cage

body seems to be super sensitive and develop allergens. I remember being put on a drip in the hospital during the birth, and my obstetrician rushing up to me nervously asked, "How are you feeling? What's wrong with you?" I was slightly stunned and answered in surprise, "I'm fine..." Have not "ah" finished, feel breathing difficulties, the scene in front of the moment blurred, immediately lost consciousness. I know that I was surrounded by a circle of doctors and nurses, do not know how long, wake up, the medical staff smiled and said to me: "All right, relax." It turned out that my whole face was swollen into a pig's head, and my eyes were swollen into a line. Fortunately, the doctor found the abnormality in time. This brush with death has kept me scared and afraid to try new things. Every time I try a new food or medicine, I will make a long mental preparation. It was also this time that I began to develop allergies to penicillin and mango and pineapple, and I have brought allergy medicine and adrenaline injections with me ever since, just in case.

In desperation, we found a new doctor in China, started taking new medicines, and returned to China regularly for physiotherapy. During the one-month stay in the hospital, I felt that I had improved significantly again. The effect of medication and physical therapy with instruments was very significant. I was very happy every day, but for some reason, along with the treatment, I began to drink too much wine, from half a bottle of wine to one bottle of wine, two bottles of wine, three bottles of wine every night... One wine wasn't strong enough anymore, it had to be mixed with a strong drink. The addiction gets worse and worse, to the point where you can't control it.

In 2019, the year I was pregnant with my baby, there was a new plan for the land in my hometown, and the government required the relocation of all the nearby cemeteries, including Zuzu's.

Zuzu's grave is on the hill, it takes a long walk up, and then you have to go through a dark cemetery. In the years before I went abroad, I used to drink

抑郁自救笔记
Notes on Depression Self-help

until three or four in the morning to go up and sit in front of Zuzu's tombstone, smoking and drinking, talking to Zuzu in a broken voice, and pouring out all my pain, sadness and anger to her. Sometimes I would lose control of my emotions, crying loudly, questioning why Zuzu left me early, blaming her for not taking me with her, and sometimes looking forward to a crack in the tomb that would allow me to lie next to her, so that I could completely rid myself of the pain and trouble of this world. However, no matter how much I cried and blamed, the round tomb was always silent. Only the moon hung high, shining on the gravestone and illuminating my face, as if to comfort me and tell me that she was always there, always with me.

  Our family is a large family with many members, but when it comes to moving the grave, Grandpa MAO put it forward, few people are willing to pay. Some people said: "I do not follow the ancestor name!" Some people even say: "My ancestors did not bless me to get rich, why should I take money to move my ancestors' graves?" After learning this, I was angry at their coolness and thinness, thinking that the cost of moving the grave was too high for them to bear. No matter how much it was, I decided to bear all the expenses myself and called Grandpa MAO to ask for details. However, Grandpa MAO told me that he only needed a little more than 40,000 yuan. I was stunned and felt even more speechless. As long as it was only forty thousand yuan, these people would not recognize their ancestors. You can make up a few hundred yuan each, right? I still remember that when Zu Zu died, they even had to share some of Zu Zu's quilts, pillows and even bowls and chopsticks. Now they say that such unconscionable words and do such unconscionable things.

  In the end, I fully covered the cost of moving the grave, but because of various reasons I could not leave to return to China, I have not yet been to Zuzu's new grave. However, Grandpa Yao and Grandpa SAN help me to worship my beloved Zuzu every year. If Zuzu knew that I was now a wife and mother, she would be proud of my growth and happiness. She would love my children as much as she loved me. I am glad to know that my daughter's name is still in the family tree of my hometown. This family tree has become the only link between Zuzu and me and my daughter, and it has been a great comfort to me. No matter how time passes, no matter how life changes, this unique feeling will always be there.

Since then, I have kept in touch with my grandpa and Grandma. However, they never receive red envelopes from me on New Year's festivals. They always ask me to take good care of myself and my children and not to worry about them. They are doing well, but my grandma's health is much worse than before. The warmth and tenacity of this family affection can always warm my heart like a beam of sunshine at some time.

In 2020, at the height of the epidemic, I gave birth to another baby. During pregnancy, for the sake of my baby's health, I stopped all medication and forced myself off alcohol, but I still continued to smoke two or three packs of cigarettes a day. While these medications have helped me in the past, I have to be very cautious during pregnancy. After consulting my doctor and learning that one of the medications I was taking had no adverse effects on the fetus, I decided to stop using the other medications for a while and only take one. Then, of course, came the emotional backlash, the restlessness and fear that overwhelmed me again.

Once, when I went for a cosmetic procedure, I made small talk with the doctor. After hearing about my condition, he suggested that I could use exercise and travel as a distraction, and also try psychohypnosis. The doctor was an ICU doctor with his own beauty studio, and I took the advice of professional doctors seriously.

When I got home, I started researching psychiatrists and hypnotists in Seattle on the Internet, and a long search led me to a licensed Chinese psychohypnotist. I went to this doctor's office with the attitude of giving it a try. The atmosphere was warm and simple, but the lighting was too bright for me. When I entered the office, the doctor greeted me with a smile. She looked in her thirties and was tall and slender, with a big smile and firm eyes. She is so determined that every time her eyes meet, she wants to win or lose. Her smile makes me feel friendly and relaxed. We started to talk and the doctor asked me some basic information about my life, work and family. But the next two visits left me feeling a little disappointed. We never got to the topic of hypnosis. The doctor just talked to me briefly. She always said, "Next time you can start hypnosis." These two consultations did not affect me much, and I began to wonder if the doctor was in name only. Perhaps she did not understand hypnosis and hesitated to continue the treatment.

During the third treatment, if I didn't get the hypnosis I wanted, I was ready to stop seeing her. No matter whether the hypnosis worked or not, I wanted hypnosis. We talked about my allergies as a result of the change in my body after giving birth. I told the doctor that I had never been allergic to mango or penicillin, but that I had developed an allergic reaction after giving birth. It made me feel extremely anxious when trying new foods, panic attacks when I was too nervous, and I even had to prepare allergy medication ahead of time just in case. I feel extremely anxious every time I try a new food and even need to prepare my allergy medication ahead of time just in case. The doctor explained that this allergic reaction was not necessarily indicative of a physical defect in me, but rather an overreaction in my body. She advised me to keep a positive attitude, gradually adapt to the new physical changes, and find suitable ways to relieve the allergy symptoms. And the allergy doesn't kill me immediately. The penicillin allergy, severe breathing difficulties and swelling are due to the fact that the allergen is directly injected into the bloodstream. The amount of food I normally come into contact with is not large enough to kill me. And there are a lot of people in the world who have allergies that are much more severe than me, but are still alive and healthy. The worst thing is to take allergy medicine, many people rely on taking allergy medicine every day to avoid the symptoms of allergies in the body.

As our conversation progressed, we turned to the specter that always hangs over my head: "There's a fine line between depression and schizophrenia..." Before the doctor could hear me out, she clapped her hands together, frowned and said, "Oh, it's really wrong. It's unprofessional to scare you when you know you're already vulnerable." This move let me hold in the atmosphere for many years a little dare to face the "next second". The doctor explained in detail the connection and differences between depression and schizophrenia. She told me that although there were some similarities between them, they were two different diseases with very different symptoms, causes and treatments. This was the first time I really came into contact with the "truth" of depression, and it was this time that I was motivated to learn more about the disorder.

By the end of the session, my feelings about allergies and schizophrenia had finally been resolved, and my trust in the psychiatrist had been established. But the hypnosis still did not take place. Hypnosis had sprouted in my mind. I wanted hypnosis.

There is a high-speed traffic jam is particularly serious, can only move at 3mile per hour. Suddenly, I was hit by a car behind me. Fortunately, the car was traveling very slowly and the impact was not serious. I turned around and asked my daughter if she was hurt or where it hurt and she said it was OK. I stopped and looked at the back of the car. There were no scratches or damage. The person who hit me didn't get out of the car, just waved and said sorry, while the car I was blocking on the congested highway honked and honked. Unable to speak English, I thought, people and cars are OK, so as not to trouble, I got on the car and continued to move forward in the congestion. But as time went by, I began to fear driving. I don't know if it was the influence of this incident on me. Later, I

抑郁自救笔记
Notes on Depression Self-help

couldn't drive at all and was very afraid of driving. The father of my child drove with me to the psychologist's clinic. When I arrived, I went upstairs by myself. I told the doctor that I was afraid of driving but I wasn't sure why. The only reason I could relate to was this time. She and I combed through everything and found the point that might cause me to be afraid. I cooperated with her in hypnosis. After the interview, I went downstairs to the car, opened the driver's door and said to the father, "Get out of the car!" He smiled and asked skeptically, "Are you sure?" I nodded in certainty, put my foot on the gas pedal and turned the steering wheel as if nothing had happened and drove home. She helped me overcome my new fear. Hypnosis is good, thank you Lala!

As autumn turns to winter and the weather gets colder, I drive my daughter to school. The heat in the car slowly dissipated, but it could not dispel the anxiety in my mind. I felt a vague sense of repression. My daughter's childish words now sounded like a chattering "hoop". My emotions suddenly broke down, and I shouted to stop my daughter: "From now on, don't talk! Don't say a word!" My daughter was shocked by my sudden sternness. Her crystal clear eyes were full of astonishment and incomprehension. She nodded and asked softly why. I shouted frantically, "Don't speak!" She "um" a quiet voice. When I arrived at the school, I rushed my daughter inside, called the father, and let off some steam. On the other end of the phone, he just listened silently, occasionally soothing a few words, but also inexplicably let me slowly calm down.

After hanging up the phone, I felt very guilty, my daughter is just an innocent child, I as a mother, but let her bear my emotional fluctuations. Remembering my daughter's face, frightened by my yelling, I saw myself as a child. The guilt and pain woke me up and urged me to seek help from a hypnotist.

The hypnotist listened patiently to me talk about the process of onset, comforted me, and then recommended a professional psychiatrist for me.

The experience of seeing a doctor in the United States is indeed different from that at home. Doctors here spend a lot of time explaining in detail the side effects, the mechanism of action and what I need to be aware of before writing a prescription. They gave me a thorough understanding of how the drugs work and even gave me the right to choose my own medication appropriately. In contrast, when I visited a doctor in China in the past, I was rarely given such a detailed explanation. It was also through the doctor's explanation that I finally learned the reason for my repeated drinking -- it was also a side effect of the medication, one of which, while treating the condition, also made me strongly addicted. This treatment experience gave me a deep appreciation of the power of the drugs and allowed me to begin to truly understand my condition. This time I would still take the drugs that cause alcohol addiction, but the amount would be halved and I would only take the occasional uncomfortable and sudden emergency.

With my doctor's guidance, I gradually learned how to choose the right medication for me and realized that I could not always rely on drugs to maintain my emotional stability. As I became more stable, my doctor guided me to gradually reduce the amount of medication I was taking until I finally stopped taking it. It was a long and challenging process, and my doctor always gave me encouragement when I was experiencing self-doubt: "What do you think is wrong with you? You're perfectly fine!" Eventually, with the careful guidance of my doctor and the company of my family, I was able to stop taking the medication.

4. "Mentor and Friend" Dr. Ma

In 2022, I was lucky enough to meet an 80-year-old TCM veteran, Dr. Ma. My friend said that she was not feeling well because of the physical tension caused by anxiety, and she was completely cured after two acupuncture sessions with Dr. Ma. After I heard that, I immediately decided to give it a try, because I desperately want to relieve the muscle tension caused by the disease. As long as I heard that there was any opportunity to help my recovery, I would try it.

After a long appointment time, I finally waited for my first consultation. He patiently asked me about my illness for nearly half an hour. In the end, he did not immediately perform acupuncture for me. Instead, he gave me a prescription of Wendan soup and asked me to take a dose after breakfast every day and come back to him two weeks later. In fact, I have some resistance to medicine, and I prefer to get direct relief through acupuncture, so that my nervous body can relax. So at my second visit, when Dr. Ma asked me to eat Wendan Decoction for another two weeks, I was a little dissatisfied and defiantly said, "Dr. Ma, you don't even dare to give me needles. You only ask me to take medicine!" At that time, Dr. Ma bowed his head and wrote down the medical record, but did not make any response.

After taking Wendan Decoction for more than a month, Dr. Ma finally gave me acupuncture. But after the acupuncture, I was still tight and felt that it had no effect. The following several times are still the same, each time a little doubt, really useful? Think back to the time when I just came to Dr. Ma for consultation and now compared with the actual improvement, continue to hold the state of skepticism to continue acupuncture.

I have a regular physical examination every year. After the results of that year came out, the doctor said to me: "Your platelets are a little small, but according to the data of previous years, there is not much change. In addition, there is some inflammation in your gallbladder that needs attention." This physical examination result made me have a new question in my heart, is the gallbladder problem caused by Wendan soup, or Doctor Ma found the symptoms before I prescribed Wendan soup?

Suddenly, after taking it for four months, the gallbladder problem got better. Dr. Ma also gave me Peaceful, a health product developed by Dr. Ma himself, which has a calming effect. Moreover, after the third month of acupuncture, I was pleasantly surprised to find that the pain of my meridians which had been bothering me gradually eased and my menstruation returned to normal, turning from dark black to bright red. In the first year of the acupuncture process, I was still a little nervous and envious when I heard the snoring of the patient next door. Now I am so relaxed that I can fall asleep when the needles are applied.

On Christmas 2022, Seattle experienced several days of heavy snow, which disrupted traffic. And the clinics are closed for Christmas. In the face of the sudden snow, I did not plan ahead to get enough medicine, resulting in about ten days in between. These days, my mood fluctuated obviously and I came to realize the role of Peaceful.

Really, the body has its own rhythm and strength. In the face of diseases and troubles, we need patience, confidence and perseverance. I suffered a lot from my hypersensitivity, but looking back I'm glad I had it.

I remember when I was in Ma Lao's consultation for a short time, I asked him, Can this disease be cured, can it be cured? He nodded firmly: "Yes, it can be cured, it just needs time to adjust, you will gradually recover." Indeed, after Dr. Ma's treatment for a period of time, the pain in my body did ease. He gave me acupuncture and moxibustion once a week, combined with medicine, and adjusted the prescription according to my condition every time he felt my pulse, and the effect gradually showed. But after all, the curative effect of Chinese medicine takes time and can not be achieved immediately.

A few days before my period, my mood is always unstable, and sometimes I have some extreme thoughts, the idea of wiping my neck and ending it all, which shocked me very much. I start to ask myself and answer: Isn't it already okay? It's been months since I've had this thought? Am I on the path to my own end? Why am I on this path? I had a life that most people would envy, and I wanted to end it? Why should I let myself be disturbed by these fleeting thoughts? I need to sort through my emotions. I need to review if something has stirred me up recently. My mind was much clearer after this. These thoughts used to run through my head every day. They used to cling to me day after day like stubborn vines, trying to harness my fragile soul. But that was then. That was then. Now, it's just my normal premenstrual mood swings combined with hunger pangs, so I need to eat something to stabilize my blood sugar, take out a purple potato and quickly nibble on it. After a while, all those random thoughts are gone. So, I always keep a few cookies and snacks handy to make sure I don't go hungry. Because I know that hunger can make me feel very unstable, like I want to yell, get mad angry, and even have cravings, which is more intense before my period.

When phasing out my last Western medicine, my family doctor once discouraged me by saying, "How are you going to fight this winter? Winter just makes people depressed. If you don't take the medicine, I don't think you can fight this winter." Now I don't remember much about how difficult that winter was. I only vaguely remember that Dr. Ma gave me acupuncture treatment and that taking health care products developed by Dr. Ma himself could help calm my mood. During that time, I insisted on strengthening my exercise and carried out the treatment under Dr. Ma's careful care. I believed in my heart that exercise would make a difference, and in Dr. Ma's ability to cure me once and for all and get me off those drugs. Dr. Ma also suggested that if I were to go off the drugs, I should taper off gradually, say to one-tenth of the amount, and then slowly stop. So I followed his instructions, step-by-step, slowly, through the spring, and finally said goodbye to the drug for good. I've been off the drug for about two years now.

Throughout the process, I believed in myself, the potential of my body, and the professionalism and experience of Dr. Ma. It was this firm belief that made me not give up easily in the process of discontinuing the medicine, and I always maintained a positive attitude even when I encountered difficulties and discomfort. Faith is not only a kind of psychological support, but also a kind of real power, which can stimulate our inner potential and help us overcome all difficulties. Now, I have completely gotten rid of the dependence on drugs, not only because of Dr. Ma's superb medical skills, but also because of the unwavering faith in my heart.

Then I contracted Helicobacter pylori, and the medication I was taking had a severe side effect, making me vomit so much that I would immediately throw up whatever I ate. In just two weeks, I lost 20 pounds and lost weight rapidly. I made several trips to the emergency room because of this intense vomiting. The doctor prescribed Western medicine to stop vomiting, told me not to eat for five hours before going to bed, and even tried not to drink water. Although I followed these instructions to the letter, a week passed and the vomiting still hadn't been alleviated. Finally, Dr. Ma treated me through acupuncture and traditional Chinese medicine. After a week, my stomach began to improve and I gradually began to eat some bland foods.

During this period, I was in low mood, because I didn't have the energy to do any exercise while taking the medicine. I was out of breath when I moved even a little, and it was very difficult for me to go upstairs. After recovery, I gradually resumed exercise and gradually strengthened the intensity of exercise. I expended a lot of energy every day, which also made my mood better and better. Sometimes I think that if someone had noticed my sportsmanship as a child, maybe I would have become an athlete and used exercise to fight off those bad thoughts.

Over the course of many treatments, Dr. Ma and I became lifelong friends. Although we are far apart in age, I deeply admire his medical skills and personality.

When asking questions, Dr. Ma would give me popular science medical knowledge in simple and easy to understand language. For example, three meals a day should not be too full (Dr. Ma has a simple diet, but eats a boiled egg every morning); Also for my Yin deficiency constitution gave some dietary advice, for example, you can eat more turtle, black beans, abalone and other Yin nourishing food, and ginseng, shrimp, red dates these warm and nourishing to eat less. In addition to medical guidance, some life insights shared by Dr. Ma can always give me a new understanding of life and strengthen my belief in treatment. However, he did not talk much, always just one or two sentences.

When I was seeing Dr. Ma for about six months, I brought up my provocation to Dr. Ma and expressed my apologies. Dr. Ma just smiled gently, wondering whether he had forgotten or just didn't care. His gentleness not only made me admire him, but also made me feel ashamed of what I had done. I realized that my provocation not only didn't help solve the problem, but made me more stubborn and narrow-minded. When faced with a problem, being more like Dr. Ma and listening to and understanding with an open and inclusive mind might make a difference. Since then, I respect and trust Dr. Ma even more.

As I write this, I suddenly realize something interesting: in nearly two years of consultations, I have never seen Dr. Ma's real face! Every time we met, we were in the clinic, and Dr. Ma was wearing a mask. This is very much in line with my impression of Dr. Ma's character. He is very reserved and doesn't say much. His speech is always to the point and goes straight to the heart of the matter. When it comes to his field of expertise, Dr. Ma once said that doctors should have their own judgment and should not be carried away by the statements of patients, because patients often only emphasize the information they think is important, which will affect the doctor's diagnosis. As for the doctor-patient relationship, he also said that patients are willing to talk to doctors about private things they don't tell others, which shows that patients trust you. In the face of life and work, Dr. Ma emphasizes efficiency, believing that things should be done quickly, not procrastinate, so that you will have time to do more things. He is like a hidden master of martial arts, reminiscent of the hidden masters in martial arts novels.

Dr. Ma is 80 years old. He is not blind or deaf. He is kind and patient with his patients. In America, you usually need to make an appointment in advance to see a doctor, but Dr. Ma made an exception for me. During that time, I was in a bad mood, with ups and downs, and he specifically told me: "Your situation is special, if there is any emergency, you can come directly without making an appointment."

His wife, surnamed Li, was also very skilled in medicine. And Dr. Li is very friendly. She always answers my questions patiently and popularizes science in detail. They opened clinics in Seattle and then in Bellevue, with two people in charge. In recent years, Dr. Ma has gone into semi-retirement and decided to practice only on Saturdays in Bellevue, but Seattle seniors complained: "You can't just dump the old patients when you have new ones." In the face of this sincere appeal, Dr. Ma felt that because of his retirement plan, he could not ignore the old patients who had always trusted and supported him, and continue to see the Seattle Clinic on Tuesdays.

When I was chatting with Dr. Li while waiting for her appointment, she said she was more specialized in gynecology and gastroenterology. When the time came to insert the needle, I asked Dr. Ma curiously, "Dr. Li said she specializes in gynecology and gastroenterology. What about you? Which department are you proficient in?" Dr. Ma's answer was beyond my expectation. He said with a touch of pride: "Every TCM is a 'golden oil', and I am very powerful in every discipline!" Ha-ha! This is the first time I have met such a boyish Dr Ma who is so confident in his profession. And so it was.

After I told Dr. Ma that I wanted to write a book. After hearing this, he supported me very much and encouraged me, saying, "I agree with you very much. Write down your experience and feelings and give them to more people like you to see. If it can help them out of their difficulties, it is a good thing." Dr. Ma's words gave me great motivation and confidence, which made me determined to write this book well.

Doctor visits, medication, hypnosis - I went through a long and difficult road to therapy. From initial confusion and fear, to acceptance and persistence, each step has been challenging and difficult. I have also come to understand that the healing process is not always a straight line, it is full of twists and turns and back-and-forth. There were times when I was frustrated by the side effects of my medication, and other times when I was anxious about the slow progress of my treatment. But it was the ups and downs that taught me patience and how to find strength in waiting.

Now, as I look back on my healing journey, I feel a deep sense of gratitude. For the doctors in my life whose expertise and care gave me hope; And to my family and friends who stood by me through my ordeal and whose support and encouragement gave me strength.

I believe that this is not only my personal experience, but also the common struggle and struggle of every soul affected by disease. I would like to share my experience with everyone who is going through a similar dilemma. May you take some inspiration from my story and find your own strength and courage. Remember that healing, no matter how difficult, is only one part of life's journey. We have the ability, and the right, to pursue health and happiness.

Chapter 3 The outline of the mind

Anxiety and depression are like shadows in the dark, affecting our lives quietly. Their presence may not be obvious, but they can profoundly change how a person feels, thinks and behaves. Knowing and recognizing these two "uninvited guests" is the first step in overcoming them.

In this chapter, I will take you inside the world of mental illness and uncover their mysteries. More importantly, I'll share some practical tips to help alleviate these symptoms. This is not only a process of science popularization, but also a soul conversation. Here, we do not set limits or judge, just to understand ourselves more deeply and face our inner feelings more sincerely. Let us embark on this journey together to draw the contours of the psyche, to discover the codes of the mind that are hidden in our daily lives.

1. The truth about depression and anxiety

All told, I've been dealing with depression and anxiety for nearly two decades. During my darkest days, I felt like I was trapped in a tunnel without light, so sad, anxious, cranky and sleepless for so long that I almost forgot about the good things in life. In recovery, I rediscovered the subtle pleasures that had been overlooked. Savoring the aroma of a cup of coffee, feeling the warmth of the sun on my skin. Recovery is a journey of the heart, full of hardship but also full of promise. Over the course of my treatment, I learned the truth about depression and anxiety, and I also learned some techniques, both from my doctors and on my own, to help with my symptoms. I share them with you in the hope that they can provide a little help and comfort to those who are going through a bad time and need a silver lining.

When we talk about depression, many people often mistake it for a temporary low mood, ignoring the complex biology and social psychology behind it. In fact, depression is a serious mental illness that casts a huge shadow over millions of people. Depression is not a simple "bad mood", but by the biological, psychological and social factors interwoven into the affective mental disorder disease. Biological factors include genetic predispositions, neurotransmitter imbalances and chronic diseases; Psychological factors, such as self-esteem, coping strategies and childhood experiences; Social factors include relationships, life stresses and major life events. These factors interact with each other to lead to depression. Patients often show listlessness, fatigue, insomnia, dreaminess, appetite loss and other symptoms, and may appear significantly depressed mood, loss of interest, depression and other emotions when alone. And anxiety disorders belong to neurosis, the main characteristics are widespread and persistent anxiety or repeated attacks of panic, often accompanied by autonomic nervous disorders, muscle tension and movement anxiety and other symptoms.

Although anxiety and depression differ in symptoms, they are also related in some ways. The two can occur in conjunction with each other, that is, at the same time or successively in the same person, as was the case with me. In addition, they also have certain similarities in therapeutic techniques.

In the face of depression and anxiety, we need to adjust our mentality to a more rational and accepting attitude. First, it's important to realize that these are common illnesses, not just mood swings. It is not a sign of weakness or a failure of personal willpower. It's not your fault that you're depressed, it's not that you're pretentious, it's not that you're weak, it's not that you're not strong enough. You're just sick, just like people get colds when it's hot and cold, just like people get sick when they eat grain. Depression is nothing more than a mental cold that needs to be professionally treated and managed by a professional doctor. There is nothing to be ashamed of.

I had a conversation with Dr. Ma about depression. Dr. Ma told me that he was very sad about today's children. In the process of educating their children, many parents will impose various requirements on their children's studies, behavioral norms, future planning, etc. Too strict education methods may make children bear great pressure. Some parents even misunderstand the child's emotional expression, regard their negative emotions as pretentious or frivolous moaning, do not understand the child's pain and predicament. If these emotions are not resolved and channeled in time, the gradual accumulation will certainly have a negative impact on children. There are also many families can not accept the fact that their children suffer from depression, thinking that it is a shameful thing to talk about. Whether it's trivialization or shame, a parent's lack of understanding and support can leave a child feeling isolated and helpless. Parents should make an effort to learn about depression and perhaps nip it in the bud when it first appears.

Recognizing and accepting these two conditions is the first step, and seeking professional help and advice is the second.

2. Reconcile with yourself

In addition to receiving medication, I have a regular counseling session where each week we discuss a few different topics. For example, in the days leading up to my period, images of scrubbing my neck often cross my mind. When I spoke to my therapist on the phone, she said she occasionally had these thoughts. A professional psychologist may also have such negative thoughts, so how can we sensitive and vulnerable people avoid them? So we should accept the emergence of negative emotions, and resolve them in time, learn to release psychological pressure regularly, find a close, trustworthy family and friends to talk or find a professional psychological counseling to open up and talk. Some of the recent things and look forward to things are sorted out a chat, after the chat will find that those pressing on the shoulder let us out of breath things are actually not can not be solved, there are many ways to choose, it is very likely that we look at things from a different perspective, limited the final choice.

I am more inclined to talk to psychological counseling than talking to people I know, because their professional knowledge can guide us to return to the right track and examine the source of stress. Think carefully about the cause of stress. Is it work stress or relationship stress? Is it a health issue or some other factor? Knowing the root cause of the problem will help you plan a solution. Even if it's not a complete solution, you can find an acceptable way to reconcile. When developing a workable solution, it may be easier to deal with the problem by breaking it down into small steps and working through them one by one.

It is also important that we learn to accept ourselves and not be too hard on ourselves and strive for perfection. Especially in this age of information explosion and beauty filters, people's definition of beauty has become blurred and distorted, and face anxiety, body anxiety and other issues are constantly emerging. Some people are addicted to their own beauty can not extricate themselves, resulting in unable to accept the reality of their own. Like myself, I can't accept aging very well. After the marathon, when I received the official commemorative photos in the mail, I was visibly gaunt and puffy compared to the photos on my phone taken years ago, which made me anxious. But sometimes when I look at the Reuters photos of celebrities in their 40s, their faces are covered with fine lines, their skin is not in the best shape, and their facial muscles are sagging. At this time, I can get a little comfort in my heart, thinking that even the stars who are talented in the face can't escape, but I am just an ordinary person, how can I resist?

Jenny, the mother of my daughter's studio classmate, is a woman who is both beautiful and intelligent. Every time I see her, I am always attracted by her elegant temperament, especially because she keeps an excellent figure with long legs and a narrow waist. However, much to my surprise, I learned from a casual conversation that she actually has a serious weight anxiety disorder. She would stare at the scale every day and get very upset if she put on a little weight. The fact that even such a talented woman can't escape body anxiety shows how pervasive this pressure is in society.

When learning English, I have a question about the date of birth. An elderly woman in my group, about 75 years old, was very resistant to answering the question. She kept losing her temper and yelling, and it was obvious that she was avoiding her age. I told her, "You can say you're 18. You're 18 every day." She laughed, squawked. Such an escape is not impossible. Although the old lady is advanced in years, her enthusiasm for learning is no less than that of the young. Although the years have left their marks on her face, she still retains her youth and vitality inside. 75 or 18, does it still matter that much?

Whether it is to accept the old or not to accept the old, we need to learn to accept ourselves. Age is just a number, it does not determine our value and attractiveness. What really sets us apart is our mentality and attitude; What really makes us beautiful is our inner peace and confidence, a love of life and a positive attitude. Although I have more wrinkles and haggard in the marathon photos, my flesh is no longer tight, but the tenacity and perseverance in my eyes make me look the same, and there is a beauty accumulated after years of precipitation and experience. I began to appreciate my indomitable spirit and the way I worked hard for my goals, and gradually let go of my obsession with "eternal youth".

Relieving anxiety and dealing with stress is a gradual process that requires patience and time. Be brave enough to seek professional help to help you cope more effectively with the condition. It is also very important not to listen to everything anyone says, but to learn to think and analyze for yourself. The psychologist who helped me solve many psychological problems once said to me that no one should be overly dependent.

3. Relieve insomnia

Insomnia is a struggle I face every night, and it's one of my most frustrating symptoms. I'm already tired. I've been through a lot all day, like working all day and running 5 kilometers, when I should be falling asleep, but my brain is awake. Counting sheep, taking deep breaths, picturing calm images... After trying all kinds of sleep AIDS, it's still hard to fall asleep. Even when you do fall asleep, you are exhausted. When I do sleep, it's as if I split into two different selves. One was trapped in an endless nightmare, while the other floated in the air and watched as I struggled through the nightmare. Not being able to fall into a deep sleep, the night did nothing to relieve my physical exhaustion, but instead caused mental anxiety.

In dealing with sleep issues, I've found a strategy with a high success rate: stop focusing so much on the process of falling asleep, and stop setting expectations about sleep. For example, demanding that you fall asleep by 11 o'clock will only increase your anxiety. Turn off the light, relax in bed rest, put a timed off soft music or hypnotic guidance (I listen to a hypnotic guidance for three years, and now as long as a play I can fall asleep in a very short time), eyes naturally open or half closed, you can think, you can turn over and over, choose their most comfortable state. Stop the anxious pursuit of sleep, and stop the rush. When we lie so peacefully in bed, we have entered the state of rest, which is itself a form of sleep. Of course, make sure that the room is dark enough to stop looking at your phone and doing things that cause your brain to be highly excited. If you drift off to sleep in the midst of such relaxation, let it happen; If you're still awake, don't worry. If you really can't sleep, just sit up and do something quiet and relaxing. Without thinking at all, doodle something with a pen, or write a little word, or write or record something aimlessly. Or close your eyes and look for those subtle sounds in this quiet, and then imagine the source and scene of those sounds, which is also a kind of meditation. For example, if we hear a faucet dripping water, we can imagine the scene. What it will look like when the water drops fall and disperse, and when the second drop will fall... Gradually, you will find that the whole body relaxes in the process, and you will unconsciously fall asleep as you continue to imagine the scene.

Your goal is simply to enjoy this restful time of rest. Don't be upset if you wake up in the middle of the night and don't check your phone to calculate your sleep time. Keep it quiet and dark, and allow yourself to continue to enjoy your rest. Even if you are awake, you can continue to enjoy the feeling of relaxation, free from external distractions. Close your eyes, relax your body, and let yourself gradually sink into the peaceful atmosphere. Perhaps you will fall asleep again and continue to have valuable rest time. Not only will you be less bothered by waking up, but you'll be better able to stay relaxed and peaceful.

You can also supplement this process with deep breathing. Deep breathing is not only a kind of physiological adjustment, but also a kind of spiritual comfort. When we breathe in deeply, our chest expands, filling our lungs with oxygen and carrying tension and anxiety with it as the blood moves through our body. Many people find that incorporating deep breathing into their bedtime routine not only helps them fall asleep faster, but also improves the quality of their sleep. Practicing deep breathing doesn't have to be complicated. Lie in bed, close your eyes, and place one hand on your stomach and the other on your chest. Breathe in slowly and deeply, feeling the bulge in your belly, then slowly exhale, letting your belly fall back. Repeat this simple process to calm your heart as you rise and fall with your breath. I now practice deep breathing exercises whenever I feel anxious or have trouble falling asleep, and it has become an integral part of my life.

4. Diet therapy

When our mood swings are high, maintaining a regular diet is crucial.

Imagine that when you feel hungry, the body's internal chemical balance may be disrupted and blood sugar levels may drop, which may cause your brain to release stress hormones such as cortisol. The release of these hormones can make you feel nervous, irritable, and anxious, lulling you into believing that you are in total control of your negative emotions, as if you will never be able to get out of this situation. This is a perfectly normal physiological reaction, and even healthy, peaceful people tend to be more irritable when they're hungry.

Therefore, maintaining a regular diet is crucial to keeping mood swings in check. Only by getting enough energy on a regular basis and maintaining normal blood sugar levels can your brain have the strength to cope with mood swings. In order to establish healthy eating habits, we can make a reasonable meal plan, for example, eat three meals a day, set a fixed meal time, and try to keep the amount of each meal is relatively consistent, which will help the body adapt to and prepare for digestion of food; Balanced diet, in terms of food choices, ensure that it contains enough protein, healthy fats, fiber, vitamins and complex carbohydrates, such as lean meat, fish, legumes, fresh vegetables and fruits; Try to avoid foods high in sugar, which, while temporarily raising blood sugar, can then cause a sharp drop in blood sugar that can trigger mood swings; And stay well hydrated, as dehydration can also affect mood and cognitive function.

Remember that mood swings are a part of life, and by maintaining a regular diet and adopting positive self-management strategies, it is better to further control these swings and reduce their impact on our lives. Instead of being afraid to ask for help or ignore your feelings, there are many small techniques that can help us gradually build a healthier and more stable emotional state, allowing us to face life's challenges more calmly and confidently.

5. The park effect

In my struggle with depression, I've also discovered a simple but powerful way to heal myself -- the "park effect." Scientific research has proven that the natural environment has a positive impact on human mental health. A study conducted by the University of Jyvaskyla in Finland found that even a short stay in a natural environment can significantly lower stress hormone levels and boost your mood. My "park Effect" is based on findings like this. No matter how busy my schedule is, every once in a while I try to find 20 minutes to take a simple walk in the park or just sit on a bench and enjoy the natural beauty around me. The transformation of these 20 minutes of nature bathing is remarkable, at first I may feel anxious or frustrated by being too quiet, but during these 20 minutes I slow down and breathe deeply, allowing the breath of nature to fill my lungs and the sight of nature to take over my senses. Over time, the feelings of anxiety and frustration began to slowly recede, replaced by an inner peace and tranquility. The natural environment provided me with a "restorative experience" where I felt like I was being "repaired" little by little.

In addition to the psychological comfort, the physical recovery was also evident. Sunlight is the body's main way of producing vitamin D. Vitamin

D plays an important role in brain function, especially in the maintenance of emotional stability and cognitive abilities. Studies have shown a strong correlation between a lack of vitamin D and an increased risk of mood disorders such as depression and anxiety. So getting more sun can help prevent vitamin D deficiency and be more effective in maintaining our mental health. Sunlight is also crucial for regulating our body clock. The body clock, also known as the circadian rhythm, is our body's internal time management system that affects multiple physiological processes such as sleeping, waking up, eating, hormone release, and more. Moderate sunlight exposure helps to set and maintain a normal body clock, thereby improving sleep quality and reducing the risk of circadian rhythm disruption, which is especially important for people with depression, as sleep problems are often linked to depressed mood. In addition, fresh air in the natural environment is rich in negative oxygen ions, which can promote metabolic activity, which in turn enhances the function of the immune system.

I encourage everyone with depression to try the "park effect." No special plans or long hikes are needed, even just sitting quietly in the park is enough to make you feel the beauty of nature. Remember that these 20 minutes are yours to immerse yourself in nature and feel its healing power.

6. Float therapy

Flotation therapy is also called sensory deprivation therapy. It's usually done in a soundproof, dimly lit floating pod or pool. The pod is filled with about 20cm of warm water, close to the temperature of human skin, to ensure comfort. Large amounts of Epsom salts (magnesium sulfate) are dissolved in the water, making it denser enough to float easily.

Being completely free of gravity and floating in a warm, quiet environment sounds like the plot of a college fiction novel, but it's actually the unique experience that flotation therapy has given me.

When I first encountered flotation therapy, I was both curious and a little nervous. As the fluid rose, so did the buoyancy, as if the whole body were being gently lifted and floating in the vastness of the universe. With my eyes closed and only the faint sound of water and my own breathing in my ears, I let myself float, feeling every cell dancing freely in the water and quickly entering a state of "emptying". The body is gradually relaxing, the mind is gradually calm. I was able to clearly perceive every feeling I was feeling, from the slight sense of touch, to the warm enveloping feeling, to the peaceful state of mind, everything was clear and real.

Floating also relaxes my muscles like never before. Enough buoyancy gave me a chance to break free of gravity and get a radical deep relaxation, from the tiniest fingers down to my entire spine; My muscles didn't have to support their own weight or resist gravity any more, an experience that is hard to feel in everyday life. It provided me with a non-drug method of pain relief. Also, the deep relaxation of the muscles is good for improving the quality of sleep.

When the float is over, I feel refreshed, as if I have just experienced a deep sleep. While it allowed me to experience physical relaxation, it also gave me a chance to briefly step away from the hustle and bustle of everyday life and speak to my inner self. I've come to realize that a lot of the stress in life is really a burden we place on ourselves.

7. Exercise therapy

There are several other remedies you can try when you're experiencing mood swings and restlessness.

抑郁自救笔记
Notes on Depression Self-help

The five senses means literally sight, sound, smell, taste and touch. Depression and anxiety tend to keep us trapped in a cycle of negative emotions, and with the five Senses method, we can take our attention away from negative thoughts and focus on sensory experiences. Each sense can be a way to relax and soothe. For example, you can take a close look at your surroundings and people, paying particular attention to their details and characteristics. For another example, it has been raining nonstop recently, which has put me in a bad mood. I will close my eyes to feel the rain outside, to imagine the picture outside the window, to see where the rain is coming from, where the rain is the loudest. Every now and then there will be the sound of a plane flying by, then I will close my eyes the same way and listen carefully to the sound of the plane, I will tell which direction it is flying to which side. And then I imagine the lights and the whole plane and the sound of it going away. Enlarge your hearing infinitely, and what might have been an irritating sound may become a grand symphony. I love coffee and chocolate, and when I get emotionally overwhelmed, I make a conscious effort to picture the aroma and taste of coffee and chocolate in my mind. I can also touch some soft objects, such as the plush toy at hand, soft cloth, etc., to feel their touch and temperature. The charm of the Five Senses method is that it teaches us how to take the most obvious feelings in the space of the moment when we are experiencing mood swings, or when we are uncontrollably anxious, and amplify them infinitely. This distraction technique is a powerful way to help us escape from the negative emotions in the moment.

Another great relief technique is breathing, where deep breathing relaxes the body and relaxes tense nerves. There are many ways to practice yoga breathing, including abdominal breathing, chest breathing, full abdominal breathing, and single nostril meridian-clearing breathing. But the most basic breathing exercises can be broken down into cycle phases: breathing in, holding, exhaling, holding again, and so on. I find a quiet place to sit or lie down, close my eyes, breathe in slowly and deeply, mentally counting from one to four, then hold my breath, and breathe out slowly, feeling the breath flow through my body. I hold each of these four counts for a very long time, breathing in anticipation of the next four. As we practice and learn to control our breathing, we can increase the amount of time we spend in each stage from four to five to six... In this way, in one breath and one breath, our attention is completely transferred from the anxious mood to the breathing, and we can regain the sense of calm and relaxation.

In addition to this, try some simple physical exercises to relieve anxiety and release tension.

Start by sitting in a chair with your legs relaxed on the floor. Then, slowly rock your legs so that the tips of your feet touch the ground lightly. Feel the muscles in your legs relax and move naturally, gradually increasing the amount of shaking. At the same time, keep breathing smoothly and focus on the shaking of the legs, letting the mood gradually calm with the swaying.

You can also try arm taps. Stretch your arm out and then gently tap or tap your arm with your other hand. Start at the wrist and gradually tap up to the shoulder and back again. Focus on relaxing your arm muscles and avoiding pushing too hard. Allow the feeling of slapping to penetrate your skin, taking away the tension in your arm and giving you a hint of comfort.

Try turning your head and neck. Slowly turn from side to side, then back to the middle position. Next, gently tilt your head to one side to feel the neck stretch before switching back to the other side. As you perform these movements, remember to keep your breathing steady and allow your head and neck to rotate naturally without straining too hard.

There are also squats and stretches. When standing, make sure your feet are shoulder-width apart. Then, slowly bend your knees into squats and slowly stand up again. Repeat, paying attention to feel the changes in your leg and back muscles. You can also increase the difficulty of the movement after several repetitions, such as lifting your heels and leaving only the tips of your feet on the ground for support. Add some simple stretches, such as raising your hands and bending down, to stretch your body even more.

You can help relax the muscles in your hand by stretching and flexing your fingers, even if you don't need to do a lot of movement. Gradually working your wrists to improve the flexibility of your fingers and wrists, or gently making a fist and then gradually opening your fingers, can also help reduce tension in your hands.

These simple exercises don't require a lot of preparation and skill, so you might want to try them when you're nervous and anxious. However, pay attention to your sensations and breathing as you exercise. These exercises should be gentle and comfortable, and our purpose is to relax the body without causing overexertion or physical pain. Personal comfort and health should always come first.

These are the experiences and techniques I have summarized in the years of illness, and I would like to share them with you who are reading. I hope to let more people realize the importance of mental health, and encourage everyone to seek help bravely and take positive actions in the face of psychological distress, hoping to give you or your family and friends help.

Now, although I still have occasional moments of anxiety and depression, I am no longer afraid of them. I know how to live with them and find strength in them. By learning to accept myself, find support, cultivate positive thinking, savour life's pleasures and set small goals, I gradually found myself back. I stopped dwelling on my past hurts. I've come to understand that everyone has imperfections and that it's not a secret I have to hide. Accepting myself has made me more true to my inner struggles, and that healing is not an end, but a starting point to redefine my life and open up to new possibilities.

Moreover, the perspective from which we view things is also very important. In the past, whenever I was driving and encountered someone speeding past on the road, even going against traffic, my first reaction was always full of complaints and confusion. I would think to myself: How could this person be so reckless and endanger their own life? How annoying! However, one time when I encountered such a situation again, the lady sitting beside me viewed it from a completely different angle. She softly said, "Perhaps they really have an emergency and had no choice but to do so." At that moment, I was deeply touched and suddenly realized: Why do I always habitually think in a negative way, only seeing the negative aspects of others' behaviors and ignoring the possible legitimate reasons or urgent situations behind them? Now, I have also started to learn to change my mindset and have learned to understand others' behaviors from a positive perspective, no longer making hasty judgments.

Healing is a gradual process, giving yourself time and space to adapt and change. It is essential to be patient and remain kind to yourself during this process. Of course, depression is a complex mental illness that varies from person to person and requires a combination of factors to develop a treatment plan. If treatment is needed, we should always follow the advice of our doctor.

Chapter 4 Refraction of Sweat

In this chapter, we will explore a powerful and dynamic subject - movement. For everyone who loves sport, it is a way of life, a way of self-expression, a way of connecting with the world; And for those who have not yet experienced the charm of sports, it will be a new journey of discovery.

1. Fall in love with sports

Six months after giving birth to my son, I was invited by a friend to try sports.

When I was working out at the yoga studio, I found the music so loud and couldn't understand why. But that experience made me feel relaxed after exercise, as if all the fatigue in my body had been cleared away. The next day, my muscles were sore and I was tired.

At the yoga studio, all the people spoke Chinese, which made me feel relaxed. After practicing yoga for half a year, I found that my stiff left hand could be lifted easily and my hunchback was relieved. To my surprise, after six months of exercise, I had significantly fewer panic attacks and became less sensitive to sound. I only found the music too loud occasionally.

But I didn't realize at the time that this was due to the exercise. It wasn't until the summer of 2022, for some reason, that I left my yoga studio and took a break from exercise. Just in time for my kids' summer break, we took a family vacation to Hawaii. It was a sun and sea breeze holiday and we enjoyed the beaches, the food and the local culture to the full, although on my second day in Hawaii I was in a terrible state due to jet lag. A good trip made me feel completely relaxed. And I always think that exercise must be in the gym, because I am afraid to go to the gym, I did not keep exercise as before. After the trip, I found myself feeling a little down. Even though I tried to adjust my mind, I couldn't get rid of the inexplicable irritability and restlessness.

Looking for a way to release my emotions, I started searching the Internet for suitable yoga studios. Luckily, I found a yoga studio with a Chinese-speaking instructor. I immediately booked a class, hoping to get in shape with yoga. During the first half of my first class, I felt a bit of anger inside me, and the noise of the instructor and other students made me feel irritated. Especially the woman next to me, always made a mockery of the sound, whenever I asked the coach some questions the coach answered, she has been issued next to the "hum, hum, hum" sound, arrogant look do not know what is humming. But as the class progressed, my body gradually settled into a familiar and comfortable state, and I began to focus on every movement of my body, feeling the stretching of my muscles and the flow of my breath. With each deep breath, I took away a trace of irritability from my heart and injected a calming power into me. Little by little, my anger seemed to dissipate as the sweat poured in. My mood became lighter and happier, and I burst out laughing.

Since then, I have realized the importance of sports. Over time, I started doing iron lift training with fitness bloggers and trying to sweat in the crossfit gym. It was a big, well-equipped gym with everything from strength training machines to cardio machines. There were also free classes from various instructors, and I was exposed to many types of exercise I had never tried before: squash, swimming, Zumba, spinning... Each presented me with a different experience and challenge, and I enjoyed them. Of course, the muscle soreness that comes with it makes it necessary for me to get a massage every now and then to relax.

I'm not sure whether it's because the acupuncture unblocked my meridians or due to my long-term running and various exercises. My hands and feet, which used to be cold all year round, are no longer cold now.

2. Thinking in motion

I found a one-on-one coach with a former professional basketball player. She developed a training plan for me that covered my back, arms, core and other areas, and lasted for an hour and a half in a non-stop super session. As anyone with any fitness experience knows, this is no small amount of exercise. She offered me a hard and easy version of each exercise, with a set of eight to 10 to choose from. In order to increase the amount of exercise and to improve the effect of the exercise, I always choose the difficult and large number of exercises. I was in good shape when I did the core exercises. I did about 15 in one sitting. I could have done more, actually, because it was a non-stop workout and there were other exercises coming up, so I stopped.

In the middle of the exercise, it was so hot that I took off my shirt, leaving only my sports vest, inadvertently showing my abs. At this time, the coach looked up and down the eyes made me a little uncomfortable, the tone is also strange, she coldly mocked: "As a professional athlete, I have a self-driven spirit." You're an ordinary man. Where did this perseverance come from? How can you have self-drive to motivate yourself?" The irony in her words made me feel extremely uncomfortable.At that moment, another staff member passed by, and she said that the one who passed was also the instructor here, a former yoga instructor. I said, I also have a yoga instructor certificate (I used to study in China). The other person responded with a cold hum and stressed: "He is very professional, with more than 20 years of experience." This seemingly deliberate effort to suppress me made me extremely uncomfortable. The gym probably has a policy of texting clients regularly, asking if members are exercising, and Posting diet and exercise plans. The trainer never messaged me again after this incident. Of course, I ignored any of her reminders and plans, because her training methods did not give me the expected results, only a loss of energy. Instead, it gave me a chance to get rid of her negative influence. I come to the gym to release my emotions and improve myself. If I get discouraged because of someone else's unreasonable oppression, wouldn't it be penny wise and pound foolish? Why don't you find another trainer? Maybe there will be a training method and plan that suits me better. 4. It would be foolish to punish yourself for someone else's mistakes.

In a word, sports have gradually become a part of my life and the most effective way for me to regulate myself. To make sure I'm getting enough exercise every day, I even occasionally set my alarm for 5 a.m. and wake up for a hot yoga class. Cardio gives me a unique sense of pleasure, like giggling when I'm running, smiling when I'm halfway through yoga, laughing when I'm doing iron lifts until I'm warm... Gradually, I was no longer satisfied with the simple pleasure brought by exercise, but more eager to understand the principle and meaning behind each movement. Why can this movement achieve such an effect? Why do we need to avoid certain wrong actions? What are the consequences of these wrong actions? What are the potential damage to the body?

It can be said that I have developed a sense of curiosity about things that interest me and rekindled my passion for life. Of course, the process of sports is not always happy, it is inevitable that some unpleasant things will happen.

After practicing Pilates for almost a year, my interest in Pilates has increased, not diminished. In order to learn more about Pilates and to be able to guide myself more accurately, I decided to get a Pilates instructor's certificate.

抑郁自救笔记
Notes on Depression Self-help

Although I have participated in Pilates class for a year, I am familiar with the movements, but I cannot understand the main points because of the language barrier. This is the reason why I want to take the instructor certificate, so that I can feel the greatest benefits of Pilates in my body. However, it was still a challenge in an all-English theoretical course and exam environment.

Yes, after all these years in the United States, I have never mastered English. Maybe I missed the best age for language learning, or maybe I have no talent for language at all. I even wondered if I had a language barrier. Anyway, learning English was not only difficult for me, but also very repellent. Even if I memorized 200 words in one day, I still couldn't recall any of them the next day. Probably because of my self-esteem and low self-esteem, in order to avoid embarrassing situations, I completely avoid it. For example, I only go to supermarkets owned by Chinese people. Sometimes when I want to eat Western food, I would rather spend more money to order it online than go to a restaurant and talk to people in English face to face.

After careful consideration, I was still willing to work hard and challenge for the love of Pilates. I gathered up the courage and signed up for the instructor training through the Pilates studio where I often practiced.

The first day of the training felt very good and very happy. However, at the end of the 6 hours of training, my randomly assigned partner suddenly said to the coach, "She doesn't speak English, so I can only instruct her to do the movements, but she can't teach me in return, and I want her to do the movements." The coach said, "Isn't the purpose of your coaching certificate to teach people? Why don't you teach her?" 'All right,' I said. The teammate not-so-happily complied.

The next day, the manager of the studio messaged me and asked me to team up with another Chinese so she could translate for me. Speaking of the other Chinese person, we met at the same Pilates and saw each other more than

Chapter 4 Refraction of Sweat

three times a week. When we did, she would greet me and leave my contact information. Later, I asked the instructor at the studio about my certification. She was there, too, and seemed very interested. After learning about it, she said, "Let me study with you so that I can translate for you." At that time, I said no: "You will make me feel indebted to you, if you want to attend the training yourself, don't go just because you want to accompany me and help me translate," and then I repeated several times to explain my attitude to her.

We returned to the second day of training, I had a strong self-esteem for a long time and finally sent a message to her, because I have no better way, afraid of other students do not want to partner with me, but also afraid of being abandoned yesterday. Happily, she readily agreed to team up with me, and said she would be late, and asked me to find a place to wait for her. As luck would have it, I texted her that day because of the traffic jam that I would also be a few minutes late. She said, "OK, I'll find a seat for you." I happily arrived at the training room and went to greet her, but she said, "I already have a teammate, you go to the Korean girl." I suddenly froze in place, did not return to God. The studio manager was right there, said it didn't matter, and told me to stay. I gestured to her teammate nearby, indicating that I could go to the Korean girl. The manager said, "You stay here, you three in a team." "All right." The manager had already said so, and I had to stick around. By this time, I had noticed that her face, which is also Chinese, was very bad, and her face was pulled down, obviously not happy with my joining.

Due to the limited space in the training room, only one student in each group can follow the coach when doing the movements, and then the student can guide another member of the group. After my partner, who was also Chinese, finished with the coach, the manager asked me to do a round. At the same time, she asked another partner to do it. The manager came and pulled me down on the mat. The other partner was also very embarrassed and politely said, "Let her do it, my abdomen seems to be a little uncomfortable, I just need to rest."

Sitting on the cushion, I was bewildered, and all I could think about was what she had said: "I'll study with you, I'll translate for you... I will translate for you, I will study with you..." "Ok, I'll find a good place for you... I've got a good place for you..." My God, what's wrong with my mind, why can't I stop thinking about these words? I feel like I'm going crazy. Really, why is that? Why was she so different in the blink of an eye? In fact, I had never expected her to translate. Why did the manager insist that I team up with her? I took a deep breath, comforted myself, focused on my study, and when my heart rate got up, I would be fine and ignore what had just happened, it was just a small thing. I try to focus on the action, trying to make myself feel tired. But no, not at all! I'm going crazy! I felt like all the people in the classroom were looking at me and they were probably laughing at me inside. The thought made me feel unbearable. I wanted to escape the scene so badly that I couldn't stay another minute. The tear ducts were sore from my tears and I tried to hold them back. It has been a long time since I cried. I even thought I had forgotten how to cry. However, now I feel so sad, and being rejected for such a reason even makes me wonder if I did something wrong. I had never intended to rely on her translator or team up with her in the first place. It was really too aggrieved! Brain very dizzy, very dizzy, feel the whole room is spinning, am I fast can not breathe? B: No, I can't go on like this. I have to distract myself or get out of here.

I got up and went straight to the Korean girl who was alone and asked her through my stilted English, "Hello, I don't speak English, can I partner with you?" She smiled and replied, "Of course, my English is not good either." Her smile put me at ease a little. The teaching continued, and the Korean girl let me learn first. This time, the movement was a little difficult, and I soon tired, and my nervous state of mind was finally relieved. As my heart rate gradually increased, the symptoms almost disappeared. Eg. This Korean girl is a little introverted, but very polite. Although we had some difficulties communicating with each other and sometimes had to use body language and expressions to express ourselves, we talked and laughed and generally had a good time.

At the end of about three hours, it was time for a break. The woman who signed up with me passed me on her way to the door for some air, and I smiled and nodded at her. To my surprise, she glanced sideways at me, raised her head and walked straight past. A: What the hell? A sense of superiority? I went to the door to breathe, and made a point of walking over to her with a smile to ease my awkwardness. Then she tossed her head again, spoke loudly in English to another fellow studio student, and walked around me. For a moment, her tears almost came to her eyes. What happened? How can someone be so different? What have I done to deserve such rejection and scorn? The constant questioning of my inner self almost broke me down. I want to go home, I want to get out of here, I am so weak at this moment, or I care too much about what others think of me.

Just then the father of my child called. When the phone answered, his gentle voice said, "How's it going? Are you very tired? A: It's been hours. Did you bring enough food? Thanks for your hard work!" I choked up and wept. He flustered and asked me what was wrong, and when he was done he said, "Go home, there's no need to insist, it's not worth it." After talking to him, the mood was slightly relieved, and the course has been half, and three hours to complete today's training, I said: "take a look at it, has completed half, so leave next time or to repeat this training." The three hours in the second half of the session went by too fast because there was too much focus and I was doing all the action.

When I got home I was very unstable, not happy about the event, my anxiety increased, and on the third day after the training I had five or six panic attacks a day. At this time, I realized that the fragile nerve injury can no longer let myself fall into the previous environment to learn, I want to change the way, so I hired a translator, after communicating with the coach, she agreed to me to take the translator to study, found several translators, said really... This phenomenon is not a person I will encounter, especially in foreign countries, Chinese people really like to fool Chinese people, the first translation can really use "what stuff" to describe, completely unprofessional, let alone the "dedication" two words and he is associated. After watching the video translation content, he said a sentence after watching the video for more than ten minutes: "This is about our skin cells." I looked at him expectantly, waiting for what he would say next, and he said, "No." What about the details, I asked? He said, "It's not even anatomy. I'm going to have a cigarette." Wha? Have a cigarette? Read a brief 14-word summary for a dozen minutes and then go for a cigarette? I thought I could solve the problem by finding a translator. Now the "translation" is the problem.

Every week I have a private Pilates lesson, and my private Pilates instructor is a beautiful white person with a nice personality and extremely beautiful turquoise eyes. After she found out what was going on between me and the Chinese guy, she opened me up and told me to be more open-minded, maybe she didn't mean to exclude me so much, etc. But it was clear that the translator was not interested in my job offer. I continued to post ads on the AD platform looking for a translator, and it wasn't long before I received a message, sending me two time slots and her home address. I replied, "I need to translate five days a week, and these times are not suitable. I only have two times a week to choose from and I have to drive nearly half an hour each way to your home, which is too far." She said, "Do you know I get paid 70 an hour in the company? I give you time, you can't come, and I can't help you if I want to." The temper of my anger did not play a place, immediately back: "The AD clearly wrote 40 dollars an hour, this is to pay for the translation, do not use the word 'help', noble as if they are doing volunteer work, with a 70 hour wage but also miss the odd 40, where the courage to let you speak wildly?"

Later, my psychological counseling introduced me to a newly graduated girl, who accompanied me to the scene to learn, watch videos together and then translate. In class, she was very serious and loved to study, even more serious than me. If she didn't understand the technical terms, she would look them up until she understood them, write them down and translate them for me. After that, she became my course partner directly, and every class was very happy. She accompanied me through all the classes that required training, and I never saw her in the training room again.

The purpose of recording this experience is to inform everyone and remind myself once again that life is like ebb and flow, and sometimes we will encounter small setbacks that may affect our emotions and our lives. However, we should not let these setbacks defeat us. We should face and solve our problems bravely. When we meet those who are negative, take advantage of us or discourage us, we should fight back bravely. Don't let their words control our emotions. Don't keep them in your heart, which will only make our emotions more depressed. Even if it is just a simple response, it can make us feel better. Of course, you don't have to fight back if you can process your emotions on your own. For me, choosing to fight back appropriately can make my emotions dissipate faster, which is purely because of my personality.

English is a big mountain, about the theory exam, I can only buy some Chinese related theory books, study hard. However, the rules of each brand studio are different, and I still can't clearly understand some of the movement taboos.

I did the final written test online through the translator, 151 questions, the correct rate of more than 80% can pass. I completely relied on the translator to complete the exam, and the correct rate was only 57%. After the exam, the Pilates instructor sent me an email telling me what I needed to make up, that I would apply for another chance to take the exam, and that I must not use the translator to aid the exam. It was true that the translator did not translate the exam content exactly, so I could not solve the questions correctly and did many of the most basic questions wrong, which is why I scored so low on the first exam. During tutoring, the little girl who had been accompanying me on my Pilates lessons translated with me, and we studied together on the spot, and she translated for me. At this point, I really understood a lot of the content, and it was not just some random translation by the translator.

After a bad study, the coach also gave me a chance to apply for another exam. During the exam, she translated the test contents to me by video and did the written test. After two hours of test, the final correct rate was 92.22%. I passed the written test! When I write this, I have already passed the final exam and got the Pilates instructor certificate. Let's all come on! For the sport we love! For a life of passion!

3. The novelty experience of a marathon

My son's principal is very inspirational. At dinner, she told me that her daughter had encouraged her to run a marathon. About a week later, she told me that she had tried to run a 4mile. I was shocked. I was so strong. I was so strong. I kept working out, day in and day out, but I could only run two and a half miles. I tried running before, but the choking sensation of not being able to breathe made me afraid that I would die from running. Each time I tried to increase my oxygen intake by opening my mouth wide, I disrupted the rhythm of my breathing. Listening to the principal that day, I secretly resolved to transcend my limitations. Half a month later, I had run four miles several times.

When I talked to the principal again, she said she had signed up for the marathon. What a courageous and amazing woman, soon to be 50 years old, who had never run before, to have the courage to run a marathon. After this conversation, I did almost no other exercise and practiced running every day, telling myself a little bit more every day, just a little bit. One day I ran 6.8 miles and didn't feel tired. The next day, as I walked by the principal's office, I asked him, "How is your marathon preparation going?" The principal said, "Just ran half a mile on Friday!" The sense of shame and anonymity surged, and I thought I'd show off my hard work of running 6.8 miles, and... Well, ignoring the fact that while I was pushing myself forward, someone else was also making progress and possibly an even bigger step. She was running 13.1 and a half miles, and I was only 6.8 miles, and I was "showing off" to her.

After coming home, I found a special free day, more than eight o'clock in the morning to go out to run, run, run, ran not long before began to side, right lower abdominal pain can not run quickly, look at the watch speed is in 14 minutes a mile, the brain has been Shouting "refueling, not to the target it is still early, can not stop." About 8mile, feel some pain around the toe, and then run more and more pain, pain some numbness, thinking: Oh! The original more than 10mile is such a feeling! Your toes will hurt. Well, come on! 3 more miles to win! Can not white pain, must be completed, you can break through to participate in the half horse, at this time under the light rain. Run ah, run ah, toe pain more and more numbness, my steps are getting smaller and smaller, almost exhausted. And the mouth is thirsty, there was a bottle of water put energy drink, because too heavy half of the half led to no water to drink, I want to have a friend at this time can pass over a cup of water ah! It is best to have applause to encourage! Maybe a cheer squad! Hahaha! After more than 3 hours of running, I finally ran to 13.22mile. I immediately took a photo and sent it to the principal for me to sign up for half a horse. My inner sense of joy and satisfaction exploded! It feels so good to be more than yourself! It was good to feel good. I came home unable to walk and with very large blood blisters on my feet. I recalled that I was really anxious before I finished my half horse, I prepared a lot of things, and bought special energy supplements, I was afraid of dehydration and low blood sugar in the middle, and I was scared when I watched short videos to learn from the experience, some people said a random talk for attention, and even before I ran, I was anxious or confused about which energy drink to buy, whether to wear compression socks, etc. After running will be a breath of atmosphere, not so, fit shoes and socks, appropriate to drink a little water is enough to deal with half a horse, ha ha.

After a week, the day of the race is finally coming. Up until the day before the race, Saturday day, I was still fighting over whether or not to run, looking at one foot that still had blisters, and thinking about the Saturday morning doctor's visit, who said that my liver and gallbladder area was slightly inflamed, not enough to medicate, but had caused a mood change and advised against running. But I didn't want to give up the first time I entered a race. I'd never had a race in my life where I'd volunteered to run, and the organizers made it clear in their email that there were professional paramedics and ambulances all along the route, and it was safe. Even so, prone to anxiety, I still had a sleepless night. Before I went to sleep, I still imagined my children waiting for me at the finish line of the race. In my dreams, I was running all about the race. On Sunday morning, I didn't want to get up very much. After fighting with myself for a while, I still got up to participate in the activity, but the conflict in my heart was floating all the time. After eating breakfast, my mood gradually became calm.

I took an Uber and went out. I was a little scared: the temperature today was only -2° and there was frost everywhere; Two big blisters when I ran half a horse last time, it has been a whole week since today, and the two big blisters have not fully recovered. Today is the second time to run half a horse, can you... I always tell myself that I will be afraid because I do too little or have not done it, I don't trust myself, and I will no longer be afraid when I am familiar with the things I often do. When I got to the activity venue, I was so anxious that I felt I could not hold it in. "Just nervous!" "I kept saying to myself.

Chapter 4 Refraction of Sweat

At seven o 'clock in the morning, it was still dark, and the city center was so hazy around the fog. I texted the principal and she brought me my race number - 6869. That's a nice number! The principal's number is 6868, which is not only "cow" but also "hair" . We take a group photo near the entrance to the track, with a striking row of porta-potties in the background. Ha-ha! Unique enough background. I was both excited and nervous. This was my first race and I was afraid that I wouldn't be able to finish it or that my speed would be too slow. After all, it took me 3 hours and 15 minutes to finish half a horse distance last time, and the maximum time to hold a placard was 2 hours and 50 minutes. Speakers sang the national anthem, while participants stretched or high-fived their peers, enthusiastic and ready to take on the challenge. The icy ground also slipped a whole bunch of runners... I felt like I was in the middle of a big celebration, like I was watching. The principal smiled at me and said, "Are you sure your feet are okay?" I winked and smiled and said, "It's okay."

The start command sounded and the runners sprinted out like arrows off the string, lighting up the track in an instant with passion and hormones. The principal and I said, "Wait for you in front of me," and ran off. I also dare not neglect, looking at the watch control speed and heart rate as far as possible to maintain the same frequency, followed. However, just a few minutes after I started running, my shoelace suddenly came loose. Well, I was already on edge, but suddenly I got even more flustered. The crowd was so crowded that I was confused. 6. Why are there so many people? Will I faint because of the crowds? Will my depression go crazy because of it? Watching them pass me one by one, I felt like I was running backwards. I began to crumble inside, feeling so awful about myself, and the fear and anxiety were almost too much to bear. At this moment, I thought I had recovered, and I realized that recovery is not an overnight process, but a process of growing a little bit and a little bit every day to become stronger and more resilient. Come on, you are the best! You have to be the way you like! Don't think about anything. Don't think about anything. Just focus on your steps. Here, let me see how you can take bigger steps and go faster. I look at the runners from the back and tell myself to control my heart rate and speed and keep it balanced. In this way, I talked to myself and encouraged myself.

By the side of the road, enthusiastic shouts rose one after another, the names of the participants were shouted, and the sound of encouragement and cheering distracted my attention and drove away my fear and anxiety. As the 1mile marker approached, I could see the supply point along the road, where volunteers were pouring water for the runners, mineral water and energy drinks. Every mile or so, volunteers and family members cheer on the runners. The whole city is shrouded in haze, hazy high-rise buildings, bustling streets, everyone is running full speed, running happily, laughing. At this moment, the fear and misgivings in my heart have completely disappeared, replaced by great happiness and excitement. The cheering shouts of the volunteers seemed to inject energy into me, making my steps bigger than usual. Whenever I felt exhausted, volunteers would appear on the side of the road to yell cheer and cheer me up.

After running some distance, a boy with dyed yellow hair caught my attention. He was at the perimeter of the track, leaning over and extending a hand to high-fives the runners while Shouting, "You're the best! You can do it!" At first, I didn't think much of it. I just thought it was the volunteer's unique way of encouraging me. The sun was out, shining through the buildings and trees, and it was getting a little hot. Then I saw the boy with the dyed yellow hair I had just left behind. He was still leaning around the corner, reaching out to give each runner a high five and offering words of encouragement. In an instant, I was moved by his persistence and passion, as if he understood the hardships and joys of each runner and went out of his way to give us strength. I don't know when he got ahead of us or how long he was waiting in front of us, but he certainly provided the motivation for all the runners to run. Unfortunately, I wasn't able to high-five him because I was on the outside lap.

During the long race, I gradually felt exhausted, and the runners behind me passed me one by one. I thought I couldn't do that. I had to set a goal. In front of a red clothes, black pants of the little sister, her clothes wet more than half, the step is also very small, looks very tired. And I have not much sweat, she should be a soft persimmon, I am sure to catch up with her! So I picked up speed and ran behind her. To my surprise, not standing shoulder to shoulder with her, she suddenly accelerated and hiss ahead. Booo! Isn't she already tired? She even had the explosive power to leave the distance I managed to catch up with. Well, I adjusted my breathing and heart rate to stay steady and not let the gap get any further.

Thirsty and a little hungry, I had a piece of bread and a small bowl of cereal for the morning. I stopped by a lot of supply stations along the way, but I couldn't drink too much water at once. Because blood flow is concentrated in the working muscles rather than the digestive system during exercise, drinking too much water can cause an upset stomach and even cause nausea and vomiting. Drinking too much water can also dilute electrolytes in the blood, especially sodium. The condition is called hyponatremia, and symptoms can include dizziness, nausea, convulsions and even coma. As a result, marathon runners often take small sips of water to gradually replace the fluid they've lost. In addition, some sports drinks contain electrolytes, which help maintain the balance of electrolytes in the body. You know, exercise helps me learn a lot. Although when I was reading, I was the kind of student who was often scolded and punished by the teacher. I always appeared at the door of the office of the principal and the class teacher. Now, I fell in love with learning through sports (in addition to English learning, of course). I not only improved my physique, but also learned a lot of common sense and knowledge, and even a little understanding of health. Thirsty and hungry 6869

抑郁自救笔记
Notes on Depression Self-help

some steps can not move, but at this time I am still running, still chasing the goal of my little sister in red clothes.

Whoaa! Water refill station! I stopped, grabbed a glass of water, and stretched my leg, which had just been cramping, by the side of the road. Several times in situ stretching, afraid of stretching time is not enough soon and cramp, and afraid of stretching time too long will be far behind. After about two minutes, I got up and took longer strides to catch up, trying to make up for the time I had just lost. Perhaps because of my long strides, within five minutes the cramps were back, even more painful than before. My toes also started to hurt, most likely from the blisters I had made during my practice last week. Even so, I still haven't seen the back of my little sister in red, let alone caught up with the light principal.

Speaking of the principal, she is a woman of light in my eyes. It not only describes her running speed, but also her flexibility and determination. Once we were talking about her experience of starting a kindergarten. The epidemic has had a huge impact on many kindergartens. Faced with many difficulties, she has endured great mental and financial pressure. After all, there are teachers' salaries to pay. During that time, she was very anxious and even suffered from depression, which required her to take medication prescribed by the doctor. However, with the improvement of the epidemic, she managed to get rid of the crisis of kindergarten operation and depression by virtue of her strong will and bright mind, and no longer needed to rely on drugs. She would get up every morning to swim and exercise. I also take medication for depression, so I know how terrible the after-effects and side effects can be. Some medications are impossible to stop and require a long tapering process. Now I am still taking a western medicine, which is already one 30th of a pill. Each reduction will make me suffer for at least half a month, of course, it is not ruled out that most of it is because of psychological effects, you know that this pill is only 25 mg. I know that some necessary drugs are in order to control some conditions, taking is inevitable. But the dangers of drug dependence are another matter. Tapering off the drug is a process of adjustment by the body, and it is the only way to avoid withdrawal when you stop taking the drug. This is absolutely necessary from a scientific point of view. That's why I'm tapering. I was filled with admiration for how quickly she was able to come off the medication. Every time I ate or talked with her, I learned something. Even though most of our conversations were small talk, every word she said was positive. How could such a light woman not make people want to be close to her?

With 1mile to go from the terminal, I strode along, trying not to think about the cramp in my calf or the pain in my toes. I was a little desperate at the sight of the downtown slope, feeling like I wouldn't be able to run up that steep incline. That's when she showed up! Oh! There comes the little sister in Red! My heart was filled with power and I started running as fast as I could. This time I really took a big step forward, and the distance between me and my little sister was getting closer and closer. Just as I was about to catch up with her, she was already picking up speed. Since we were going to finish the race in five minutes, it was time to prove that we could outdo ourselves. And guess who I saw at this point? Yes, the boy with yellow hair! This time because it was almost the end, I ran the inside lap early, and as I got close to him, I jumped up and gave him a high-five, Shouting, "Thank you!" I had a big smile and ran fast, passing one woman after another, feeling like the wind and whizzing past. Over the loudspeakers came the names of the runners who had passed the finish line... I almost stopped when I heard my own name as I galloped, though I had always hated the name my biological father gave me. In my excitement, I thought I had crossed the finish line, only to realize I had a few more steps to go when I saw the banner ahead of me.

Come on! Smile to meet the victory! When I crossed the finish line, I got the medal of the race. The time was frozen at two hours and 33 minutes. The atmosphere was so exciting that I ran 42 minutes faster than I did on my own! Oh my God! It's progressing so fast! I have blisters on both big toes from last week, but my heart rate and speed are very even. I conquered myself and it felt really good to surpass myself. The anxiety and depression seemed to have moved away from me. I found that they were afraid of me, afraid of my growth, afraid of my inner strength. As our hearts gradually become stronger, we may find that the anxiety and depression we once had are no longer as frightening as they used to be. They become a part of life, still present, but no longer insurmountable obstacles. Growing up and being strong allowed me to accept my imperfections, just like in this marathon, where the principal finished in 2 hours and 23 minutes, 10 minutes faster than me. Next time, looking forward to the next time I run with her, I will fight to catch up with this woman who was once so afflicted with depression that she had to take pills to steady her mind.

I used to see people running on rainy days, running on the roadside, running in the park, I feel that they are really full of food and nothing to do is not too tired to panic, why do so toss themselves? Now I understand, not tired, not full of support, is the temper. Tempering our will, let us accept anxiety and depression. Depression is just an emotion, we have to learn to accept it, and then gradually fade it, do not let it take root in the heart. Inner growth is not about getting rid of all pain, but learning to dance with it. Emotions that were once so daunting become part of the inner strength, even most of it. It is these experiences that give us a deeper understanding of the meaning of life. In strengthening, we gradually find an understanding of ourselves, accept our past, and move toward a fuller, more confident future. So don't be afraid of your inner anxiety and depression, they may be the key to making you a stronger person. Believe in your own strength and rise to the challenge, you will find a stronger self.

The cold feeling in my body, the cold sweat in my palms, and my shivering body are all reminders that I need to exercise. Yes, it was time to step out of my comfort zone and do something I'd never tried before. Even if you don't achieve anything great in the end, just being able to push yourself into unfamiliar situations and accomplish something that has never been done before is invaluable. That's where recovery begins. I began to take steps to run, go shopping, eat in crowded places, and say hello to the kind elderly people in the park. Care about the people around me, care about them at the same time also warm themselves; When I smile at them, they will respond gently to me, and that smile can cure all worries and anxieties. Gradually, we will be surrounded by these smiles. Hey, when you smile at someone, it's like giving them a little mood gift. A smile is an expression of kindness that doesn't require words. When someone returns your smile, you seem to establish a tacit understanding and a feeling of mutual understanding. Together, you create a small world full of warmth and understanding, and heal each other. Of course, there is a limit to how much you care. Excessive caring may cause stress or even discomfort to the other person. Everyone takes it differently, and some people may prefer to enjoy their own world and be less comfortable with excessive care from others. So, we need to be flexible when we care about others and pay attention to each other's reactions. If the other person appears nervous or less open to attention, it may be necessary to moderate restraint. In general, showing concern requires a deep understanding and respect not only for the other person's feelings, but also for their independence and personal space. In this way, caring can work best as a positive and pleasurable experience.

My story may be just one of thousands of ways to find redemption through sports. If you are a sports enthusiast, this chapter may provide you with a new perspective on how exercise is not only a physical exercise, but also a healing of the mind. Whether you're on the track, on a yoga mat, or in the pool, remember that every effort is a step toward a healthier, happier version of yourself. Experience familiar exercises with a different mindset and discover new meanings together. If you haven't been involved with sports at all before, I hope my sharing will ignite your curiosity to explore the world of sports. Start with a light walk, take the first step, and experience the physical and mental changes that sports bring!

Chapter 5 Beyond the Island

Perhaps each of us has at one time or another felt like an island in the midst of a sea of humanity. This feeling is especially strong in the shadow of depression. When I was very ill, I felt more alone than I had ever felt before, cut off, misunderstood, cut off and alone. There was no one who fully understood how I felt, no one who felt my pain, and no one who could offer me sincere spiritual support. During that time, I longed to find a friend who understood me, who could empathize with my pain, who could give me sincere spiritual support, but there was none.

When we talk about the importance of friends for people suffering from depression, we are actually talking about an invisible power. This kind of power is like a bridge that crosses the gap of the heart and connects one island to another. This kind of power, though invisible, is powerful enough to ignite the spark of hope in the heart of the patient, and inspire the courage and strength to fight against the disease.

1. An old friend who knows his time

Through a mutual friend, I got to know Li Qing, who has a lot in common with us. We are both frank and careless people. We soon became good friends.

We like to drink together, even in the small tofu stall on the side of the road, while eating small tofu and blowing beer bottles can also talk until the morning, often talk about the excitement of the spit stars flying, we looked at the flying spit signal tofu on the tofu stall... Looking at each other, while covering their mouths and laughing.

Li Xiaoqing is an extremely crazy yan control, see handsome men can not walk the road, the degree of lechery full level.

We all like to play mahjong, but it is a pity that her technology is too poor, touch cards, cards always look for a long time, every "gambling" will lose, but also feel that they play very well, always want to call friends to play for a while, can be said to be "food and love to play". This has been many years ago, maybe she has now become a chess master, it is not known.

Li Xiaoqing university is an English major, every time she drinks too much, she stands up and points in one direction to speak English.

She is also a bit nervous and always can't remember names, but she especially likes to ask others to drink at the wine table. When the family name was clearly Liu, she said, "Sister Li, have a drink", and after a while became "Sister Wang"; Someone else's contact lens fell on the floor, she helped them pick it up and blow it, let them put it on again, saying that she blew it was equivalent to disinfection; After drinking too much must let others drink milk bubble scallops, said can cure; In Jiuzhaigou, obviously already high upside down, still in the " 嘻 唰 唰 " and friends drinking Qingke wine boxing...... However, she was very bright and enthusiastic. All her friends liked her very much, and no one minded her bold lines.

We will also have disputes, I have a quick temper, occasionally angry at her, she is always tolerant of me, hey hey smile, and then coax me: "You don't be angry." Before I got sick, Li Qing invited me to stay with her for a few days. She smoked and drank and bragged every day. She took care of me like a grandpa. Her mother would often cook the noodles and bring them over. We ate the delicious noodles, crossed our legs, idly lit an after-dinner cigarette and waited for her to pour me a glass of water. Putting away the dishes is her job, too. It's all about being a quality partner. In those years, I slept until 2 or 3 p.m. every day to wake up naturally, and then went out to eat and drink, and then went to the bar, if you still feel not happy then went to ktv singing or dancing, in short, the nightlife is rich, often go home to rest until dawn. Every time I asked Li Qing to go out in the evening, she always said she had something to do and rarely went with me. At that time, I didn't understand why she had so many things to do. Life is all about eating, drinking and having fun. Now I understand, work, family, dreams... There's always so much going on.

Li Qing is engaged in the tourism industry. Before going abroad, she always likes to take me everywhere to play and experience all kinds of new things. For a while, my aunt wanted to travel, and Li Qing happened to develop a new tour route near my hometown, Gaohe River. We hit it off immediately. Li Qing offered us a cost-only tour and we helped him test the new route. So my aunt's family, Li Qing and I went to Gaohe River. That evening, in addition to my aunt and uncle, several of us young people went to see the night scenery. Five of us drank 12 jin of rice wine, and we were all a little drunk. I have always hated my cousin's girlfriend, she has a tough personality, always bossing my big cousin around, and the tone is full of commands. Eg. Through drinking, we had a conflict. In the process of fighting, she and I pushed and pulled up, pushing harder and harder, plop, we both fell into the river.

"Yo son, I'll save you!" Don't look at Li Qing drink too much, the reaction is very fast, Shouting directly into the river.

The big cousin who can't swim saw us falling into the water and shouted in panic: "Save my sister quickly, she can't swim." The same cousin who can not swim also shouted, looking for tools to rescue. The water was very deep, and my cousin's girlfriend kept stepping on my body to get herself out of the water. I couldn't get out of the water at all. At this time, Li Qingyou came to me and shouted, "Don't step on her anymore. I'll push you up!" Then he said to me: "So you don't mess up, I hold your chin and swim to the shore." Fortunately, the woman who used my feet was quickly pulled up by me, and after a lot of tossed, everyone was on the shore without any danger. Looking at the wet Li Xiaoqing, I really hate and love, hate her regardless of their own safety, love her sincere feelings for me. Let me think of once we drink too much with the next table guest conflict, Li Xiaoqing is the same, and the next table fight, people help out with a knife, her first reaction is to let me "run quickly". Very smart, beat but run. The next day, the wine has not scattered we listless, early in the morning to drift. Not too much for a while she saw handsome man immediately spirit and passers-by to play water fights, even drifting for 9 hours, days dark.

Li Qing is really the cutest, bravest and kindest drinking maniac I've ever met!

Another time, a bunch of us went to Xijiang Miao Village to play, in order to better understand the Miao village, Li Qing also found us a local guide. At the dinner table, Lu Meili, Qingge, Li Qing and I were dazed by the endless singing and toasting of wine by local Miao girls. They have a custom that a person should not touch the wine bowl when toasting others, otherwise he or she will have to drink all the wine. Those beautiful Miao girls fed us bowl after bowl of wine, and looked at a table of delicious dishes we could not eat. The tour guide saw how much fun we were having and joined us in the drinking. Near the end of the dinner, the guide told us that he had another group to stop by. At the end of the dinner, five people went to the top of the mountain drunk to see the night scene, and drank a lot, before and after a total of more than ten catties of rice wine, are drunk confused. Especially Lu Meili walk to help, she also insisted on only go to the men's bathroom.

Drinking leads to urination, and Lu Meili and Li Xiaoqing frequently urinate, but they are still far away from the toilets at the top and foot of the mountain. At this time, we found a large truck parked on the side of the road, which was suitable for shelter. Lu Meili squatted down first, Li Qing also deliberately took off her coat to help Lu Meili cover. The sound of water just sounded, "dudu dudu" , the truck started slowly and drove away! Probably we all drank too much, no one noticed that there was someone in the cab, did not hear the sound of the truck starting. Lu Meili was left alone in the wind. Hahaha!

Down the mountain to walk a place, the scenery is good, Lu Meili with everyone to take a family photo. After taking the family photo ready to go back to the residence, turned into the path leading to the hostel, we found a person lying in the bushes on the side of the road, is the guide! He was so drunk that he fell asleep on the side of the road. I don't know where he had thrown his wallet and documents. Everyone carried him back to the hostel and gave him a nickname of "Xi (wash) Yangyang" . Back to the residence, we several continue to drink, Li Xiaoqing completely drunk, has been Shouting: "boss, please fry an egg, I want to eat one-sided!" I want to eat six!" The next day I got up to see the family photo taken by Lu Meili... Only one do not know whose toe, and blurred.

......

I really have too many good and happy memories when I was with Li Xiaoqing.

It was Li Qing who discovered my illness. At the party at Li Qing's house, we all had a good time. Li Qing said that I was particularly silent that day, when the noise was loud, I lay near the window to smoke, my eyes did not focus, straight into a daze, called me several times before there was a response. She asked me what was wrong, my response was also very slow, deal with two sentences and began to daze. When I forced a smile, the corners of my mouth were vaguely twitching.

After I arrived in the United States, we gradually lost contact because of the time difference between home and abroad and the busy work of each other.

抑郁自救笔记
Notes on Depression Self-help

And I don't want to burden my friends by dumping emotional trash on them unilaterally, so we have fewer and fewer opportunities to confide in each other and stay in touch far less frequently than before. Whenever we talk on the phone, food is always the topic of conversation. We both love food, but Li Qing likes to cook it himself. When I talk to her about food, she can always talk to me about the preparation process. She also likes to take advantage of the time difference and send me food videos and scary sound effects just before I go to bed, either to make me hungry or to scare me.

Until we talked on the phone a few days ago, Li Qing actually said that she had committed suicide because of depression, and then got a tattoo on it to cover the wound. I can't believe it. In my mind, she has always been open-minded, optimistic and cheerful.

Here is Li Qing's own account of this experience:

Depression, I never thought it would have anything to do with me. Until I got cranky and irritable over a piece of paper or the sound of whatever it was that made, or even woke up every day thinking about death.

It is no exaggeration to say that every morning I would get up, my family's nerves would be on edge, I would throw tantrums because the water was not hot, I would throw glasses at a word.

I knew there was something wrong with my mind, then one day, a small thing happened, I chose to commit suicide, when I cut my artery with a blade, I felt a relief, I felt a relief in my heart.

My best friend saved me from death. After going to the hospital, the doctor said that there was only 0.5 mm to trouble. My bestie was afraid that I would do anything stupid again. During that time, she always accompanied me and enlightened me.

I was grateful to her in my heart, but I couldn't be happy. I felt so miserable and struggled in my heart.

I decided to go home and saw that my mother had a lot of grey hair all of a sudden. I began to wonder why I had become so negative.

Relationships, work, and family are issues that everyone has to face. It's just that some people live through it and figure it out.

I, on the other hand, got myself into a dead end by being anxious.

I had to change. I had to save myself.

So I bought a cat and I told it every day what I wanted to say in my heart. Some people ask, why don't you talk to someone and get your heart out, at least a friend can enlighten you and talk to you?

What can a cat do? And heal people. That's impossible.

The point I'm trying to make is that it's not as simple as having a cat. It's about what I've learned from owning a cat. We are a process of healing each other. We just need to be a good listener.

But people are very strange, used to love to go out and chat with friends, said useful useless business, but when everyone has their own family, work, everyone is busy for their own family, who has time to listen to these, even if it is listened to, their position is not the same, get the information is not the same, over time, you do not love to say. And family said, it will not have the same resonance.

And me and my cat, I have nothing to say, although I am talking to myself, but it has been with me, just listening silently, without any opinion. I get a kind of verbal catharsis inside of me.

There is also a sense of responsibility. When the language, emotions have been cathartic, my heart began to slowly happy up, a lot of people do not understand, I now understand that a lot of things are from the lack of love.

Parents' love, is the love of course, is a kind of love that will be ignored by us. The love between friends is the love of friends in need. The love between lovers is the love in which we yearn to belong.

No matter what level we start from, we end up searching for this love, wanting to be loved, and in the process losing ourselves, losing our soul.

And I thank my family and friends around me for their concern for me, and let me slowly get better.

With the end of the epidemic, I began to work, traveled to many cities, and saw many good things.

I found that life from another perspective, in fact, is very beautiful. You have to find the positivity in life.

First, you have to get rid of your anxiety and control your emotions. When you are emotionally stable, you are less likely to be swayed by external events.

Do your best work again. Even if the job is not the industry you love, keep a good attitude to treat it.

And love yourself. When you love yourself well, nothing else will affect you. And you will find that if you love yourself, you will regain self-confidence. Having a healthy body is more than anything else.

Get rid of your junk on a regular basis. Exercise, drink, do whatever you feel you can to let off steam.

Make a plan to travel every year. To see the beauty of the world, to discover the beautiful things.

This is how I do it. Slowly, I don't get depressed, I don't dwell on negative things, I don't even get angry so easily over the smallest things.

On the contrary, I now look at a lot of problems, are a steady state of mind to treat, you will find that the once cheerful I come back. I sincerely for the future life and work harder.

It was complicated to see my former best friend in the same depression as me. On the one hand, I felt empathy and understanding, because I know the pain and helplessness that depression can cause. It fills my heart with pity that such a bright and cheerful girl like Li Qing needs to go through such suffering. It is even more regrettable that I was not there to give her some care and comfort during her most difficult and supportive period. This absence fills me with deep guilt. On the other hand, I felt genuinely happy for her to come out of the dilemma strong. I know that it took a lot of courage and determination. Her success is not only an affirmation of herself, but also a great inspiration to the rest of us.

In Li Qing's self-description, the experience of owning a cat especially caught my attention. This kind of communication with pets, although seemingly one-way, actually has a non-negligible effect on emotional stability and recovery. Although cats can't talk, they are excellent listeners and can provide us with a safe, stress-free environment where we can freely express our emotions and thoughts without fear of being judged or criticized. For people with depression, loneliness often worsens the condition, and an adorable cat can be a companion in our lives, providing us with great warmth and comfort. This constant sense of companionship plays an important role in the recovery process. And a cat's soft fur and warm body, including their bonding behavior, are healing agents in themselves, helping us release our body's "happiness hormones" like oxytocin and dopamine. These chemicals help relieve tension and boost mood. In addition, owning a cat increased the amount of exercise and activity patients did. Caring for a cat requires regular feeding, changing water, cleaning the cat's body, cleaning the litter box, etc. These tasks make the patient's daily life more fulfilling and help establish more regular habits, while also increasing their amount of physical activity, which has a positive impact on both physical and mental health.

Li Qing, who is still working in the tourism industry and recently opened a hotel-style nursing home, has managed to keep her career and life in good shape. This is how she managed to overcome depression through self-reflection, self-adjustment and actively seeking help, which is quite remarkable.

Hopefully, Li Qing's sharing can bring hope and courage to those who are struggling with depression.

2. An old friend whose heart has been lost

In the early years, there was a girl who helped me with all the details of my life. During that time, my depression was so bad that I avoided going out all the time, sometimes not going out for months at a time. She bought everything I needed for the house and accompanied me to anything I needed to do in person. In this process, the friendship between us gradually deepened. In the United States, such friendship is especially rare. In China, most of our friends are known since childhood, and it is easy to communicate with each other, but here, people are often not easy to reveal their innermost feelings, as if they will be taken as a joke after dinner. So I cherish the friendship between us very much.

The girl is younger than me, but she is very sensible and capable. After she lost her job, she asked me where she could find a job. Naturally, I invited her to work in my company. She could invest as much of the company's existing stock as she wanted, be directly involved in the management of the company, or choose to take a cut.

In the beginning, she worked very hard and got a lot of things in order, which is why I felt more comfortable leaving everything to her and letting her make decisions. Gradually, she unwittingly mentioned several times that she wanted her husband to work in our company. After much thought, I finally agreed. So she and her husband both worked in my company. However, after a period of time, their working attitude gradually became lazy, which caused dissatisfaction and complaints from other colleagues. I checked the surveillance video and found that her husband often sat idle in the office area during working hours, playing for a while and then leaving.

She was there to watch the security footage with me, blushing and sheepishly glancing at me from time to time to see if there was anything wrong with my expression. When I was done, I gently mentioned that the company was overspending and needed to lay off staff. She also saw in the video that her husband had really been slacking off and offered to let him quit. The day after our conversation, I had dinner with the couple and others. Of course, we didn't mention the layoffs during the meal, which was between her and me. The next day, she started a rumor that her husband did not know that he was going to be fired at the dinner table. If her husband knew the news at that time, he did not know how he would react and might make some shocking actions. She also said that she had held up the entire company by herself during her tenure.

Indeed, a lot of things in the company are in her hands. Whenever she comes to me with a problem that needs to be decided, such as how to do this or how to deal with that, I usually ask her for her opinion first. After she expresses her idea, if it is correct, I will agree with her and encourage her to boldly go ahead and do it. It's true that I was very sick at that time and didn't have much energy to deal with the company affairs, but I didn't expect that my encouragement and trust in her would eventually turn into her "holding up the company by herself". I almost mistook her for having founded the company.

Somewhere along the way, something happened that made me very uncomfortable. I have a tool shop of my own, and the company buys all the tools it needs directly from my shop. Then she found a manufacturer in California that sold the tools we needed for about $1.50 less than mine. To make the difference, she drove to California herself, buying tens of thousands of them at a time. In addition to selling them to companies, she would sell them to other people, at the price of $1.50 more at my tool store. One day, she told me she couldn't work and was going to California. When I asked her what she was going to do, she said she was going to buy some tools for someone and the company was short of them. Then she calculated the account for me and said that she could earn a difference of more than 20,000 yuan in one trip.

After hearing this, I felt very uncomfortable. She was flagrantly wasting public funds. After much thought, I called her to talk about the problem. She responded that she just wanted to buy cheaper tools to save the company money. I countered that whether it was buying the more expensive tools on my end or going to California to buy the cheaper ones, the profits would be mine in the end. In doing so, she took more than $20,000 out of my pocket and flaunted it in front of me. I told her it was illegal and a waste of public funds.

She explained that her original intention was to save the money and give it to me. I felt very confused. I owned the tool shop and the money was mine. What was the purpose of changing hands with her? If I wanted a cheap tool, I could buy it somewhere else.

During the operation of her company, I trusted her with all the core matters, such as cash flow, finances, and receipts, and I trusted her 100% without holding any guard. However, such trust collapsed in an instant and I lost everything at once. What I call "nothing" not only refers to the material loss, but more importantly, the trust, tacit understanding and friendship between us no longer exist. Maybe she has a plan to start her own business for a long time. She has contacted my clients behind my back many times, but the clients ignored her completely and told me that I pretended not to know.

I said to her, "When I first met you, you were so sensible and lovely. And since we were close friends, I don't understand why you have become so fussy now that you can't even count every penny." She raised her voice and opened her eyes wide. "That's just the way I am," she replied.

We were friends who trusted each other and told each other everything. When my spirit is the most difficult to endure, her silent care and help let me feel the warmth. Unfortunately, in the face of interests, seemingly indestructible friendship or become fragile. This is not because the friendship itself is not strong enough, but because in the real world, the complexity of human nature often exceeds our expectations.

We tend to divide human nature into black and white, good and evil, good and bad. However, in real life, human nature is often more complex and changeable. Sometimes, a person may show a kind and selfless side at one moment, and then reveal a greedy and selfish side when the temptation of profit appears. Life is what it is and it doesn't change just because of our expectations and ideals. In this complicated world, the only thing we can do is learn to face the reality, learn to deal with all kinds of complicated interpersonal relationships, and learn how to find a balance between interests and friendship. This is not easy because it involves one's own values, morals, and definitions of "success" and "happiness".

In the process, we may experience betrayal, disappointment and pain. But above all, we must not beat ourselves up or doubt our worth. Our feelings and happiness are the most important. They should not be influenced by external judgment or the actions of others. We should not blame ourselves or doubt ourselves because of others' betrayal. We deserve to be treated well and loved.

3. The Friend Filter

I admit that I did go through an unspeakable period of sadness, anger, and disappointment after dealing with my friend's betrayal. Even when I talk about it again, it still brings me to my heart. But we can't always live in the shadow of the past. It doesn't do us any good to keep looking over the hurt. Self-healing and re-choosing friends are both important issues that I have to face.

I began to reflect on what role I had played in the friendship and what had led to its end. I realized that I needed to pay more attention to communication and understanding between my friends in future friendships. I will learn to communicate with each other's thoughts and feelings sincerely to avoid misunderstanding and estrangement. In the same way, I will establish healthy boundaries and learn to say "no." I need to learn to say no, to protect my own interests and feelings, and to stop sacrificing myself to accommodate others, so that I can build friendships based on equality and respect that help me avoid potential harm.

I have also become more careful in choosing new friends. I take the time to observe and learn about their character and values. I will no longer be eager, but will be willing to take the time to test a person's sincerity. While a friend's betrayal pains me, it doesn't mean that all friendships do. I believe that there are many other sincere and kind people in the world who deserve to be known and cherished. 10. I will not close my heart just because of one hurt. I am still willing to be brave enough to love and trust. I believe that sincere friendship is one of the most valuable assets in life.

I compare how you choose your friends to the process of drawing a picture of your support network. First, add people who "get me" -- people who know about my depression and, far from judging it, are willing to be understanding and caring when I need them. And in this group, one friend's story is particularly worth mentioning -- the friend who accompanied me to Nanjing for medical treatment mentioned above. During that time, he always listened carefully to what I had to say and would give me feedback immediately after I finished. For example, he would tell me that he had experienced some of my symptoms, even though his condition was not as severe as mine. He would encourage me: "Really, I think you're going to be fine." Maybe he didn't fully understand my inner struggle and pain, but the sincerity in his words made me feel less alone and gave me a glimmer of hope.

Next, I hope to add some color to the painting, namely, people who have the same interests or views as me. They can be my friends who laugh and talk with me, or they can be my friends who share my sports experience with me. Getting along with them makes my life more colorful. When I was younger, I used to fantasize that I could be friends with rich people, naively thinking that I could become rich because of this. But as I grow older and experience more, I gradually realize that real wealth is not easily acquired through simple social connections. The truly rich have often worked hard and accumulated their wealth over a long period of time. Their success also hides a lot of bitterness and dedication, but these efforts are often hidden from the outside world. Only by trying to become a good person can people gain wealth, otherwise there is no great sense in getting close to rich people. When we succeed through our own efforts and talents, our social circle automatically rises.

After thinking about this logic, I gradually lost interest in those who only pursue famous brands and luxury goods, and even had no common language with them. We used to get together to talk about the latest handbags, popular colors and brands, and discuss who bought more Kelly and who bought more Birkin. Now, however, these materialistic pursuits have lost their appeal to me. It's been a long, long time since I've gone into a Hermes store, because I've found that they're not what I really want. I now pay more attention to my own comfort and inner satisfaction, rather than external evaluation and material accumulation. The clothes I wear can be ten thousand yuan a piece, it can be one yuan a piece, as long as it is comfortable and I like it, I don't care about its price.

In the same way, I am more inclined to make friends with people who have a rich spiritual world. Some people may be rich in material things, but they may be poor in spirit. On the contrary, there are some people who are not so rich in material things but are full of spirit, and communicating and working with them is more satisfying.

Of course, the painting also needs some bright colors to represent those positive people who bring me positive energy. We can feel the positive sunshine emanating from his body, as if surrounded by a dazzling halo, there is an invisible appeal and drive, so that people around are involuntarily attracted to him, feel the beauty of life. Jenny, the mother of my daughter's studio classmate, is such a person. She always looks at things from a positive perspective. Even if it seems to be a negative thing, she can also discover the positive side. The occasional complaint is an objective way of sharing bad things, rather than simply conveying negativity: "Look, there are such bad things!" Soon she shows the other side of the story, showing us that we can have a good life even when bad things happen in our lives. She is undoubtedly a quality friend.

And my ESL teacher, Jean. Mentioning Jean in this chapter seems a bit off topic because she was my teacher; But fitting, because her encouragement and support gave me a lot of motivation, and she is the best teacher in my heart. Looking back on my learning journey, if I hadn't experienced the pain of having my ear wrenched as a child, perhaps I wouldn't have been so resistant to reciting my multiplication tables; If I had had a loving teacher like Jean when I was in school, I might have been more enthusiastic about learning.

Jean is different from my previous teachers. She is gentle and patient. She always smiles and explains things patiently. Although most of our students tried hard to express themselves, they could not say a whole word for half a day, and even if it took several minutes, they could only squeeze out a hard word. No matter how difficult the process was, she listened patiently until we had finished our clumsy but determined attempts. She always encouraged us: "I will help you", "this is a really difficult word, that's why you have a hard time reading it", "Don't be afraid, it will get better in the future" ... I have attended ESL classes six times in the US, but each time it didn't last more than ten days. I always get bored and resistant quickly and leave school. But in Jean's class, I found the motivation to stick with it. These warm words really gave me great encouragement and inspired me to become a better myself.

Please also note that this painting is not about adding elements endlessly, we need to be careful about the people and things that intersect with us. Relationships that seem to add color at first glance can lead to fatigue and stress in the long run, just as messy lines in a painting can ruin the overall harmony and beauty. Friends who often pour out their negative feelings to us endlessly, with little or no regard for our feelings and needs; Friends whose communications revolve around material comforts and superficial entertainment, but lack any real emotional connection; Friends who approach us with a purpose and try to get some benefit from us...

In the process of drawing this picture, also remember to give yourself some blank space to represent our personal space and privacy. After all, everyone needs some alone time to self heal and reflect.

Finally, don't forget that this painting is only a part of life. While the support of a friend is important, professional psychotherapy or medication is also indispensable. They are like picture frames that protect and support our "support network map."

So, choosing friends is really about carefully building our social picture and making it work best in our lives to help us better cope with the challenges of depression.

4. How do you deal with people with depression

In this fast-paced, high-stress society, depression has become a mental health issue that cannot be ignored. When a friend or family member around us is

抑郁自救笔记
Notes on Depression Self-help

struggling with depression, how can we reach out and accompany them through this difficult time?

First of all, we need to understand that depression is not a simple feeling of depression, let alone a complaint, it is a disease that needs to be understood and paid attention to. Put yourself in their shoes to understand how they feel, rather than rushing to judge. We may not be able to fully empathize with their inner pain, but the best support is to listen and feel their needs. Let them know that their sorrows and joys deserve to be heard, and will be heard. Reach out and let them know that they are not alone in this fight. A simple "I'm here", "I'll be there for you" can sometimes be more powerful than any words. So, if you know someone who is going through this, don't hesitate to hold their hand and tell them "I am here" and be willing to accompany them through this journey.

In addition to listening and being there for them, we should also try our best to provide them with substantial help. For example, offer to help them find and connect with a professional counselor or psychiatrist. Depression is an illness that requires professional treatment, and professional medical professionals are able to provide the most accurate diagnosis and the most effective treatment options, the earlier the better. Even small actions can make a big difference. Whether it's walking them to the doctor, reminding them to take their medicine, or doing cardio. This practical help helps them feel warm and cared for.

At the same time, we should also pay attention to their emotional changes, give them enough care, often support them with positive and encouraging words, and avoid any negative language that may make them feel worse. People with depression often avoid social activities due to low self-esteem or anxiety, causing them to feel more lonely and closed off. We can take the initiative to invite them to some social activities, such as dinners, parties or trips.

Even if they start to feel better, don't let your guard down. Recovery takes time, like waiting for a flower to open. Stay patient, believe in their strength, and accompany them step by step into the light.

Depression, this seemingly bottomless whirlpool, is not invulnerable. With the company and support of our friends, it is as if we are given a solid shield. They do not just listen to you, but truly understand you, accept you, and can give you a light of understanding and support in the darkest moments of helplessness. I also hope that readers who have friends with depressed people can be more understanding, attentive and supportive. Depression is not a shameful illness, but a mental health issue that needs to be cared for and treated. Your presence, listening ear and encouragement are invaluable to the sufferer. Please do not ignore their feelings, your care and understanding, may change a person's fate, bring them a new life possibility. May you in the journey of life, can be a beacon for others, illuminating others' islands.

Chapter 6 Small Hands Hold Big Hands

In life, there are always some people whose existence is like a shining gift, just the thought of it makes my heart shine. And that is exactly what my two little friends are like to me. They took our big hands with their small hands, and guided me out of the dark corners of my heart with the power of innocence and trust, so that I learned how to love and how to cherish. Their innocence and pure emotion made me look at my own life in perspective and realize how important it is to keep my zest for life. It's not so much that I nurture them as that they heal me.

1. Diametrically opposed siblings

My daughter is very lively and has an uninhibited childlike spirit that brings me endless joy, but also sometimes makes me feel a little helpless.

She has a mild form of ADHD, is particularly energetic, and has an even more surprising curiosity and thirst for knowledge, both similar and different from me as a child. She was smarter than I was, but she was also a rebel like me, a woman who said you must touch what you can't touch, who said you must test for yourself what is dangerous, a woman who never looks back. Whenever she annoyed me, she would purse her cute little mouth and signal to me, "Mm, mm, mm." The message is obvious. She wants to give me a kiss on the lips. After joining the swim team, her hyperactivity improved and her concentration improved significantly. She is also very athletic and often asks to practice, and I am worried that she will be overloaded. At nine o'clock in the evening, the practice of the swimming team was over, and she asked me to play table tennis with her. The old mother said that she really could not move.

My daughter has a little friend in the studio, the little girl's mother looks very beautiful, she is curious about what the father looks like, I must drive her to the little friend's home. Coincidentally, the little girl's father was the same doctor who gave me tachyphotons and suggested that I seek help from a psychologist. To satisfy my daughter's curiosity, I actually took her to the father's studio and told the receptionist that I had a friend to introduce to Dr. Guo. The receptionist smiled and explained my purpose. I took my daughter and met Dr. Guo in the meeting room. He seemed very friendly and kindly came over to say hello to my daughter. I still remember my daughter's thoughtful expression as she looked at Dr. Guo. Children's world is really full of curiosity and surprise, and a small discovery can make them happy all day.

My daughter has always wanted to keep fish at home, so we bought some tropical fish to keep downstairs in the living room. When we got them home, the father said that the fish could not be put in ordinary tap water, and needed a special kind of water. Incredulous, my daughter and I asked him, "How do you know?" The father said, "Because I have a good father and he told me..." This really touched me. His father told him about it, and he told his daughter. Isn't such a small transmission of experience a transmission of love and warmth? This small sense of happiness fills me with satisfaction. Time goes by without us knowing it. If we don't recall these beautiful moments often, they will quietly disappear in the long river of memory. As time goes by, we may forget that we ever had these wonderful moments and feel that we are not happy. That day. The daughter was very active in helping to change the water, the special water her father called, and stayed in front of the small fish for a full two hours, while pointing to one of the colorful fish, excitedly Shouting: "Look, how beautiful this fish is!" For a while, he looked at a few fish playing in the water with surprise. Her little face was full of excitement and her eyes were bright all the time. The next morning, as soon as the little girl woke up, she ran downstairs to see the fish. Halfway down the stairs, she saw several small fish in the fish tank floating motionless on the surface of the water. Yes, her beloved little fish were all dead. The poor daughter cried bitterly.

Before, I was also a curious child, full of the desire to explore everything around, even others kill eel I would go over to see what it is. However, with the growth of years and repeated illness, I eventually became an "indifferent" adult, becoming less and less talkative. During treatment, I did what the doctor told me to do, and I took what medicine I took, no longer like a teenager. For quite some time, I also very calmly accepted this change, thinking that it is an inevitable process of growing up, we must abandon those naive curiosity, in order to become a mature adult.

However, my daughter's childlike innocence and curiosity made me re-examine myself and realize that curiosity is not only for children, but a state of mind that everyone should maintain. I hope to explore this wonderful world with my daughter in the days to come. In her company, I can find myself full of curiosity and expectation for the world again. At the same time, I also hope that I can be her partner and supporter in exploring the world during her growing up.

Recently, hyacinths have grown in my backyard. They are very beautiful. They come in dark purple and lavender. My daughter finished her homework early, practiced the piano, and then went to the backyard to pick a lilac hyacinth, especially fragrant. I suggested, "You can send this lovely scented flower to your teacher. He will surely feel your heart." My daughter nodded and said yes, but my speech caught me off guard. She said seriously: "Mom, I think about it, I don't want to give it to the teacher. I want to put this flower in front of you when you die." All at once, I felt a mixture of emotions that I could not describe. Is it gratifying? Is it moved? Or an unspeakable breakdown? The flower was beautiful in her heart, and she wanted to save the best for me, and I knew it was a pure unadorned love. But why could she not show her love to me with this flower while I was alive? Even though she has ADHD, I patiently guided her to understand the principles of the world, including the natural laws of birth, age, disease and death. I put a lot of effort into teaching her. The frustration of this education broke me briefly. It may also be that she thinks that good things should be given to her mother, but I have never given myself a birthday, so she thinks that the only time to send something to her mother is the day that her mother leaves, or that day is more special so she wants to send flowers, it is not excluded that the gift is flowers when I saw on TV to send a deceased person, etc., in short, I was devastated when I heard her childish language.

  I took her to take part in a physical training class. When she first went, she faced a challenge: goat jumping. Standing on the side of the jump box, she took off while resting her hands on the box and straddling it like a horse. That jump box is a little too high for her, and she tries many times and can't jump over it, always riding straight over it. But, she never gave up. After maybe four or five lessons, I was pleasantly surprised that she could already perform this move with proficiency. It was incredibly gratifying and touching to see her progress. At the same time, I feel worthy of my own efforts, but also feel the tenacity and growth of my child.

  It is in this interweaving of breakdown and healing that I have come all the way, each setback, each confusion, to understand my children more deeply, to observe their needs and reactions more carefully. Education is not something that can be done overnight. It takes time, patience, and trial and error. I hope that in this process, my child and I can grow together and become a better version of ourselves.

My son and my daughter also have completely different personalities. The contrast between the two children is obvious. For example, don't touch the jack. When I emphasize this to my daughter, she will touch it deliberately. If she can't touch it, she will find a small object and insert it. And my son, after listening to me, will ask me, "If it's so dangerous, why don't you find something to stuff it?" He's more inclined to make sense of the world through logic and reason than through adventure and challenge.

There are three boxes of mineral water under the cabinet in the living room, which are piled on top of each other in order not to bend over to take them. Pull the remaining half of the top layer of water, and what little mineral water is left inside will be dangling. The son seemed to find a new pleasure in it, and stood beside it and kept pulling it. Looking at the look of the mineral water swaying, worried about falling down and hitting him, I consciously restrained my impatience to lose my temper, and took a deep breath and patiently told him: "You don't do this. After a while the mineral water will fall down on your feet, very painful oh!" Listening to my exaggerated tone, he thought for a moment, moved two steps to the side, stood at what he thought was a safe distance, and continued to reach and pull with one hand to make the mineral water shake. "You can't do that," I said, "because you're not strong enough to fall and hit your foot. You have to push harder to fall." He thought about walking to the front of the mineral water with both hands to push the shaken mineral water back into the original position. After finishing, clap his hands, a very hard and relieved look: "Well, so that you will not hit everyone!"

He is not only very safety conscious, but also knows a little about health. Because I told him that when the weather is bad, for example, when it rains, he should wear small leather shoes that won't seep through water, and when the weather is good, he will remember. Every time he leaves the house he asks me, "What's the weather like today?" If the answer is that it's raining, he puts away his favorite pair of soft, breathable shoes. When he goes out, he must keep his hat on and zip it up. Also, he only drinks warm water. This serious look, really like a health care little old man!

I occasionally tell my children that "if they don't study, they will become useless" . When he didn't want to go to kindergarten, he would tell me, "Mom, I want to be a loser today." I was amazed and amused by his childish voice. If he caught me in a brief moment of laziness, he would teach me, "Are you trying to give up? Do you want to be a loser?" Well, I have a cutie pushing me behind my back!

A three-year-old has a bright brain. Every Thursday his sister goes to the studio for an hour and a half, and he wants to go, but he's too young and the studio doesn't accept him, so I take him to Pilates with my friends and I do sports with my friends and he checks his phone. One time my friend canceled our date because he had something to do. He said, "Mom, I want to go to the gym with you." Because he can look at my phone while I am doing sports. I answered him, "Baby, it takes two people to make a reservation at the sports side." He thought for a moment, "Mom, aren't you and I just two people? One more would make it three, you know?" The moment made me feel that this boy can develop into science.

I told my daughter and son a story about the lazy bird effect. There were two little birds. One was diligent from childhood and never slack in practicing flying. The other was very lazy and stayed in bed all day, relying on the diligent birds to bring food. After a long time, the flight skills of the diligent bird became very, very good. The lazy bird still lived a comfortable life, waiting for the food to come. One day there was a fire in the forest. The flames flew high and high and spread very, very fast. In the face of the fire, the diligent bird flew out with its strong wings and successfully escaped. However, the lazy bird was unable to fly because of the lack of exercise for a long time, and finally was burned to death.

At the end of the story, my son played a super logical thinking, said: "Mom, we have to learn every day, we are growing every day, dad always lying in bed looking at the mobile phone, then he is a lazy bird?" I answered with a smile: "Yes." He said firmly, "Then I'm going to work at the fire station. I want to be a fireman. I want to have a fireman's car. I want to have their tools. I want to be a fireman. If Daddy Bird gets burned, I want to save him." In an instant, a certain place in my heart seemed to be hit, and suddenly turned into a spring water, warm and soft. How can there be so much love, how can such small details be so warm? Suddenly my brain keeps searching back to my own youth. I don't know if I said anything at that time to move my family, or if my family has a moment to capture my childlike innocence and love.

My son is so sensible. He shows such maturity beyond his age that sometimes I even forget that he is still a child and treat him as an adult. When I get along with him, I don't always try to coax him, and I don't hug and kiss him too often, even to my sister. Maybe it's because I haven't been exposed to such displays of intimacy and affection myself since childhood and am not used to them. My daughter sometimes says to me, "Mommy, I want a hug," "Mommy, I want a kiss." At these times, I actively satisfy her by giving her hugs and kisses. But sometimes when I am in a bad mood or she acts naughty, I may unconsciously reject her, which will make her sad and cry. This is something I need to work on.

My brother's maturity often gives me the illusion that in two years, when he starts primary school, I may not have to worry about him anymore and he can handle everything on his own. I don't know where this confidence comes from.

Although my brother is mature in thinking, he is still a child after all because of his age, and his occasional naivete and childishness are very lovely.

He likes cars very much. Every time he goes to the supermarket, he has to "mention" all kinds of new cars. He often simulates traffic scenes and dubs cars

Chapter 6 Small Hands Hold Big Hands

with milk and gas. He is also a picky eater, candy and chocolate attraction to him is quite strong, every time he eats something in his mouth, or he sings.

Once, my aunt was on vacation, and I was too lazy to go out, so I decided to cook a bowl of noodles for them at home. The noodles were mixed with vegetables, poached eggs and sliced meat. They looked delicious and delicious. However, when my daughter tasted the noodles, she suddenly made a strange sound and spat out the noodles. When my son witnessed the scene, he immediately covered his mouth with one hand and swung the other hand in the air. His body involuntarily ducked back, expressing the intention of "no". He watched me, choosing his words for fear of hurting me: "Mom, I really love you, but I can't eat it. I'm so scared. Can I not eat it?" Seeing him like this, I really can't laugh or cry.

Although in most cases my brother is a very healing child, there are moments that break my heart. While I was working out at the yoga studio, he happened to be in his drawing class. His class was over and I wasn't done with my exercise, so to keep him from running off, I found his favorite Spider-Man on my phone.

However, as I finished my exercise and prepared to leave, he said, "I'll watch it a little longer." To be fair, I proposed to play rock-paper-scissors: "If you lose, we'll stop watching and go home; If you win, we'll watch an extra minute." He readily agreed, but sadly lost, but he was unwilling to accept the result and asked to play again. I firmly refused his request, after all, it was after eight o'clock and we needed to go home. But he cried and screamed and even hit me. I ignored him.

Then we went to the car to wait for our daughter. Her teacher took her out to eat and do some homework, and then dropped her off. When her daughter got into the car, she asked her brother curiously why he was crying. I tried to tell the story as calmly as possible, but my voice broke with frustration and exhaustion. I did my best for these two children every day, helping them arrange all kinds of after-school activities they wanted to learn, taking care of their daily life and diet, and taking care of their emotions. Now, my son is beating me because he refuses to let them look at his phone.

When my daughter heard the grievance in my voice, she could not keep up. She burst into tears and grabbed my arm and said, "Mom, you must not write it down in the book. We will be very sad to see it later."

However, as a habit of keeping track of my life, I decided to write it down in a book. I understood my daughter's concern. She knew what my brother was doing was wrong, and she wanted our family to be harmonious and happy. But I know that what my son did was just a child's subconscious behavior and that he did not mean me ill. The real record allows us to better review and reflect, and I believe that when my children and I read this story again, we will surely see the growth and change of each other.

2. My children teach me to learn

When I was a child, I witnessed the elders with their legs crossed and cigarettes in their mouths playing cards, mah-jongg and cards in rooms where the smoke filled their eyes. Smoking, drinking and staying up late were the norm. It seemed that no one would leave society and keep up with the trend, spending money frivolously and never taking money seriously. Under the influence of such a family environment, I also learned to live up to expectations of these habits, fingers gently across any mahjong card is not out of touch, my mother and I live under the same roof, often busy with their respective card game, wine bureau about one or two months will meet. I also think that money is to be used, money is spent anyway are won. And I believe that life is meant to be enjoyed to the fullest, that is, to play cards and smoke and drink. On the contrary, I can't understand why adults must ask us to read and study, smoking and drinking do not use the multiplication table, right?

At that time, I did not understand what was meant by family responsibility and family values. I never thought that family and marriage should be maintained, nor did I think that people need to communicate to reach a consensus, but simply thought that marriage was to get a marriage license, then have children, and live in the same house. There is no concept of raising children. Do parents still need to accompany their children? Do they need to nurture their children? When you have a baby, you have a baby. How the child grows and develops is up to the child. These are the values of family and parenting that the previous generation left to me.

Until my daughter changed me.

When my daughter was three or four, I started looking for a preschool and came across one that was highly recommended as excellent. However, because all the staff spoke English, I had no way to communicate with them and eventually gave up. Looking back now, I realize I didn't make the right decision. After all, in an English-speaking environment like America, it was important for her to have a solid English foundation early on. At present, the main reason why my daughter is struggling in her studies is that she does not understand English and has difficulty understanding it.

At the age of five, she became interested in dancing and drawing, showing a strong desire to learn. But at that time, I was too sick to get out of it. I was very resistant to driving, let alone communicating with training institutions and teachers in English. So I had no choice but to send an advertisement asking a Chinese-speaking teacher to come to my home and teach her singing and dancing.

As she grew older, she saw that her classmates had mastered many skills, and she was eager to learn them. Her thirst for knowledge grew stronger. I was infected by her attitude of loving to learn. She was eager for everything, which made me realize that I must create a better learning environment and conditions for her. No matter what, I must do something for her more or less. Then look at her painting day by day more beautiful, watching her can write more and more day by day, watching her grasp of knowledge day by day richer, I feel that people do need to learn, to some environment, can really grow up.

Once, because the next class is very close, I went to school ten minutes in advance to pick her up. Who knows, as soon as she left the school gate, she began to shed tears and said very aggrieved, "Why do you want to pick me up so early? The class is not over yet!" Having dinner with a friend, my friend has three children at home, and my daughter especially likes to play with them. At the lunch table, the children happily discussed the toys, my daughter ran to my friend, asked the other person a math problem, my friend said: "You don't drive her crazy, she came to ask me she can't do math problems." This really does not blame me, she is not the first time to ask others when eating math problems, usually like to play watch in the computer. And drawing. Because of her ADHD, she was disturbing the other kids in the studio, and the studio didn't want her to stay. When she found out, she had tears in her eyes and said, "Mom, I will never run to talk to my classmates or run around the studio again. I want to paint." That innocent, wistful look really made my heart sour and soft.

Watching my daughter's growing enthusiasm for learning, I could not help but think of my own resistance and resistance. Every time I faced the learning of new skills, I was always very nervous, afraid that I would not learn, afraid that I would make mistakes, afraid that others would look at me differently and laugh at me. I never go to the car wash alone because I can't get on the tracks at the car wash, the people behind me honk constantly, and I can't understand the automatic payment page in English. In addition, as a deep coffee lover, I was afraid to buy coffee from the store because of the language barrier, so I had to buy a coffee machine to make my own undrinkable coffee at home. All these are because I am afraid of the inconvenience caused by study.

I think it's time for me to try to learn some new skills. Not only for my daughter, but also for myself. The more I played sports, the more I realized the importance of learning and began to try different sports. In addition to yoga, I also tried running, squash, Zumba, swimming, etc., even though I was afraid of water. There are so many interesting things in this world, no wonder my daughter likes to learn.

Recently, I have been thinking about a question. With the development of society, electronic and intelligent has become a part of our daily life. Our generation is lucky to have a certain understanding and contact with electronic devices and systems. However, for some people older than me, they may never touch a computer, or even know how to turn it on and off. Of course, this does not mean that they have no knowledge and culture, they may be highly educated and have deep knowledge in a certain field, but they don't know anything about computers. This kind of comparison makes me wonder, in the past, people in their 40s and 50s May feel that they are entering the sign of old age, starting to move on to the second half of life. In this era of information explosion, the growth of age no longer means anything, no matter how old, the pace of learning can not stop. The change of knowledge is so fast that what we learn may soon be out of date. This requires us to constantly learn new knowledge and upgrade our skills in order to keep pace with The Times.

Increasing age no longer means decreasing ability or decreasing desire to learn. Instead, it should serve as motivation for us to continue exploring and growing. Living in this era of rapid change, we need lifelong learning and constantly updating our knowledge base to remain competitive and adaptable.

And after watching The Courage to Be Hated, I accepted that I don't speak English. Everyone is good at different things. There are so many things to learn

抑郁自救笔记
Notes on Depression Self-help

in the world. I can't speak English, and you may not speak Chinese. I can play mahjong, but you may not know it. So I started trying to wash my own car, even though the cars behind me honked their horns because it took me too long to pay. I went to the store to buy coffee and typed the name I wanted in a translator. I went to western restaurants and found the food I liked according to the pictures on the menu. Go to various supermarkets... I began to embrace life positively and bravely.

My son observed that both my daughter and I were working hard, and especially when seeing his sister paint, he offered to learn to paint as well. When he saw his sister taking Chinese lessons, he insisted that we arrange the same lessons for him as well. The point is that a three-year-old can sit in front of an iPad for an hour, intently learning Chinese from the teacher, and answer all the questions the teacher asks. Regardless of whether he got the answers right or wrong, I was amazed by his enthusiasm and concentration.

The atmosphere in the home has a huge impact on a child's development, something I am only now realizing. If the child is not born very self-discipline, we do not create a good learning environment for him, but do nothing all day, cross legs, smoking and playing majao, how can we expect the child to calm down to study, or even to achieve a career? This is absolutely impossible. They can be studying hard one minute and playing games the next, completely unable to face up to their future plans.

Sometimes I wonder if I have so many lessons for my daughter that she doesn't have time to play. But when I think about it, it is not my initiative to give her such a full schedule of classes. All the courses are those she is interested in and actively asks to learn. Sometimes even at 9 o'clock in the evening, she still hopes that I can arrange some more classes for her.

Many people think that a child's childhood should be about having fun and having fun. This is true, but I look at her in class, tutoring that happy smile,

I think, she in class is not already playing it? Every time after mastering a knowledge point, the smile on her face, the sense of satisfaction, is really like a harvest. Perhaps learning and play are not mutually exclusive. After all, every child is unique and has his or her own way of understanding and experiencing the world. As long as we give them enough love and support, they will naturally find their own way.

I once saw a particularly naughty child do something that I thought would be severely reprimanded by adults. I thought to myself, this child must be miserable, wait to see what his parents will do to him. However, to my surprise, things didn't work out the way I thought they would. Instead of punishing him, his parents treated him with treasure and communicated with him. I was puzzled at that time, I didn't understand how any parents could teach their children like that. If what that child did had happened to me as a child, I would have been punished, maybe even beaten to death. I even had a picture in my mind of being beaten as a child for being naughty. When my daughter makes a mistake, I often think in my heart: Only I, a good mother, can forgive her and tolerate her. But the child incident made me realize that harsh punishment is not a common phenomenon.

I reflected on why I felt this way, and it may have something to do with my experience of being beaten up from a young age. I thought this way of being treated was the norm and everyone should experience it. But now I understand that the way I was treated was not the same as the way everyone else was treated. Every family is raised differently, and spanking is not something every family does.

I accompanied my daughter to a little boy's birthday party. The atmosphere was pleasant. The children were playing and the mothers were chatting together, mostly about school. When it came time to cut the cake, the child's mother said some words to express her gratitude to the child, praising him for being sensible and taking care of his brother. This scene made me feel very much, my initial idea is that being a mother should be like this, using praise to let the child know some things and grow up.

But when I got home, I thought about it, and I thought I might have been wrong. Education is diverse, and each family has its own unique way of education. Because different families have different cultural backgrounds, educational concepts, children's personalities, growth environment and other factors. Some families may pay more attention to cultivating their children's independence, encouraging them to actively participate in various activities and social occasions, and exercise their communication and collaboration skills; Some families may put more emphasis on academic achievement and knowledge, and provide their children with abundant learning resources and guidance. Others may pay more attention to their children's emotional education and mental health, and strive to create a warm and harmonious family atmosphere for them. As for my children, I hope they can focus more on their own happiness and growth at their current age, rather than taking on the responsibility of being sensible too early. Of course, this is not to say that we do not guide and educate children, but we should pay more attention to the inner needs of children, so that they can grow up in a happy atmosphere. For example, my daughter's birthday party, what she wants most is a super big cake and a video to follow the whole process, hoping that the whole party is full of mermaid elements. I tried my best to fulfill her wish by placing the lollipops that she rarely eats, so that she and her friends could have the simplest happiness in a joyful atmosphere. For another example, I am a very anxious person, in raising children, I naturally hope that they learn more things, understand a wider range of things, and can be used in the future. At the same time, I also hope that they can have more social insight, the so-called more to see the world. This means that I hope they can come into contact with more diverse people and environments, understand the diversity and complexity of society, so that they can better adapt to society in the future. Every

Wednesday, Ian, my daughter's tutor, takes her out to dinner, whether it's a fancy restaurant or an everyday restaurant. I want her to see different aspects of life in the process, and to understand that our family can provide her with such a rich variety of life experiences and let her enjoy these wonderful times. My intention is not just for her to experience material superiority, but also for her to develop independent, sensible values. I don't want her to be easily misled by others in the future because of a few fancy restaurant dinners or some seemingly glamorous appearance in the circle of friends.

The diversity of parenting styles brings some challenges and opportunities as well as references to parents. The challenge is how to find the most suitable parenting style for their children, not only to avoid overindulgence, to ensure that the children will not become spoiled, but also to ensure that they can deeply feel the warmth and love from the family, so as to build a healthy emotional foundation; Preventing an overly harsh parenting style that can lead to depression and frustration, and ensuring that they are upright and develop a personality that is both disciplined and creative.

3. An equal parent-child relationship

My son's character is very different from mine. He always hopes that others will reason with him. Every time he tells him something, he will stare at you with two eyes and listen carefully to what you are saying. After listening, he will think for himself. After thinking about it, he will also raise some relevant questions and feedback. I also express my thoughts directly. "I'm angry," "I'm unhappy," "I don't like what you're doing" ... In the parlance of the day, it's never internal. Before my period, hormones are in full swing, hormones are completely out of control, and I occasionally lose my temper with him. He would also burst into tears, clasping his hands to his chest: "Huh, I'm ignoring you." But then he comes to me again, "Meow... I'm a Kitty..." This is for "reconciliation" . It melted my heart. It was very warm. Thank you for turning into a cutie to defuse my anger after being scolded. So I realized something about my son: Not all problems need to be solved with violence and loud scolding. On the contrary, as long as we explain patiently in a gentle tone, and make clear the harm and importance of the problem, the child can understand and understand.

Although I understand this truth, it is really hard for me to do this rationally when things happen.

For example, my son wakes up first in the morning and a few moments later I hear my daughter talking in the bedroom. I told her downstairs to brush her teeth and wash her face quickly, put on her school uniform and send her to school. That day, the aunt at home just rest, after finishing breakfast, I have to prepare my daughter to take lunch to school. A whole morning, I like a top, busy round and round. And I hate cooking so much that I get upset when I walk into the kitchen.

By the time I've got everything ready, I haven't seen my daughter come downstairs. When I went upstairs and saw her lying in bed pretending to be asleep, the anger inside me was instantly ignited. I tried to wake her up by patting her in spite of my anger, but she still pretended to be asleep and didn't move. "Did you really not hear me call you?" "I raised my decibel level, my tone serious. She opened her bleary-eyed eyes: "Mom, I really didn't hear it, I just woke up and fell asleep again." Despite her explanation, I was still upset and urged her to hurry up and wash up. When we got to the top of the stairs, I went back and accused my daughter of dragging her feet and having no sense of time.

When I went downstairs, my son broke the tense atmosphere: "Sister, you see mom is so hard today, there are a lot of things to do." He approached his sister and asked, "Sister, are you very tired today?" Someone is concerned, the daughter's mood can not be stretched, wet eyes: "I really fell asleep."

Looking at her grievance, I suddenly felt sorry for herself, whether she was too fierce, but I know that my character is very impatient, it is difficult to keep calm in anger.

After breakfast, my daughter volunteered to put away the dishes. She knew that my aunt was not here today and wanted to share some housework for me. In fact, she is already a very sensible child.

After all, children are children, they have their own nature and rhythm, we can not ask them to think and act like adults. If we ask them to be as disciplined as adults, they can do anything, which is unfair to them.

It really hit home to me when my daughter was taking a bath after a swim. I saw two overlapping fuchsia teeth marks on her right back shoulder. One was light, the other was deep, and the bite was purple. It seemed that she was trying hard to get down. When I asked my daughter what was going on, she said they had been bitten by a classmate. "People bite you, why don't you stop it? And two bites in a row! ' 'I asked eagerly. My daughter was aggrieved. "They wouldn't play with me, but then I was in so much pain that I told him to stop. When I was in really, really bad pain, I asked him to stop." When I heard this, I felt a mixture of anger and heartache. What she meant was that she had to put up with the pain in order to please the other children, so that they could play with her. I dread to think what would happen if it got worse. If my daughter reaches puberty and someone threatens her in a similar way, you can play with me, but you have to give something, will she buckle?

After comforting my daughter, I communicated with my teacher. After I calmed down, I began to reflect on my parenting style and found that I was deeply influenced by my childhood in the treatment of my children. My childhood was an unhappy one, filled with the anger and petulance of adults, who always communicated with me in a rough and impatient way. Now I am exactly the kind of person I hate, and although I remind myself every moment to raise them with love, I can't hide the little things I have experienced as a child. I put too much emphasis on rules and discipline in my interactions with my children, and not enough on the transmission of emotion. Sometimes I may communicate with my children in an imperative tone that makes them feel oppressed.

I have to change my relationship with my child in time. I have to communicate with my child in a gentler, patient and understanding way. I try to use more hugs and encouragement to let her know that I will be there for her no matter what she does. Sometimes I think that I should treat myself as a child, get along with the children from an equal perspective, and integrate into them. I should listen to their ideas and opinions carefully and give them positive feedback in time. Even if their opinions are different from ours, respect their rights and encourage them to express their opinions.

This has been a challenge for me to change my temper and the habits I grew up with, but I hope to build a healthier, more loving home environment where my children will grow up in an atmosphere of support and encouragement.

Six months ago, my daughter came to me to talk about her troubles. She told me that she found herself different from other children, felt strange and even didn't like herself. Hearing these words, I felt very confused, surprised, sad, and anxious. I immediately gave her my support and encouragement and tried my best to convey to her the importance of loving myself. I was thankful that I had the time to reflect on the last time my daughter was bitten, and to adjust the way I dealt with my children so that my daughter could be bold enough to share her thoughts with me. There was still enough time to nip this negativity in the bud. After this, I also discussed the issue with her tutor, Ian. I'm sure he talked to her about it too. Although I don't know exactly what they talked about, I do know that the conversation and encouragement had a positive effect on her. I asked her again if she liked her and she replied: "Yes, we are all different individuals, everyone is different, to accept their own shortcomings, for example, I am very slow and procrastinator, but this is me, I still love my procrastination." A: Wait! She says she drags! Suddenly, her newly relieved heart is filled with new anxiety. My daughter seems to be telling me that she knows she procrastinates, accepts all her shortcomings and has no plans to correct them... Well, at least she knows how to love herself.

She is entering a drawing competition soon and is in the idea stage. I asked her, "Can you share your idea with me?" She replied, "Everyone is an imperfect version of themselves, everyone is flawed. But we have to love ourselves." I said, "So how are you going to draw it?" And she said, "I'm going to draw a little girl who doesn't love herself and is confused and looks like she's going to fall into a pool. Then when she figures it out, she'll sprout wings, become colored, and fly out of the pool that's trapping her." The next words shocked me even more: "She is beautiful, and no matter how imperfect she may be, she is her own person, and she will accept her imperfections." This painting symbolizes her acceptance of who she is, and I am comforted by her growth, from a confused child to a brave girl who knows how to love herself. No matter how many flaws and inadequacies a person has, he is unique and deserves to be treated with tenderness and love.

4. The Me in my child

My daughter always says that a cute brother makes for a funny mom, and a funny mom makes for a weird daughter. Since last year, she has wanted to get married at every turn. She made a pact with a little boy in her community who she had met only once or twice to get married when she grew up. While chatting, tell her teacher, "It's time for you to get married." I asked her, "Daughter, why do you want to get married? Do you think getting married is a happy thing?"

She said, "Yes, marriage is a very happy thing. In the future, I will be good to my babies. If they want to learn to draw, I will arrange lessons for them to learn to draw. If they want to swim, I will take them to swim. If there's anything they want to do, I'll arrange it for them..." I continued, "How do you make money?" "At this time, you are already making money, I am a restaurant owner! I will cook a lot of delicious dishes, and then let my husband take to the restaurant to sell, earn a lot of money. I can use this money for my baby to share with them, give them lessons, buy them delicious food..."

Looking at her, I realized in a split second that children are like a mirror, reflecting our appearance, learning and replicating our behaviors and traits. In her idea, our family is happy, the mother is love to learn, the mother is especially love the baby, the baby to do what the mother will take them to do. What she feels is that mother is very happy and happy to do all this, so she looks forward to the future is also like this. I am grateful that I have created a positive and happy home atmosphere for my children, providing emotional support and a sense of security. Of course, I blame myself a little bit. I was still deeply sick when my daughter was young, and I missed out on many important moments with her. At the same time, because of my own resistance to English, I sadly missed out on her early childhood, when she had a solid English foundation. Now, looking at my lively and lovely son in front of me, I often try to remember whether my daughter had such a lovely side when she was young, but I only have a little sense of picture. I am annoyed at myself for being so troubled by an invisible disease that I miss my daughter's precious childhood growth. I can't make up for it, but I know that I should cherish the moment, accompany my children wholeheartedly, create new memories together, and never be absent from their growth.

The learning of various skills and knowledge may be beyond my ability, so I can only find professional teachers to guide them, but it is the responsibility of parents to shape the spiritual level. What we need to do is not only verbal encouragement or temporary encouragement, but we should show the right values and positive attitude towards life through our own actions. Children learn from our actions. They observe how we face challenges, how we deal with difficulties, and how we maintain a positive attitude.

On March 31, 2024, at 8:15 am, I accompanied my daughter to finish her first 5km outdoor run. Before she ran out of the neighborhood, she fell down and skinned her knees. I asked her if she could carry on. She cried and said, "I'm okay mom, I can finish it." At the end of the run, her Apple Watch gave her 5 sports MEDALS, she was very happy, her little face was full of happiness, as if she had conquered the world. Every time I saw the smile on her face, my heart became very warm and soft.

After that, I took my daughter to participate in a marathon. This time, my mentality was completely different from the nervous and hesitant I had been when I participated in the marathon myself. Last time, the day before the race, I was tossing and turning and couldn't sleep. Even when I got up the next day, I had some resistance and hesitated to go. But this time was different. I made a point of driving more than an hour a day earlier to pick up my marathon number card, which was more than two hours round trip. At 6 am the next morning, I got ready and drove my daughter to the starting point of the marathon. There was no slack in the whole process, but I felt that it was a rare experience to experience the charm and atmosphere of the marathon with my daughter.

My daughter is really good. The first time we ran together, she ran six kilometers in one go. I couldn't believe it. My brother is only 4 years old now, but he can run with me a little. He also offered to run with me, saying, "Mom, train me to run. Long distances are too hard for me. I run short distances. I want to run marathons with you someday. I am very happy that because of my influence, children can love sports so much from an early age and have a healthy body.

Of course, the influence goes both ways. I try to be a positive role model for my children and lead them on a positive path in life. At the same time, they continue to inspire me and make me more determined to move forward in a better direction. We influence each other and grow together, forming a positive interaction and feedback.

"Lucky people spend their lives being healed by childhood, and unlucky people spend their lives healing childhood." Unfortunately, I fall into the latter category; But luckily I have two lovely little friends - my daughter and son. Big hands holding small hands, trust, dependence and love are passed between them. In the process of accompanying them to grow up, it is as if I have walked through my own childhood and raised my childhood self again. I was always struck by their innocence and childlike innocence, one of the few holy places of purity in the world. When I am with them, I feel as if I am in a flawless world. I can take off the armor of defense, look inside myself, and let all the anxiety and fickleness go to peace.

Chapter 7 The Revolution of the Self

We like to walk in the light, but sometimes the most powerful light comes not from the outside world, but from our own inner revolution. Every challenge, every change in our mindset, is a step in our own redemption, a revolution in our own self. Life is like a never-ending practice, in which I stumble, but also in which gradually mature and strong. Looking back on the past, I can see that the confusion and confusion I once had have now become a precious treasure.

In costume dramas, the young masters of the school are possessed by evil spirits. The evil spirit is the former servant of his father, who intends to use the body of the young Lord to strengthen himself and save his imprisoned master, the Young Lord's father. At the critical moment, a celestial from the outer heaven came and cast out the evil spirit from the little Lord's body, allowing the Little Lord to recover his sanity. When the little Lord talked with this celestial being for a long time, another voice suddenly sounded in his head, which gave him a splitting headache and made his heart struggle. When confronted with this, the celestial said, "It seems that no external force is trying to invade your body and control your will. Sometimes it is your own inability to control your inner turmoil that turns you against yourself."

Those words struck me deeply. It is true that many of the troubles and struggles in life are not caused by external pressure or interference, but by our inner fears, doubts and insecurities. It is only when we learn to master our inner self that we can truly emerge from difficult situations and embrace a brighter future.

抑郁自救笔记
Notes on Depression Self-help

1. Be the master of your emotions

In our daily lives, we often encounter a variety of emotional triggers, and anger is one of the most intense and difficult to control. However, learning how to properly deal with anger and stress is an important issue that all of us must face. Let's discuss how to deal with anger and stress correctly, using a series of trivial things that I experienced some time ago as an example.

I bought some local products of my hometown in China and asked my friends to send them to my selected Courier company for transfer to my destination. This express company will compensate the lost goods according to the price and refund the freight. I have also confirmed with her again and again whether the compensation terms are true. The previous two mailing processes were relatively smooth, and I received the packages without any danger. However, the last package did not arrive, and there was no news. When I contacted the Courier company to ask about the situation, they insisted that only two cases had been sent and that I had only paid for two cases of transfer.

My friend clearly sent me 3 packages weighing 85 jin, but I only received 2 packages weighing 30 jin. In the face of my repeated questioning, the Courier company began to make vague statements. First they told me it was stuck at customs, then they said they needed to send it through another slower channel. But I didn't know anything about it. When I asked again, they began to avoid answering. This went on for half a month, and my patience wore thin as the urge to get something fast, the thousands of expensive airfreight costs and the resulting extreme frustration and anger, aside from the value of the item, reached its peak. In the heat of the moment, I sent the other party a text that bluntly pointed out the irresponsibility of the other party's behavior, even the most basic honesty. To my

Chapter 7 The Revolution of the Self

surprise, she turned on me and eventually blocked me.

I understood that the reason why they were so arrogant was that they thought I was abroad and could not deal with them face to face. Even in China, how many people would go out of their way to negotiate with them face to face for an express delivery? Faced with this dilemma, should I just sulk on my own?

We moved to a new city because of our daughter's schooling. The day before we moved into the house, Ralph, the owner, went over every inch of it and took pictures of every damage or mark to make sure I returned an identical one when I checked out. I made it clear that if there was any damage I would be responsible for repainting the entire house to make sure it was back to its original state, but the attentive Ralph insisted on taking photos of each one. Perhaps because I am used to being careless, I feel a little uncomfortable with this extremely meticulous approach. I think it is too troublesome and untrustworthy. But I also understand that everyone has his own way of life and principles, Ralph may just be used to this way to protect his property, so I still choose to respect and try my best to cooperate.

This Ralph just bought the house and rented it to me, so he has not lived in this house himself, so he is quite strange here. Of course, the result is that the house has not been thoroughly repaired and maintained, so I have to deal with all kinds of little problems. According to the rental practice here, he is responsible for repairing any problems in the house, no matter how big or small, and it is also stated in the signed rental contract that Ralph repairs the house and the outside. Tenants can only cherish the house. Seeing that the weather was going to be hot soon, I found that the window screen of the house had been removed and had not been installed, so I called the renovation master. The master said that the handle of the screen was broken, and the part of the mesh was also damaged, and I needed to buy a new one to replace it. When Ralph heard this, he said he would see if he could fix it himself. He came to check, taped up all the holes, and bought a new lock to replace, but the new lock was the wrong size and model. After hours of trying to fix it himself, he went home and tried to buy a new doorknob.

A short time later, when he got a new, better fit, he asked me, "Can you install it?" I said, "I can't, I've never done any of this and I don't want to." He said, "Would your aunt do it?" I said, "Auntie is in her 70s, do you think she would fake it?" He said: "This is very simple, you just ask her to learn it." I said, "Sorry, my aunt has to cook and wash clothes, and she does all the housework by herself. She is already very hard and has no time to learn this." And since she's in her 70s, I don't think she has the obligation or the ability to learn how to put together a window screen.

One day, an employee from the water department dropped by and did a detailed leak inspection of the home. After making sure that all the taps were closed, the officer said the meter was still running slowly, indicating a hidden leak somewhere in the home. After a careful search and investigation, we finally found the location of the leak. There was an outdoor faucet that was broken. Although it was closed tightly, it kept leaking. After identifying the leak, Ralph immediately purchased a timer and came to install it himself. I wasn't home when it was installed, so when it was time to use it later, Ralph showed me how to use the timer by video call while reading the instructions himself. However, the video instructions were not so clear and effective. The steps were cumbersome and difficult to understand. You had to click on a menu, hold down a function key for five seconds, then jump to another selection key, then untap the left outlet pipe and switch it to the right one... In short, it takes a series of operations to complete the water smoothly. Wait, please pay attention here, change the faucet to another outlet, this timer has two outlets, can easily twist the water outlet I think it is rare.

In this regard, I am somewhat dissatisfied, the housework in our home is taken care of by a 70-year-old aunt, she can not even use simple electronic

Chapter 7 The Revolution of the Self

products, and can not even use wechat to send videos, let alone such a complex operation. I am very confused, why can't Ralph directly replace a tap that is easy to operate, and the water will come out directly after a twist, which is not good for simple and practical? But he said he couldn't find it, and so on. I still can't understand the specific reasons. Now the water has been leaking, then I have to bear the extra water bill?

In short, I have no choice but to temporarily agree to use a timer, at least to solve the problem of leakage first, to avoid water waste and unnecessary water charges. I think it is really not possible to use this faucet every time before the operation by me to open, and then let my aunt do the follow-up content such as watering flowers, and it is manual watering flowers. According to the law, the tenant only uses the automatic watering system and is not responsible for watering the flowers manually. Who knows the plumber Ralph went to the next day didn't use the timer, he took it off, didn't put it back on, and the faucet kept leaking. I could only text Ralph again to ask for a solution, only to find that his words said that I had complained about the leak and that I had been complaining.

I was curious what part of my message made him think I was complaining all the time. After all, I pay the water bill, the faucet has been leaking, of course I will be annoyed, this problem has not been solved, it is a problem for me, after all, the water bill is paid by me, because of the leak, I have paid more than $1,000 water bill, you know, normally 2 months water bill is about 200.

In the process of communicating and solving the faucet, Ralph and I also had disagreements over the replacement cost. I asked the repairman how much it cost to replace a simple faucet that is used in everyday families. The other side said that the cost of manual materials was 200 dollars, but Ralph said that the repairman told him that it was 100 dollars, and it only took 50 or 60 dollars to install the timer, so he chose the timer instead of replacing the faucet. I am not sure that the repairman will tell him 100 dollars, because with the price of labor in the United States, it is impossible. Later, I reviewed the chat records with him and his clear words said that the two faucets were replaced for a total of 300 dollars, which reminded me of the first day we moved into this new home. At that time, I had a cleaning company do a thorough cleaning of the entire house, including deep pipe cleaning of the central air conditioning, carpet cleaning, various pipe cleaning and other things. I have always asked this company to help me clean my house. Last year, I spent 700 dollars to clean my house. Then this year, they told me that I needed 1000 dollars for this house, because the area of the house has become larger, the cleaning work is much longer, and the amount of work is much larger. The day after the cleaning, Ralph asked me how much it cost and I said 1000. He looked surprised. He said how could it be? He told me it was 650. At that time, I was confused, I thought to myself that I have a good relationship with the wife of the cleaning company, how can I say 650 to you and 1000 to me? What's more, when I was cleaning at my house, I paid 700. It's not possible that it got cheaper, right? These two price differences, as if I deliberately high prices can profit from the same, then again, the cleaning money is my own and Ralph has nothing to do with the difference in the amount of my heart is very uncomfortable.

I temporarily solved the faucet leak, and there was a problem with the door at home. One of the doors went off the rails. The door was made of solid wood and was very heavy, and my aunt and I tried for a long time but couldn't fix it properly. What worries me most is what to do if such a heavy door suddenly falls down and accidentally hits the children. After I communicated with Ralph, he said that he was not in the local area, and I did not ask the specific time to repair the door. A few days later, another lock was also broken, which could not be opened and could not be twisted at all. I used something to pry loose the lock and shook the lock with all my strength for a long time before it was opened. When the door lock finally arrived, I found that the model was wrong. Another derailed door simply pushed the track back on, not realizing that the track was loose because of years of use, which could easily collapse again due to the weight of the door. Sure enough, as soon as we pulled, the door fell back down again. Concerned about the weight of the door and the safety of the children, I advised Ralph to call a professional repairman to fix the problem once and for all. Instead, he confronted me about whether the door was being used properly and whether the children were pulling the door hard while playing? Isn't the proper way to use a door to pull it open and close it? And are children strong enough to pull a solid wooden door that adults find difficult? Ralph began to scold me. "I come over every week and fix things for you... You can't even do the basic thing of taking the faucet off and switching it to the other side, you need someone to help you..." These words really make me laugh, repeated home repair is not because the house is too old and not professionally repaired? Isn't it because you repeatedly buy the wrong parts? From window screens and faucets to now door locks, the problems are endless. I have no complaints that such back-and-forth repairs will take up my time and affect the normal life of my family. I pay the rent on time every month, and Ralph is certainly responsible for making sure that the facilities are in good working order. Why should I change my lifestyle just because something is wrong with your house?

"Earlier, he had also said to my aunt," You let her do it, she's still so young. She was referring to me, which made me feel deeply offended and uncomfortable. Aside from the fact that it was a family matter, he was in no position as the owner to interfere; Even if I was willing and able to handle the chores, why would I hire a babysitter? Everyone has a limited amount of energy. I have to take care of the kids, keep busy with my job, and now I just moved and have to fix up the house. I really don't feel like I can handle it all in my stride. What's more, I have to keep an eye on and take care of my emotional and mental health to keep my life in balance, and all this clutter makes me feel even more exhausted.

This is clearly not an irreconcilable contradiction, but a matter of attitude. If Ralph had carried out thorough maintenance and inspection of the house before handing it over, instead of spending a lot of time taking pictures to facilitate the division of responsibilities later, I believe the conflict between us would have been greatly reduced. Similarly, if Ralph can choose accessories more carefully during the maintenance process to avoid increasing the difficulty and complexity of maintenance due to the wrong purchase, I believe I am not an unreasonable person. Wouldn't it be better if the easiest way was to get a professional to deal with it? Many renters who come across any naturally broken or aging accessories will call the landlord directly to have them dealt with. What I can do by myself, I try to do by myself. When we first moved in, there were a lot of small areas that were broken, so I asked the master to fix them myself. For example, one of the blinds needed to be replaced. Ralph said go ahead and work out the cost with him then. I also did not quarrel with him, because the cost of replacing a blind is only about 200. I think it is not necessary to quarrel with such small problems. I also paid to repair the pipe falling out of the dryer before, and there are many other repairs. And now he's... I also thought about fixing 200 faucets myself and calling it a day, but I don't want to keep indulging him like this.

When it comes to attitude, it reminds me of picking up my daughter from school. As soon as my daughter got into the car and we were about to leave, a car pulled up to park in the space next door. It was a narrow space and I had a feeling it was going to rub up against me. When I tried to warn the other driver, the woman gave me a look of hatred. Well, I decided to stay still and wait for her to complete the stop. As expected, it hit, her mirror clipped mine, making a "clang" that took a bit of paint off. However, she only glanced at me before leaving with a look of hatred and contempt in her eyes. Now it's my turn to wonder. Shouldn't you apologize for bumping into me? Are you going to "kill" me with a look and turn away? When she parked, I opened the window and asked her in

Chapter 7 The Revolution of the Self

stilted English, "Do you know you just hit me? "(Do you know you just hit me?) "She responded," Yes, I hit you, but it didn't look serious, just a light scratch." I followed up with, "And then what? Do you owe me an apology?" Then she smiled and said, "Oh, I'm sorry." I responded, "That's okay, leave it at that." And then I left.

Actually, the seriousness of the matter often depends on the attitude of the other person. The woman apologized promptly, and I instantly felt that even if she shaved my mirror badly, it wasn't too much of a problem because her attitude was very good. If she continued to look at me with that hateful look and didn't apologize, I might choose to call the police, even if it made things complicated. I just want to have an outlet for my inner emotions, but I don't want to get any substantive compensation. In the several frictions between Ralph and him, he kept accusing me and even tried to dominate me, not only beyond his proper limits, but also ignored the respect and rights I should have as a tenant. In life, no matter it is a small friction or a big conflict, with a peaceful and understanding heart to deal with, with a positive attitude to communicate, often can solve the problem invisible. However, those who face problems negatively and try to avoid responsibility only make things more complicated.

I was under Ralph's influence for the next few days and was not in a good mood. On the way home to pick up my daughter, unable to concentrate, my mind was filled with messages from him: "I thought it was hard for you, but now you take others for granted... I just can't believe that you've been in the United States for so many years and still have such a big girl mentality... I can't believe that instead of being grateful, you just get worse..." These words distracted my attention. The speed limit was 25 miles per hour on that road, but I was doing 30 miles per hour when I was stopped by a policeman on the side of the road with his lights flashing. I stopped the car and when the policeman got out of the car, I was surprised to see that he was the same man who had been in my house the other day. That day, my friend parked his car on the side of the road instead of in front of my house, causing a misunderstanding among the neighbors, which resulted in two police cars coming, and he was one of them.

I tried to break the awkwardness with a lighthearted tone, bringing up previous events and trying to introduce myself and my situation in broken English. The policeman smiled and, remembering the day too, nodded and said, "Yes, I remember." I asked him in broken English, "Are you going to give me a ticket?" He hesitated, then smiled and said, "Let it go this time, but don't drive so fast next time."

At that moment, I really felt my inner growth. Ten years ago, I was also ticketed for speeding. I was taken to court and ordered not to have any infractions for seven years, or they would take away my license. At that time, I was silent. I just obediently handed my license to the police. However, now I dare to use my poor English to communicate and fight for my rights and interests. Even though I can only squeeze a few words out of my broken English as I recall that day: "my home the car park... no no good. "But the important thing is that I am no longer afraid to communicate in English. This is not only a language improvement, but also a sign of my inner growth. This experience made me deeply realize that inner strength is more important than any external strength. It enables me to keep calm and express myself bravely when facing difficulties and challenges.

Although this brave expression gave me a great sense of achievement, the conflict with Ralph still affected me to some extent. The very next day, I was once again unable to concentrate and drove without paying attention to the speed limit. I was speeding again and got a $217 ticket.

Power differences can really change a person's perception of who they are. Recalling his initial messages to me, his words emphasized his help and kindness to me. It was not an ordinary reminder, but an indirect suggestion that I was the one in need of care and help, vulnerable, flawed or inadequate. Instead, he occupies the position of power and person in the relationship. In such an unequal relationship, I gradually came to believe his evaluation and definition of me, unconsciously believing that his views and output were correct, and even forced to be extremely grateful to him for his behavior, although in fact he was only fulfilling his obligations under the contract. I remembered some of the things he had said to me, such as: "Not only are you not grateful, you are pushing your luck..." I felt a pang of guilt that I still can't fathom. I often wonder if I am insatiable, unreasonable, out of line, etc. But thinking about the requests I communicated with him, such as fixing a fallen door frame and (other examples), were really about the safety and basic needs of my home and my family. These conflicting emotions, I think, are what make me feel sorry for him and grateful for him as the "strong person" in the relationship, manipulating my thoughts and emotions. For example, every time I responded with a polite "thank you," he would follow up with some lengthy message emphasizing that I owed him gratitude, as if I owed him a great debt of gratitude. This series of actions made me so fearful and afraid of him that when he attacked me with insults and harassment, I did not dare to make any response, for fear that I had gone too far and was not satisfied and grateful enough.

 I also tried to change the bad relationship between us, but in return, I only seemed to get more terrible emotional kidnapping. As I slowly realized that I was losing control of my emotions, I tried to show him that his behavior was causing me fear and I was afraid to even click on his texts anymore. His reply was actually, "Well, I'm afraid to click on your messages either for fear that something might be broken." At this time, I strongly felt that my statement was not recognized, and I was also accused of a more serious crime. He used this form of evasion to try to make me feel guilty, as if I had unilaterally caused our problems. The communication that followed was this: I said that my problems were keeping me awake, he said that he couldn't sleep either because he was worried about me, and that no matter what I said he would always retaliate with my words, which really made me feel speechless and isolated.

In short, the whole process of moving into a new home is not very smooth, there are always one thing or another. But life seems to give us a constant stream of sudden changes that often take us by surprise, and before we know it, our mood is affected by bad things. Just as old problems are sorted out, new ones are created. Life is like dominoes, falling in a series and piling up quickly, which can be overwhelming. During that time, the words "stagnation in the heart" were very embodied in my body. Those unsolved problems and accumulated troubles, like a boulder piled up in my heart, made me gasp for breath. They are like invisible thorns, constantly stimulating my emotions.

In the past, faced with pressure and frustration, I would certainly choose to escape and try to hide myself in a safe shell and sulk alone. This way seems to punish myself, not only does not help to solve the problem, but also makes my heart heavier, so that the problems can not return.

To ease my anger and dissatisfaction, I've learned to vent appropriately. Sports became an effective way for me to release my emotions, such as running. Every step I took was like stepping on my worries and pressure. With the flow of sweat, those negative emotions were gradually discharged from my body. For example, playing racquetball, I swing my racket hard, the ball is hit against the wall one by one, and then suddenly bounce back. With each swing and bounce, you beat your anger and discontent out of your body and let it dissipate into the air as the ball moves. Of course, catharsis does not mean allowing ourselves to indulge in emotions, after the emotions are released, we still have to calmly face the problem and seek solutions. Although the mountains are high and the rivers are long, I can't solve the dispute with the express company personally, but I can rely on the power of friends to help me to call the police, provide all the relevant evidence and chat records, so that they can help me. Although after more than half a year, the Courier company still did not give me the refund I deserved, and only gave me some piecemeal compensation, I have been freed from this shameless dispute. I must defend my rights, but I will no longer punish myself with anger.

The problem is solved, the knot will naturally open. Even if it is really difficult to solve the problem, we can also seek professional psychological counseling, do not sulk alone.

In addition, I have found that the key to controlling emotions is to distinguish between subjective cognition and objective facts under the influence of emotions.

When anger comes, our subjective perception tends to be swept up in the waves of emotion. We may feel that the whole world is against us, that everyone is bad for us, and this bias in our subjective perception can lead us to make bad judgments and decisions. For example, we may say hurtful words or act impulsively out of anger, which will make us regret when we calm down. Therefore, the first task of controlling our emotions is to learn to stay calm and rational when anger comes, and not be swayed by our emotions. In the face of sudden emotional surge, we can calm the excitement by deep breathing, temporarily leaving the scene, meditation, etc., so that we have enough time and space to recover calm.

At the same time, we also need to develop the habit of looking at problems objectively. After anger, we should try to look at the incident from a different Angle, to understand the whole picture and the truth of the matter, and avoid being misled by subjective cognition. By collecting more information and evidence, we can evaluate the situation more objectively and then make a wiser and more reasonable decision.

In the journey of life, we will always encounter such troubles and setbacks, perhaps from the Courier's mistakes, perhaps from the other party's backtrack, but no matter what, they are the sharpening of our growth on the road. Every patient communication, every time to actively seek solutions, are my positive attitude towards life and the brave face of the problem. I believe that only when we truly master the wisdom of coping with emotions can we move smoothly in life and enjoy more happiness and satisfaction.

Now, I don't care what anyone thinks of me, whether they say good or bad things about me behind my back or to my face, I feel that those things are irrelevant, my only pursuit is to live my own happiness, and I now avoid all kinds of parties, enjoy the time alone - indulge in healthy delicious food, Accompany children to play in their little world. I try to avoid causing trouble to others, and I do not like to be disturbed by others, especially those tedious social activities, which disturb the calm and simple rhythm of my life. As I moved away from these distractions, I found an unprecedented clarity in my heart, and my worries seemed to dissipate. In the past, even if it was a simple walk or shopping, I used to go with a partner; Now, I can relax alone. Tasting seafood dinner alone, enjoying the fun of Hot pot alone, each bite tastes mellow, more comfortable than eating with others. I do what I want, I don't have to negotiate or compromise with anyone, I have my own time. The world is afraid of loneliness, but I have found a fertile ground for self-growth in this loneliness. Loneliness, for me, has become a profound art of self-exploration and independent living, a way of being completely self-owned without attachment, and I have found inner peace and strength in solitude.

2. New connotations of sensitivity

I seem to have been born with a keen quality, and if I were to choose my career over again, I believe that only a detective could use this trait: if I were given the slightest clue, I would follow it and pursue it until I had uncovered the whole story.

My sensitivity is not limited to problem solving; it's more of an all-encompassing sense. I often have strong premonitions about various things in my life that tend to happen exactly as I imagine them to, with surprising accuracy.

But at the same time, this sensitivity has caused me some problems. It makes me feel the pain and loss even more deeply when going through difficulties and challenges. It also makes me overly concerned with the reactions of others, and overly concerned with the appropriateness of my own words and actions. This excessive concern sometimes makes me nervous and cautious in interpersonal communication, and even affects my confidence and expression. What's more, when my body shows even the tiniest signs of discomfort, I can immediately detect it and unconsciously start over-interpreting the signs. Then I became trapped in a cycle of self-speculation, constantly searching the Internet for possible illnesses that might be related to these symptoms. Each day I bounced between different symptoms and tried to diagnose myself, often ending up scaring myself half to death and exhausted from my imagination before I'd even seen a doctor.

I knew that this internal friction was not conducive to my condition, but my innate sensitivity and paranoia were hard to shake off, and for a long time I resented my "sensitivity." But in fact, sensitivity is like an open window, letting in the pain and troubles, but also allowing me to more clearly capture the subtle happiness in life.

For example, I am often moved by small details in my interactions with my children. When I go for a run, my daughter chases me on her scooter, and when I turn around, I see her rosy face. I smile and yell, "Baby, chase me, short legs!" This simple and pure interaction with my child fills my life with happiness.

Sensitivity also allows me to be more sensitive to the needs and emotional changes of my children. Before, both kids slept in their own beds, but some time ago they got sick, so they both came to my room. My son is especially clingy to me and has to touch me when he falls asleep at night. If he can't, he wakes up immediately, rolls over and runs out, calling "Mommy" as he goes. Once, his cold snoring was so loud that I couldn't sleep at all. When he and my sister fell asleep, I went to sleep in his room. But in the middle of the night, I heard him running along the corridor with his little feet clomping and screaming "Mommy mommy". I quickly opened the door to call him, when he entered the door, he fell down on the bed and slept soundly. It looked like he was too sleepy to do. After a while, he probably slept restlessly and began to move about. I patted him and said, "Mommy's here, don't be afraid, don't be afraid…" He immediately calmed down and went to sleep again.

As long as I say: "Mom is up, you sleep some more." Immediately, he would sit up in a daze, look at me with half his eyes open and say, "No, I'll get up too." I would ask him, "Will your mother stay with you for a while or will you get up?" He hugged my neck and said in a coquely manner: "Sleep for a while." My son's innocence and love ignited the warmth of my heart like a fire. The night before, I had reprimanded him for being naughty.

This hyper-sensitivity has saved my life several times in critical situations.

Once, shortly after my arrival in the United States, I was almost saved from death by my own ignorance and carelessness. At that time, I had to use an insecticide for my job. The insecticide was used by closing the doors and Windows and opening the jar and filling the room with smoke to kill the insect. I had never touched this product before, and because I didn't know English, I couldn't understand the instructions. I just listened to others describe how to use it. But the important thing is that no one told me that people could not be kept indoors during use, no one said that they had not thought about it and no one had common sense.

After following the instructions, it wasn't long before I felt dizzy and had

Chapter 7 The Revolution of the Self

trouble breathing. I realized something was wrong and struggled to move towards the door to escape the space as quickly as possible. There was only one thought in my mind at the time: I can't just die like this, no one knows I'm here, I have to get out on my own. But before I could walk a few steps, I lost control of my body, fell to the ground and lost consciousness.

When I woke up again, I found myself lying outside on the grass with the door open and half of my body crawling outside. Using my survival instinct, I managed to get outside before I lost consciousness. Although it is impossible to recall the exact escape process, it is certain that it was a strong desire to survive that drove me to escape Heaven.

I slowly climbed to the farther grass to rest, and was fully conscious. Dragging my half-recovered body, I got up and got back to work. Over. Go to a tool store and buy the tools you need. The owner noticed my anomaly and was surprised to ask me why my face and neck were red. I just smiled and said nothing more. It was a thrilling experience that left me with a profound feeling that I can't even describe in words to this day.

Perhaps it was the happiness of the rest of my life after the disaster. The helplessness and fear of being in the closed room, surrounded by toxic smoke, struggling to breathe and blurred consciousness, are still vivid today. When I regained consciousness, I was surprised to find that I had escaped from heaven. Life is so fragile that it can be lost in a moment. But at the same time, life is so tenacious and tough, even in the desperate situation, can also burst out the survival instinct.

My life, like a candle being re-lit, although weak, but tenacious. It was another witness to the resilience of life, and I had no reason to waste it.

The other time was many years ago. I had to transfer to my hometown after getting off the plane in Chongqing, but since it was the end of the year and the time was so late, there was no other means of transportation available except black market cars. I had no choice but to get into an 11-seater car and take a single seat in the second row behind the cab. It wasn't long before a girl got on the bus and sat in front of me. During our chat, we learned that she and I took the same plane. What's more, our hometown was in the same place. She was in a small county near the city. We both felt a lot of fate, so we added wechat to each other. As everyone was getting on the bus, one person caught my attention. He had a fishing bag with him, and with consummate skill he slipped it under the two rows of row seats directly opposite the door. Following his movements, I noticed that a hollow iron bar had been placed there. Then he went to the end of the car and chose a single row seat. When he sat down, his eyes wandered around the car, glancing at everyone from start to finish. His eyes are like a scanner, recognizing the value of each person's outfit.

It wasn't long before another boy came up. As soon as he got on the bus, the boy appeared to be playful and kept on laughing, laughing so hard that one shuddered. He also made a point of glancing under the seat where the fishing bag was lying, and that was the only look that alerted me. And I noticed that he had a very strange look at the man who had put the bag under the seat. What made it even more unusual for me was that even though the car wasn't really noisy and everyone was chatting away at random, every time the smiling boy sent a message, the phone of the man with the fishing bag went ding-dong. And every time the man with the fishing bag replied, the smiling boy's phone ding-dong. Caught by this tiny detail, I sensed something was amiss and immediately became alert and texted the girl sitting in front of me.

After reading my message, the girl also took a closer look to confirm the situation. A few minutes later, she replied to me and said, "Yes, something does seem wrong." The girl decided to test the smiley boy. She deliberately asked him some questions, such as where he lived, where he was going, where he was from home and so on. Although the boy's answers seemed composed, the girl, who is a local of the place he was answering, knew the obvious discrepancy and texted me to tell me that the funny man did have a problem. Fortunately, everyone on the bus was chatting and the boy was completely unaware of the girl's attempt.

Soon, we arrived at the gas station. While we were filling up, everyone went to the bathroom or got out of the car for some fresh air. The girl and I also learned from the staff at the gas station that mugging is a common occurrence in this area, which is to put a carload of people under anesthesia and then rob them. Upon hearing this, we both decided not to get in the car again and the girl immediately called her dad and asked him to pick us up in his car. About 40 minutes later, the driver called me in a very quiet environment and asked if we had started yet, saying that they had arrived at their destination. According to the time, it would take them at least two and a half hours. It was impossible for them to arrive right now. Add to that the uncharacteristically quiet, eerily quiet environment on his side. By this point, we were almost certain they were in cahoots.

Looking back on this experience, I am deeply impressed with how important it was for me to be keen and act decisively. Perhaps there are two sides to the coin. Sensitivity gives me the ability to perceive the world more deeply, but it also makes me more vulnerable and influenced by the outside world. I wish I had a switch to control my sensitivity, so that I could enjoy life delicately and gently, and at the same time, I could laugh away the hurt and unhappiness. I still have a long way to go before I can get along with sensitivity. I hope we can all switch between sensitivity and uneasiness.

3. Break the old and break the new to free your mind

When we drop our daughter off at the swim team, we always park our car in a fixed spot and go in a big circle through the front door. She's been at that pool for two or three years now, and for nearly three years we've used the front door. Until the other day, I suddenly realized that our parking position is the side door, and we just need to push the door open and we can go directly to the car. I was very surprised and asked my daughter, "Baby, do you know that you can also enter through this door?" She said, "Yes!" 'Then why do we have to go so far every time? It's more convenient to use the side door!" "I know you can get out here, but we're used to the front door, aren't we?"

It was this simple thing that made me rethink habits. "Habits" often make me feel comfortable and at ease. Positive habits can also help us maintain stability and continuity, and become a driving force for us to move forward. However, once a habit is ingrained, it may prevent us from having a better choice.

When it comes to habitual thinking, I can't help thinking of Jenny, my daughter's mother who is in the same studio as her classmate. She always keeps an open mind when facing and solving problems. Even though her husband is a Western intensive care doctor, when she had a headache, I suggested that she go to see Doctor Ma, a Chinese medicine doctor, and she readily accepted and actively tried. She is always curious about new things. We both fight in the same boxing gym. I told her that there is another gym with a better atmosphere, and she will try it quickly without being stubborn. Seeing how open she is to new things, I was inspired to think that I should be brave enough to try new things, otherwise I might miss out on a lot of good things.

Habitual thinking is a common phenomenon in our life. It is like a mindset that makes us tend to use past experience and knowledge to solve new problems when facing them. When we are stuck in a rut, we are reluctant to try new methods and ideas. For example, on short video platforms, some people wear white lab coats and soak goji berry water with a thermos cup. We are always accustomed to thinking that they are doctors and believe their words and products. This is the work of habitual thinking and stereotypes.

In patients with depression, negative habitual thinking is more common. It is like a negative tape that plays on a constant loop, repeatedly emphasizing the patient's incompetence, feelings of worthlessness, and failures. It constantly eats away at the patient's sense of self, making it difficult for us to see our strengths and achievements, or even question the meaning of our own existence. Under the influence of this kind of thinking, patients may have a negative attitude toward everything they do, regardless of whether it is truly worthy of affirmation or not.

Habitual thinking can also be an insurmountable obstacle when people with depression seek and accept new treatments. People with depression may have tried a treatment before but it didn't work well, so they have preconceived notions about it and all that goes with it. This bias can cause us to overlook other treatments that may be more effective, limiting recovery options. For example, I was so distressed by the side effects of medication that I avoided medication as much as possible in my subsequent treatment.

So how can we avoid habitual thinking? First of all, keeping an open mind is key. When encountering new ideas and suggestions, don't be too quick to dismiss them. During her two or three years on the swim team, my daughter may have tried to share a shortcut to a side door, only to be cut off by my "impatience." Second, we should try to think from different angles and positions. Just like standing in the position of stadium designers, we will understand that how can such a large swimming stadium only have one entrance and exit? Finally, continuous learning and growth is the key to avoid habitual thinking. Through continuous learning and accumulation of experience, we can broaden our vision and cognition, enhance our flexibility of thinking, and actively adapt to changing environments and challenges.

Habitual thinking may be a natural tendency of our brain, but that doesn't mean we can't overcome it. Hopefully, we can all keep a curious mind and keep exploring and learning to become a better version of ourselves.

4. Chocolate Inspiration: Cherish the moment

A friend brought back a box of chocolates from Dubai for my daughter. Each small chocolate bar is individually wrapped and comes in purple or silver. The silver chocolate has a slightly bitter taste, while the purple one is a little sweeter.

My daughter and son loved it after trying it, especially the sweet purple. So I decided to allow each of them one piece a day. At the end of the day, there were only two silver chocolates left in the box. When I brought them to my son, he was very upset. "Why the nasty silver ones? I will never eat silver again. I want purple. Purple is so sweet. I'm very unhappy right now."

Watching his furrowed brow and pursed mouth, I try to steer him in a different direction. I asked softly, "Baby, are you happy that you still have two pieces of silver chocolate to eat? If you don't have these two pieces of silver chocolate, you will be even more unhappy?" He thought for a moment, nodded and said, "Well, yes, there are two silver chocolates left to eat."

Watching my son contentedly eat that piece of silver chocolate, I couldn't help but admire my own wisdom in avoiding a "dispute" with just two words. At the same time, I was surprised at the change in my own mentality. In the past, I would have reacted the same way as my son in such a situation. Because we are often driven by the instinct to pursue the good and avoid the pain, it is easy to ignore and complain about those things that do not meet our expectations. Dissatisfaction with silver chocolate is simply a natural response to life's imperfections. But as I've lived my life, I've come to realize that beauty isn't limited to our beloved purple chocolate. The less eye-catching silver chocolate is worth savoring and cherishing as well.

This small conversation about chocolate led to a thinking about "living in the moment and cherishing the present".

Living in the present and appreciating the present is a kind of life wisdom, which requires us to focus on the present, not to be troubled by the regrets of the past or excessive worries about the future, and enjoy the beauty of the present. The afterlife can't be waited for, the past can't be pursued, and the only thing we can really control is this moment. In fact, there is no lucky or unlucky life, it is only the comparison of two different circumstances. The saddest thing in life is to miss happiness in comparison and to miss the best time in hesitation. There will be "better", but the "best" must be the present within our reach.

Living in the present and cherishing the present also requires us to maintain an open and optimistic mind. The world in the eyes of pessimists is always a little less colorful, a little more heavy, easy to feel depressed because of small disappointments, lack of confidence and expectations for the future, just like me. Optimistic people, on the other hand, draw different strengths from the same situation and see the positive side in life. When they see the remaining piece of silver chocolate, they feel a surge of gratitude and happiness that they still have two pieces of chocolate to eat, which is happiness in itself. They have the ability to appreciate the good in life and to be resilient and optimistic in the face of difficulties, like me right now.

Can not help but think of the "Forrest Gump" in the famous line about chocolate: "Life was like a box of chocolates, you never know what you're gonna get." Life was like a box of chocolates, you never know what you're gonna get. Life is full of unknowns and variables. We can't control the color of each chocolate, but we can choose how we want to taste it.

抑郁自救笔记
Notes on Depression Self-help

5. Trust in the goodwill of the world

Yesterday, I had a little trouble going shopping. When I was trying to pay for myself, I accidentally pulled out my card early and couldn't make the payment. The system told me I needed to do it again. But the process was a little too complicated for me. I spent a lot of time at the self-checkout machine, which was supposed to be really busy, and no staff immediately came to help me. An off-duty employee walked by and noticed my predicament. He voluntarily stopped and asked if I needed help. After I explained the situation to him, he patiently guided me through re-entering the information and trying to pay again. Also, when he didn't succeed the first time, he immediately helped me make a second attempt until I finally made the payment.

I've been going through a lot lately and I'm feeling a little down. But in that moment, the kindness of seeing a stranger, even when off duty, still willing to take the time to help me was very heartwarming and touching. After all, in the American culture, off work is off work and you won't be given any more attention. That's true of most people. He was willing to lend a hand not because of the demands of his job, not because of any special concern for me, but because he was a good person, a helpful person.

Just this morning, while moving out to get my Wi-Fi service, I met a very responsible woman. The way things work here, customers have to wait next to the staff, even though it may take hours, or they won't help you. I've been doing this for over an hour with the help of this woman, and I still need to contact another company to help with some procedures, such as switching lines. The whole process was extremely cumbersome and the other company was very slow and kept us waiting. Fortunately, the staff member was patient and dutiful throughout

Chapter 7 The Revolution of the Self

the process. Soon, however, my alarm went off to remind my daughter that school was over. I could only explain the situation to the woman and say that I had to go pick up my daughter. She was immediately understanding, saying that she too was a mother and could understand my situation. I asked if I could have a three-way call with her so that she could continue to handle my business without me present, and she readily agreed. Eventually, the business was done and I didn't have to wait to pick up my daughter from school.

These little kindness not only solved my immediate problem, but also made my heart warm. They remind me that no matter what background we come from, kindness and a willingness to help can always transcend barriers and warm others. Life is full of moving and surprising moments, as long as we try to see and feel the beauty around us. These wonderful things and people will make us love life more and will make us more determined to move forward into the future.

6. Allow yourself to be easy

The other day, I accidentally twisted my lower back. It happened to be the day of the weekly home massage, and after Wayan's massage treatment that night, my pain was slightly relieved. But by the next day, I was still worried lest I hurt my bones, so I went back for the massage treatment. This time it was a male masseuse, and he had a lot of strength. Although it felt comfortable at the time, the next day the pain was worse and left me in agony. I went for an X-ray and the doctor told me it was just a muscle strain, not a bone. In the end, I went to see Dr. Ma and the problem was solved.

A few days later, I was on the verge of calling 911 again because of my sore feet. My feet may have gotten a little bigger around that time, but I had to drop my kids off at piano lesson in slightly tighter shoes for about three hours.

抑郁自救笔记
Notes on Depression Self-help

On the drive home, the instep of my left foot was particularly painful. I thought I'd be home in half an hour. Let's hang in there. When I got home, the pain in my instep got worse and worse. I was a little annoyed and blamed myself for not wearing a pair of shoes that fit, knowing clearly that the foot has become bigger but still insist on squeezing into the small shoes. When the pain was unbearable, I suddenly developed symptoms of anxiety. I began to feel chills, shivers, cold sweats, palpitations, nausea, thirst, the need to go to the bathroom, and even my chest turned red. My first instinct was to call 911, fearing that I might need to be rushed to the hospital. I was also worried about what would happen to my two children if I went to the hospital. I couldn't predict when the doctors would send me home.

In frustration and panic, I searched the Internet for pain relief and emergency treatment, and contacted a beating doctor I had seen in the United States. He told me how to deal with the emergency and made an appointment for me at the clinic the next morning. As I calmed down, I realized it was probably just a regular sprain, or a pinching pain caused by my shoes being too small. The anxiety dissipated as I thought about it.

I knew that I had been overstretched in my life. Every time something unexpected happens, I am always too tense and I have trouble relaxing even in small things. Just now, the pain in my feet made me think of death. This is largely due to fear of the unknown. I often feel like an idiot when it comes to common sense. On top of that, it has to do with excessive expectations of results. My constant fear that things will go wrong or not turn out as expected keeps me from relaxing. Not only did this stressful state of affairs affect my mental health, but it also put unnecessary stress on my body.

I badly needed to "take it easy". Relaxation significantly reduces the body's stress response, helping to slow the heart rate, lower blood pressure, and reduce muscle tension. I've found deep breathing, meditation and yoga to be the most effective "relaxation techniques." I can clearly feel the gradual release of tension and fatigue in my body, and the quality of my sleep improves. Relaxation not only relieves physical tension, but also gives me huge psychological benefits. In moments of relaxation, I am able to put aside my daily worries and stresses for a while and truly free my mind.

A person who is used to being tight will not be able to completely relax overnight. It takes time, it takes patience, and it takes self-awareness and adjustment. Hopefully, I can gradually make myself more comfortable and comfortable.

7. Desire: The balance between pursuit and satisfaction

Desire plays a complex and powerful role in the human mind. It is the engine that drives us forward and the source of many of our inner struggles. This simple word carries with it the pursuit of knowledge, the desire for achievement, and the yearning for family, friendship and love. It can not only stimulate my potential to constantly exceed myself, but also inadvertently become my shackles, trapping me in endless pursuit and comparison.

For example, I have been taking ESL classes for three or four months, and someone once told me that it would only take three months for me to master English and communicate freely. However, the reality is far more complicated than the expected simple promise. My current listening skills, as measured by standardized test grades, are about four. When faced with real communication scenarios, I feel powerless to communicate fluently, and more often I have to rely on a translator, which often fails to fully and accurately convey my intention. This frustration made me question myself and hesitate to continue the ESL course.

Just two days ago, I needed to deal with a series of transfer procedures for electricity, water, garbage, etc., because of the move, I was pleasantly surprised to find that it was a little difficult for me to fully understand the content of the page, but I was able to understand some of the sentences. I suddenly realized that I was not without gain. I had signed up for ESL with a progressive attitude, hoping that I would have the courage to overcome my fear of language. But as time went on, I found myself losing my normal mind when my learning state didn't live up to my expectations.

There are many similar situations, I tend to question my ability, and even have some unrealistic fantasies, hoping that I can have super powers, such as becoming a group of outstanding abilities like vampires, with strong learning ability, physical fitness and eternal youth; Or I can have a chip implanted in my brain and become fluent in spoken English overnight. But the reality is, none of us are superhumans, and these ideas are just an excuse to escape from reality. Learning is a long and difficult process, and it takes time and effort to see results. With this in mind, I choose to continue my ESL learning journey. Although I was really busy, only the morning hours of my day were free, and the afternoon hours were almost taken up by the children's activities. But I still insist on using my precious morning time to study English. I told myself that even by learning just one word, one sentence pattern, or practicing one expression every day, I was deepening my memory and understanding. Of course, such persistence is not only to improve my language ability, but also to enjoy the process of learning and growing. Appreciate every brave attempt you make, whether successful or not, and don't let desire and materialism get to your head.

In my quest for self-improvement, I have often set extremely high standards and expectations for myself. This inner drive is sometimes, inevitably, projected onto my children as well. As a mother, I sincerely hope that my children will be healthy and happy, but as they grow up and reveal their talents and potential, I can't help but feel a special sense of expectation.

Record at this time, although my son is only 4 years old, but contact with every teacher will praise him, said that he is very smart, especially the concentration is very good, three years old can sit there firmly, seriously on the ground to finish an hour of class. No matter what kind of questions the teachers put forward, he could answer them calmly. This makes me expect more and more from him. I'd be surprised if he didn't know that one plus one equals two, because in my mind, he should have already mastered it. I patiently taught him to use his fingers to understand addition and subtraction up to ten. Slowly he learned that he could add and subtraction single digits by twisting his fingers to get the correct answer. Happily, I imagined that maybe tomorrow he would learn to add and subtract two-digit numbers in a more complicated way. Without realizing it, I began to impose my own expectations on how fast he would grow.

The previous two years, my daughter's swimming teacher suggested that she join the swim team. But the practice time was too late, and given her need for adequate sleep, I didn't agree. As a result, my daughter persisted and said she really liked swimming, and I eventually decided to support her interest and let her join the team. She got faster and fitter, which was a great surprise. The coach often complimented her on her talent for swimming, which made my initial desire for her to swim happily stir up a little. For another example, my daughter has been learning painting and has also participated in some related competitions. Recently, I received an email from the competition agency informing me that my daughter's work had been selected for the National Selection of Children's Works after a rigorous selection process. The email specifically explained that the anthology would feature the best work of children from all over the United States, that not every child's work would be included, and that I would approve of their use. Although I had hoped that she would stand out in the competition and I had confidence in her, I was still very surprised and pleasantly surprised to learn that her works would be included in such a prestigious collection, as if all the efforts and expectations had been answered at this moment. This honor not only affirms my daughter's artistic talent, but also paints a brighter picture for her future. Her love for mathematics also gives me high hopes for her academic success in the future.

My daughter attends a private school, which is known for its academic excellence. For example, if the child is in the first grade, the school uses the textbooks of the second grade, which creates a gap between the educational standards of the school and those of ordinary schools. My daughter is now in Grade Two, and her head teacher told me after the mid-term exam that her English level is only equivalent to that of pre-school. This news is unacceptable to me. My daughter's preschool years are at this school, she has been here for three years in a row - preschool, first and second grade, and now tells me that her English ability is only preschool, and the school also claims that they value academics above all else.

The impact of this news on me was huge, and I felt unprecedented pressure and anxiety. After all, in an English environment, if she could not keep up with her English level, I worried that it would affect her study in other subjects and even affect her interpersonal communication. In order to help my daughter improve her English, I began to find private tutors for her after class. After about half a year of intensive tutoring, my daughter's English level finally reached the level corresponding to her grade in the latest exam.

During the six months of my daughter's tutoring, my heart was full of anxiety, and I often wondered: Why has her score not improved significantly? When will she reach the level I expect? I was too eager to see the results of the tutoring, as if expecting her to make leaps and bounds overnight. I overlooked the fact that learning is a gradual, incremental process. Just like when I was learning English, I was anxious and always felt that my progress was slow. But in fact, both my daughter and I are making progress little by little. And, by comparison, my daughter's learning speed is much faster than mine.

Because of this incident, I had the idea of transferring my daughter to another school. After much deliberation, I chose a public school that everyone wanted to go to. This also meant that if we wanted to apply to the public school, we had to move to the same district as the public school. To be honest, I had never considered public schools before because everyone said private schools were so good. And with half the student-teacher ratio, teachers have more energy to pay attention to each student, so I never really researched which school was best for her until my teacher told me that she was in grade two but only had the English level of her interest class. This public school will provide a better learning environment for her to develop in all aspects, and with her younger brother going to school soon, it is an important choice that will benefit both of their futures.

After moving to my new neighborhood, I went out running like I used to. Despite being in the same neighborhood, the houses here have a distinct hierarchy based on location and quality. As I ran, I reached the most luxurious area. I could feel a strong desire burning in my heart. The houses were so spacious that the yard had more floor space than the whole house I was living in now, and the gate alone looked extraordinary. As I ran, I couldn't help but imagine trying to buy land here and build something bigger, with tennis courts, racquetball rooms, a heated pool for my daughter to swim in, an oversized gym... But then I thought, even in a mansion like this, someone else has a better house. If I blindly continue to pursue a higher material life, my heart will always be in a state of dissatisfaction, and I will always struggle in the whirlpool of chasing desire.

It occurred to me that I needed to be still and reflect on my desires, both for myself and for my children. I was going to learn to control them.

My transmission of these expectations to my children may not always have the most constructive motives. It fuels my deep concern for their future and my desire for them to have a successful and happy life, which is the most common phenomenon of all parents. But these expectations should not become a burden on their children's path of growth. I don't want my desires to rub off on my children and make them feel stressed or insecure. Every child is a unique individual with their own interests, talents and speed of growth. I can only try to adjust my mindset and try to see my child's growth from a more peaceful and rational perspective. Instead of simply pursuing them for quick mastery of skills or knowledge, focus more on whether they feel happy and fulfilled during the learning process. Encourage them to explore areas that interest them, even if they may not reap the rewards of fame and achievement.

Love and understanding may be more important than any expectations. I can only do my best to provide my children with a loving and supportive environment where they are free to grow up and be who they want to be and choose the life they want to lead.

Desire is what drives us forward, but excessive desire only causes us to lose our way and forget our true goals and values. So, we need to stop and start, constantly examine our hearts on the way forward, be able to look at life more rationally and peacefully and make sure that our desires are under control. If we go too far beyond our limits, we can only expect to be destroyed.

This "self-revolution" is not only a reshuffle of the inner world, but also an indomitable strength to find in the challenge of depression. I learned how to face my inner fears, how to break the shackles of my mind, and how to develop a more resilient and positive self in the face of adversity. With each success of my own revolution, I stand at a new starting point on my journey of growth.

Remember, no matter how the outside world changes, we all have the power to lead our own "self-revolution" and become the masters of our own destiny.

Chapter 8 Miscellaneous Feelings

In the long course of human history, depression, as a profound spiritual experience, has inspired countless artists and writers. From classical literature to modern film, painting to music, the theme of depression runs through various art forms, serving as a window into human nature, emotions and social reality. Each work is a unique universe that tells the story of humanity in different ways and reflects the diversity of life.

In this chapter, I will record the echoes of these works in my heart, whether it is deep thinking or simple moving, it is a real dialogue between me and these works. Here, there is no strict theoretical framework and no fixed analysis mode, only sincere emotion and random brushstrokes. Together, we will explore the movies and books that touch my heart and share the inspirations and insights they bring to me.

After reading The Courage to Be Hated

"The Courage to Be Hated" is a book by Ichiro Kishimi and Shiken Koga, which introduces the psychological theories of Austrian psychologist Adler. The book takes the form of a dialogue and tells the story of five days of conversation between a young man and a philosopher. It presents the core ideas of Adler's psychology in a concise and in-depth way. It encourages us to take control of our own destiny and courageously pursue self-fulfillment and perfection.

The courage to be hated, by definition, is the ability to accept being hated by others. We want to have the courage to be hated, because we want to be a free person, and freedom here does not mean to break away from the family, the group, the society, but to be able to pay no attention to the evaluation of others, not afraid of being hated by others, do not seek to be recognized by others, we all look forward to having such a free lifestyle.

The dialogue between the "philosopher" and the "youth" in the book seems to be the dialogue between me and my own heart. Adler's psychological ideas made me re-examine my own life and depression. Adler taught me that depression is not caused by past experiences, but by our reluctance to move on from the past. We are constantly looking for reasons not to move forward, trying to find comfort in past experiences.

Psychological trauma, I used to be deeply troubled by it. I was always looking back, trying to figure out what caused me to fall into depression. But, Adler told me, "Whatever happened in my previous life has no bearing on how I'm going to live my life." It's who you are in the "here and now" that determines your life.

Accepting who I am is a concept I've never tried before. I had been trying to run away from myself, from the imperfect me. I would never go to the car wash alone because I couldn't get on the track at the car wash, the people in the back would honk constantly, and I couldn't read the payment method because I didn't know any English. In addition, as a deep coffee lover, I was afraid to buy coffee from the store because of the language barrier, so I had to buy a coffee machine to make my own terrible coffee at home.

But the first step to change, Adler told me, is accepting yourself and having a strong sense of self-identity and values. No matter how unsatisfactory the reality is, I have to tell myself that I allow myself to be this way. Because only by truly accepting myself can I find the motivation and courage to change. The first step in accepting myself is accepting that I don't speak English and acknowledging my resistance to language learning. Because I was afraid of making mistakes in the learning process and being looked at differently, I denied myself in advance and refused to learn English to prevent this from happening.

With this in mind, I tried to focus on what I could control instead of focusing too much on the external environment and other people's comments. I started trying to wash my car by myself, even when the cars behind me honked their horns because it took me too long to pay. As I went there more often, I became more adept at the process. And I have found that many native English speakers sometimes have trouble getting things done and need to call staff to help them.

I mustered up the courage to sign up for ESL's online course. ESL, which stands for English as a Second Language, is a specialized English language course offered in the United States, Canada and other English-speaking countries for people whose first language is not English. Each class is two hours, sometimes two and a half hours, the teacher usually reads a paragraph in English for the first hour, I always listen very confused. This feeling of "not being in control" aroused my resistance again and I wanted to give up many times. In the next hour, the teacher explained these contents clearly. After I understood and absorbed them, the feeling of pressure and being out of breath was relieved. I am glad that I just did not give up and learned something new today, otherwise my own growth will be delayed by myself.

I still remember that one class taught a grammar that I could not understand. I handed in a blank paper for the homework after class. Later, the teacher left the correct answers in the comments. I filled in the answers and submitted them again. The next day, when I looked at the "100 marks" the teacher gave me, I had no memory of what I had written yesterday, let alone the grammar.

While reviewing for the exam with my Pilates translator, I took out this question and asked her to help me explain it. The translator first explained two example questions to me and then asked me what I should fill in the question. I said I didn't know. "Yes, you do! "She sounded a little firm. "I really don't know." "Yes, you do! I was a little aggrieved by her over-certain tone, and I really felt like I didn't get it. I forced myself to look at the question carefully one more time and tell her the answer. "Yes! Can you do it or not? !" At that moment, I really want to cry, some self-blame, feel that they have not used the heart to learn English this thing to feel that they can not do it, did not pay all the efforts.

This incident also confirms the "responsibility" mentioned in the book. We should be responsible for our words and deeds, admit the impact of our choices and decisions in life on ourselves, and be willing to take responsibility for these impacts. I chose an "undeserved" 100 and an easy learning process, and I have to accept the consequences of not being able to learn this grammar. Learning is a process that requires patience and perseverance, and there is no way to achieve it overnight. Even if we learn something, it takes constant communication and practice to become really good at it. Otherwise, we can easily fall into a vicious circle of "learning, forgetting, and forgetting to learn again".

When I was young, I always felt that I was young and in good health. I indulged myself too much and didn't take good care of my body, which now causes me some pain from time to time. I guess the pain may have something to do with my behavior back then. For example, I cut many wounds on my arm and even cut the tendons in it. Now I always feel a particular pain in the meridians of my left hand. Sometimes it feels like I haven't been stretched enough, and sometimes it even feels like the whole meridians have been broken.

Looking back now, I really regret something, that is, when I was young, I did things too impulsively, blindly pursued short-term happiness and satisfaction, did not care for my body, and hurt my body. Now, my physical pain is a direct consequence of my impulsive behavior in my youth, and I deeply experience the cost of irresponsibility. True maturity is not only about making choices, but also about taking responsibility for those choices. This means that before making any decision, we should think it through, anticipate the possible consequences, and be prepared to live with those consequences. Now, I value my body more and actively work out to compensate for the urges of my youth.

I was also inspired by the book's discussion of relationships. "Relationships are the source of all your troubles and bad emotions." Faced with the complexity of relationships, we often find ourselves caught up in the annoyance and anxiety caused by the contradiction between the expectations of others and our own needs.

The concept of "subject separation" mentioned in the book provides us with clear ideas for better handling of interpersonal relationships. Project separation is the distinction between what is your project and what is someone else's project. To put it simply, everyone has their own problems and challenges to face. We don't have to get too involved in others' problems, nor do we have to let others get too involved in our problems. We just focus on ourselves.

Of course, although I understand and agree with the importance of "subject separation", in real life, especially when dealing with my children, I tend to forget this principle and over-restrict them. Perhaps it is because, as parents, we naturally want to protect and educate our children, to avoid dangers and detours. However, this over-protection may become a stumbling block to their growth, preventing them from thinking independently, solving problems independently, and experiencing both failure and success. They need our guidance and protection, but they also need freedom and space to explore the world and to exercise their independence.

One thing that stuck in my mind was that my body was sick because of Helicobacter pylori, and I even vomited blood. Two ambulances were called to my family. At this tense moment, my daughter, who seemed to be watching a good show, excitedly leaned over the window and shouted, "Wow, two ambulances are here!" I couldn't laugh or cry. It was the younger son who wondered what had happened to his mother and why she was in the ambulance. My daughter was always so active, and even at such times she would play without fear, which made me deeply anxious. If she has always been so innocent and unaware of human suffering, will she be able to cope with the difficulties of life on her own if I am afraid that I should die suddenly now? She was such a kind child. She easily forgave those who hurt her. She always took everyone's word for it. If I am not there, will she be able to deal with the complicated relationships and solve the difficult problems? Now, I fully understand what Zuzu said to me: "What will you do when Zuzu is not around you?" I deeply understand Zuzu's anxiety.

These worries have made me more aware that I need to teach my children to be independent and how to face the difficulties and challenges of life. When we find ourselves overcontrolling our children, we need to stop and reflect on our actions immediately. We need to ask ourselves, are we acting out of protection for them, or out of our own anxiety and fear? Or do you want your children to be the way you want them to be? Only when we truly recognize our motivations can we make a change. The practice of "project separation" is difficult but important, and I hope I can keep it up, both for my children and for myself.

In short, the whole book conveys the idea that we are encouraged to be ourselves! In the treatment of depression, this "be yourself" way of thinking is especially important, and can be liberating for people with depression. People with depression often get caught up in a spiral of self-denial and anxiety, and they are so concerned with the opinions and evaluations of others that they neglect their own inner needs and emotions. The concept of "being yourself" encourages patients to accept their true state and pay attention to their inner world, without deliberately catering to the expectations of others or distorting their true feelings in order to please others, requiring them to find themselves again and bravely show their true selves.

In this process, we will gradually find that the real self is not as perfect as others expect, but it is the most real, the most natural, the most powerful, is worthy of love and respect. When we begin to accept and value ourselves for who we really are, the burden and anxiety within us will gradually ease. In the pursuit of our true self, find the hope and courage to cure depression.

Feeling Back in New Jersey

"Back to New Jersey" is a small budget independent film that Zach Braff wrote, directed and starred in, which made him well received by the American film critics of the year. The wave of positive reviews made me curious even as a person who doesn't pay much attention to movies, and I heard that it was a lighthearted romantic comedy with quirky content, so I opened it after the kids were asleep. Unexpectedly, I was rewarded with a warm night.

The story revolves around the hero returning home for his mother's funeral. 26-year-old young Andrew has a dream of acting in his heart. He has struggled for many years in Los Angeles alone but has run some solo roles. He is always at odds with the bright and bright Los Angeles and is ridiculed by guests when he works in a restaurant. Just as Andrew is confused about his future, his "psychologist" father calls, and his mother, who has been paralyzed for many years, dies. It was a terrible shock to Andrew, but as he said, he didn't shed any tears. He could not cry for the world.

Andrew's childhood was not a happy one. It was a dark and sick time. Because he was too naughty when he was young, his parents were very strict with him and even thought he had some problems. In order to restrain him and control his emotions, his father put him on medication for a long time until today. These drugs have taken a toll on his physiology. Unable to stand his parents' excessive interference, Andrew even had the idea of letting his mother die, and in one accident, led to the tragedy of her life in a wheelchair. So his father sent Andrew to a boarding school. There, his classmates saw him as an outlier, and he felt it too. After graduating from high school, he left home, said goodbye to his friends and headed to Los Angeles to pursue his dream of acting. During this time, he never returned home and his relationship with his father became increasingly strained. The word "father" -- a word that should be filled with warmth -- meant indifference to Andrew.

At his mother's funeral, Andrew runs into his childhood friend. These friends take him to all kinds of lively parties and meet all kinds of people. However, the shadow of his childhood still seems to linger in his mind, and he always feels that he is bound by an invisible force. At this point, the heroine Samantha comes into Andrew's life. The girl is neurotic, even hyperactive, but that doesn't stop her from being attractive. She is kind and loving, and has adopted many small animals. Moreover, she had great skills and the potential to become an Olympic champion, but she never advertised it.

Andrew's inner world is filled with doubts about self-worth and conflicts over family affection. His childhood experiences have left him strongly conflicted with his parents, indirectly leading to his mother's tragic accident. Such psychological trauma became an inescapable shadow for him, forcing him to constantly seek relief. His dependence on drugs is an irrational way for him to escape from reality and heal himself. This is not only a true portrayal of people with depression, but also a profound reflection of everyone who feels lost in the modern society.

In just a few days, friends created an environment where Andrew could reveal his heart, get off the drugs, and truly face his heart. Gradually, Andrew learned to let go of his inner constraints and forgave his father for his harshness and misunderstandings. He stepped out of the cycle of his life and began to see himself and the world around him in a new light. The experience not only led him to find true love, but also to rediscover the meaning and value of his life.

As the film came to a close, I also began to reflect on my life and my heart. In Andrew's story, I get a glimpse of a man who is Shadowed by his past and who finally breaks free and finds meaning in his life, much like myself. I have experienced all the symptoms of depression that the hero experiences: chronic insomnia, tossing and turning at night, staring at the ceiling until dawn. Anxiety is a constant shadow, accompanied by a racing heart and shortness of breath, a sense of suffocation and even panic attacks in ordinary everyday life. Headaches, stomachaches, muscle aches -- they come to you for no physical reason. Depression is a common occurrence, stealthily robbing us of all joy and excitement. The most tiring thing is that people lose interest and motivation in life, once hobbies and pursuits become boring, even simple daily tasks become unbearable, and they just want to avoid all social activities.

Not to mention, to this day I still can't reconcile with my biological father the way Andrew did.

Andrew's story gave me the confidence and courage to say goodbye to my past in my own way. Instead of dwelling on their mistakes or expecting them to change, I chose to let go. Life is for growing -- for appreciating and growing, not for holding grudges and dwelling on them. People can't stay in the shadow of the past forever. Continuing to dwell on what they did will only make themselves resentful and unable to move forward. Just keep some distance, avoid too much overlap, and focus on your own life.

Samantha and her friends are undoubtedly the salvation of Andrew's life. They bring warmth and care to Andrew in a long time. We may all feel lost and alone in this noisy world. But as long as we are willing to open our hearts to those who are willing to come into our lives, to understand and tolerate different voices and perspectives, we can eventually find our own warmth and strength. Life is lonely and cold, if someone can bring you a little power to overthrow the past, let you feel that life and emotions become tangible, this must be the most moving feelings in the world.

This movie is not a simple romantic comedy, nor is it just a depiction of depression, but rather a paean to humanity, love and redemption. It's worth watching no matter what state of mind you're in right now.

"Sports change the brain" after reading

In our busy life, we often neglect the importance of exercise for various reasons. When stress, anxiety, depression and other negative emotions hit us, we tend to look for drugs or other external solutions, and overlook a simple but extremely effective way -- exercise.

With vivid writing, rigorous scientific research and a wealth of real-world examples, the author of Exercise Rewires the Brain shows us how exercise rewires the brain and how it can help us better cope with life's challenges. When it comes to aerobic exercise, the book elaborates on its role in improving cognitive function. Jogging, swimming and cycling, for example, can promote blood circulation in the body, increase the heart and lung function, help the brain get more oxygen and nutrients, and improve the brain's work efficiency. In addition, aerobic exercise can also stimulate the growth and connection of brain neurons, enhance the brain's cognitive reserve, help delay cognitive decline and improve memory. As for strength training, it is not only able to improve muscle mass and improve the body's strength and endurance, but also can improve emotional state and reduce anxiety and depression symptoms by promoting blood flow and releasing brain hormones. Strength training can also enhance the connections of neurons in the brain, improve the brain's processing capacity of information, and help improve cognitive function. And balance training, such as yoga, tai chi and dance, can help protect the brain from damage by improving stability and coordination and reducing the risk of falls. The book also mentions the Pilates exercises I have been studying, such as Pilates bending, which improves coordination while also promoting the connection and communication of neurons in the brain, which helps improve cognition, reaction speed and concentration.

Exercise also plays a positive role in the prevention and treatment of some mental illnesses. For example, exercise can be equivalent to a certain dose of psychotropic drugs that can help treat psychological disorders such as anxiety and depression. Exercise can also provide effective help for those who are trying to quit smoking, stop drugs, or kick addictions. For example, John, who is a professional, often feels extremely stressed and has severe mood swings. By running every morning, his anxiety and stress are alleviated. This is a simple and effective way to reduce stress and anxiety in the workplace. Then there's Amy, a young woman who has been challenged academically and feels her ability to learn is declining. By increasing physical activity, especially aerobic exercise, Amy saw improvements in her concentration and memory. This case shows that exercise is not only good for physical health, it is also essential for learning and cognitive function. As for middle-aged David, the weight gain and depression caused by sitting at a desk for a long time because of work can also be alleviated by regular exercise. Older Lady Lily, on the other hand, joined the community sports group, made many new friends and became more cheerful and optimistic.

Each case shows the positive effects of exercise on brain health. In addition, there is one protagonist whose experience impresses me the most. He separated from his wife because of an extramarital affair, his work was not smooth, his life rhythm was completely disrupted, and he fell into a state of depression. He himself had problems with hyperactivity and inconcentration. The doctor gave

抑郁自救笔记
Notes on Depression Self-help

him medicine for this, but the side effects of the medicine made him feel very uncomfortable, and he had a variety of uncomfortable symptoms such as muscle pain, headaches, and stomach pains. The doctor then suggested a new medication for his condition. While discussing the effects of the new medication, he began to vomit endlessly. He did not like the discomfort of the drug and decided to stop taking the vomiting medicine and to exercise to adjust his body. His next visit came two weeks later, during which time he continued to run every day, and the doctors saw changes in his physical and emotional state. Then, a month later, he was almost fully recovered, and his new job and life became more organized.

He resented the side effects of his medication, just as I felt at the time. In the early fall of 2021, my family doctor advised me not to stop taking Western medicine, believing that the rainy seasons and winters that followed in Seattle would make me even more depressed. I said to my family doctor, "No, I can't stay on medication anymore. I'm going to phase out the medication, and I'm convinced that exercise will help me change that." Therefore, I know very well how dependent people with depression are on drugs, so when he decided to stop relying on drugs and completely rely on exercise to improve his physical and mental state, I truly admired his determination and perseverance.

Not long before I read this book, I had just stopped taking the last thirty percent of my medication, and by this point I was completely out of the situation of relying on Western medicine to maintain my mood. I am now in the habit of exercising regularly. Whenever I have some free time, I go for a run or play squash. I also take advantage of my children's time to go to interest classes. Even if I have to run for 20 minutes to pick up my children, I am content to enjoy the pleasure and freedom that sports bring. Through sports, I feel the harmony and balance of my body and mind. I no longer rely on drugs blindly and get nervous when I lose drugs. Instead, I learn to release negative emotions through sports. Sports make me more confident, optimistic and strong, and also make me cherish and enjoy every moment of life more. Of course, it cannot be ruled out that the reason why I have to stop taking the medicine so small has a great relationship with my sensitivity.

The book's protagonist, who had a similar or even more difficult recovery, made me realize that there are millions of people in the world who suffer from depression and other illnesses, and their experiences may be even more unfortunate than ours. I hope that my recording of this story and insight will help more people to read the book "Exercise Remakes the Brain" and understand the importance of exercise for physical and mental health. Maybe his close friends, maybe his relatives, were touched to encourage and persuade him to start exercising, to help him have a chance to get rid of the pain.

Objectively speaking, there are some things in the book that I don't understand. For example, some theoretical knowledge is rather esoteric, and a large number of medical terms may be difficult for non-professional readers to read. In addition, although the book lists a large number of experiments and cases, the descriptions of individual cases may not be detailed enough for readers to fully understand the scientific principles behind them. But that doesn't stop it from being a good read.

Of course, I am not advocating that patients who are taking medication stop taking it and blindly exercise and fitness. All the rehabilitation process should be carried out under the professional guidance of doctors.

In these essays, I share my feelings and thoughts, which may not be perfect, but are real and profound. I hope these words will inspire readers' empathy, and maybe in a casual moment, you will find your shadow and feel the touch of your heart.

Life itself is a rich and colorful work in which each of us is a writer and a reader. I hope that in the coming days, no matter what kind of story you encounter, you will experience it with an open heart, to feel it, and write your own chapter in the big book of life.

Postscript

When I put a final full stop on this book, the emotion that surged up in my heart is beyond words. This is not just the end of a book, but also a milestone in my personal journey. Looking back, it seems like only yesterday that I struggled with depression, but now I am at a new beginning. There may be more setbacks in the future, but I firmly believe that I will not be defeated by any negative emotions.

Looking back, depression has been a deep scar in my life. It made me miserable, confused and even lost my love for life. However, it was this experience that gave me a deeper understanding of the fragility and strength of human nature. I learned to find strength in every adversity and light in every darkness.

When I took steps and no longer confined myself to my own house, the world felt so beautiful and wonderful. The taste of freshly baked pizza was unparalleled, and the handmade pasta cooked in the restaurant was much more flavorful than the take-out version I could bring home. As I went out more often, the anxiety in my heart gradually faded away, becoming weaker and weaker. The increasingly diminishing sense of anxiety made me feel as if I were about to harmoniously blend with the world. Even though I don't speak English, I can do many things, I can live a happy life, and I can eat delicious food.

In the process of writing this book, I went through a lot of self-analysis and reflection. Each chapter and paragraph reflects my thoughts and feelings about that experience. I hope that through my story, I can arouse more people's attention and attention to mental health, and bring some comfort and courage to those who are going through difficult situations.

I would like to thank my family and friends for their love and companionship, which gave me the strength to face my past and the strength to move on from that dark time. Your understanding and support have been the greatest motivation for me to make it through this journey. At the same time, I would like to express my heartfelt thanks to the doctors who helped me. It was your expertise, selfless dedication and patient listening that made me gradually find myself again. I want to thank the therapist who healed me over the phone every week, even after 9pm -- her non-working hours -- and calmed me down when I was feeling really bad. And special thanks to Dr. Ma, who is not only a healer for my body, but also a guide for my mind. Thank you to everyone who has supported and helped me on my journey to recovery. It is you who have made me believe that no matter how hard life gets, there is always hope and light waiting for us ahead.

And finally, thank you to everyone who is reading this book. The fact that you took the time to learn my story is a precious connection in itself.

"The sea of life, the mountains and the rivers, is not enough." Life may be full of twists and turns and thorns, but please believe that every fall is an opportunity for growth, and every darkness is a harbinger before the dawn. Just like the haze of depression, it is the dawn of re-embracing happiness and hope. May we all be brave enough to face our inner challenges and learn to find strength in adversity.

Remember that no matter how rocky the road ahead may be, there is always a ray of light waiting to be found.

www.ingramcontent.com/pod-product-compliance
Lightning Source LLC
Chambersburg PA
CBHW081152070526
44583CB00021B/2810